TM

References for the Rest of Us!®

BESTSELLING BOOK SERIES FROM IDG

Are you intimidated and confused by computers? Do you find that traditional manuals are overloaded with technical details you'll never use? Do your friends and family always call you to fix simple problems on their PCs? Then the ...*For Dummies*® computer book series from IDG Books Worldwide is for you.

...*For Dummies* books are written for those frustrated computer users who know they aren't really dumb but find that PC hardware, software, and indeed the unique vocabulary of computing make them feel helpless. ...*For Dummies* books use a lighthearted approach, a down-to-earth style, and even cartoons and humorous icons to diffuse computer novices' fears and build their confidence. Lighthearted but not lightweight, these books are a perfect survival guide for anyone forced to use a computer.

> *"I like my copy so much I told friends; now they bought copies."*
>
> — Irene C., Orwell, Ohio

> *"Quick, concise, nontechnical, and humorous."*
>
> — Jay A., Elburn, Illinois

> *"Thanks, I needed this book. Now I can sleep at night."*
>
> — Robin F., British Columbia, Canada

Already, millions of satisfied readers agree. They have made ...*For Dummies* books the #1 introductory level computer book series and have written asking for more. So, if you're looking for the most fun and easy way to learn about computers, look to ...*For Dummies* books to give you a helping hand.

TM

IDG
BOOKS
WORLDWIDE

APPLESCRIPT® FOR DUMMIES®

by Tom Trinko

IDG Books Worldwide, Inc.
An International Data Group Company

Foster City, CA ◆ Chicago, IL ◆ Indianapolis, IN ◆ New York, NY

AppleScript® For Dummies®

Published by
IDG Books Worldwide, Inc.
An International Data Group Company
919 E. Hillsdale Blvd.
Suite 400
Foster City, CA 94404

www.idgbooks.com (IDG Books Worldwide Web site)
www.dummies.com (Dummies Press Web site)

Library of Congress Catalog Card No.: 95-81819

ISBN: 1-56884-975-3

Printed in the United States of America

10 9 8 7 6 5 4 3 2

1E/RX/QZ/ZY/IN

Distributed in the United States by IDG Books Worldwide, Inc.

Distributed by Macmillan Canada for Canada; by Transworld Publishers Limited in the United Kingdom; by IDG Norge Books for Norway; by IDG Sweden Books for Sweden; by Woodslane Pty. Ltd. for Australia; by Woodslane (NZ) Ltd. for New Zealand; by Addison Wesley Longman Singapore Pte Ltd. for Singapore, Malaysia, Thailand, Indonesia and Korea; by Norma Comunicaciones S.A. for Colombia; by Intersoft for South Africa; by International Thomson Publishing for Germany, Austria and Switzerland; by Toppan Company Ltd. for Japan; by Distribuidora Cuspide for Argentina; by Livraria Cultura for Brazil; by Ediciencia S.A. for Ecuador; by Ediciones ZETA S.C.R. Ltda. for Peru; by WS Computer Publishing Corporation, Inc., for the Philippines; by Unalis Corporation for Taiwan; by Contemporanea de Ediciones for Venezuela; by Computer Book & Magazine Store for Puerto Rico; by Express Computer Distributors for the Caribbean and West Indies. Authorized Sales Agent: Anthony Rudkin Associates for the Middle East and North Africa.

For general information on IDG Books Worldwide's books in the U.S., please call our Consumer Customer Service department at 800-762-2974. For reseller information, including discounts and premium sales, please call our Reseller Customer Service department at 800-434-3422.

For information on where to purchase IDG Books Worldwide's books outside the U.S., please contact our International Sales department at 650-655-3200 or fax 650-655-3297.

For information on foreign language translations, please contact our Foreign & Subsidiary Rights department at 650-655-3021 or fax 650-655-3281.

For sales inquiries and special prices for bulk quantities, please contact our Sales department at 650-655-3200 or write to the address above.

For information on using IDG Books Worldwide's books in the classroom or for ordering examination copies, please contact our Educational Sales department at 800-434-2086 or fax 317-596-5499.

For press review copies, author interviews, or other publicity information, please contact our Public Relations department at 650-655-3000 or fax 650-655-3299.

For authorization to photocopy items for corporate, personal, or educational use, please contact Copyright Clearance Center, 222 Rosewood Drive, Danvers, MA 01923, or fax 978-750-4470.

 is a trademark under exclusive license to IDG Books Worldwide, Inc., from International Data Group, Inc.

About the Author

Born in Chicago, **Tom Trinko** has lived a deprived life, never once having butchered a hog. In an attempt to improve the quality of life in Chicago, he pursued his higher education in Pasadena, California, at Cal Tech. He moved to Wisconsin for the better climate and picked up his Ph.D. in physics, graduating with the official title of mad scientist. His first smart move was marrying a woman who worked at Apple and who had an Apple IIe. With that, he was able to extend his professional programming career, which began in 1972, to home computers. His long-suffering wife brought a Mac home in 1984, which marked the start of Tom's enthusiasm for the only OS for people who want to get work done. He's ordered the Mac around in Basic, Forth, C, Pascal, and about a billion or so scripting languages. Back when Apple didn't know any better, he did contract work for Apple's Developer University. In real life, he works on other platforms, ranging from supercomputers to UNIX workstations, which continually remind him of how spiffy the Mac really is. His current main objective in life is staying more computer literate than his kids, at least until they hit 6th grade.

ABOUT IDG BOOKS WORLDWIDE

Welcome to the world of IDG Books Worldwide.

IDG Books Worldwide, Inc., is a subsidiary of International Data Group, the world's largest publisher of computer-related information and the leading global provider of information services on information technology. IDG was founded more than 25 years ago and now employs more than 8,500 people worldwide. IDG publishes more than 275 computer publications in over 75 countries (see listing below). More than 90 million people read one or more IDG publications each month.

Launched in 1990, IDG Books Worldwide is today the #1 publisher of best-selling computer books in the United States. We are proud to have received eight awards from the Computer Press Association in recognition of editorial excellence and three from *Computer Currents'* First Annual Readers' Choice Awards. Our best-selling *...For Dummies*® series has more than 50 million copies in print with translations in 38 languages. IDG Books Worldwide, through a joint venture with IDG's Hi-Tech Beijing, became the first U.S. publisher to publish a computer book in the People's Republic of China. In record time, IDG Books Worldwide has become the first choice for millions of readers around the world who want to learn how to better manage their businesses.

Our mission is simple: Every one of our books is designed to bring extra value and skill-building instructions to the reader. Our books are written by experts who understand and care about our readers. The knowledge base of our editorial staff comes from years of experience in publishing, education, and journalism — experience we use to produce books for the '90s. In short, we care about books, so we attract the best people. We devote special attention to details such as audience, interior design, use of icons, and illustrations. And because we use an efficient process of authoring, editing, and desktop publishing our books electronically, we can spend more time ensuring superior content and spend less time on the technicalities of making books.

You can count on our commitment to deliver high-quality books at competitive prices on topics you want to read about. At IDG Books Worldwide, we continue in the IDG tradition of delivering quality for more than 25 years. You'll find no better book on a subject than one from IDG Books Worldwide.

John J. Kilcullen

John Kilcullen
CEO
IDG Books Worldwide, Inc.

Steven Berkowitz

Steven Berkowitz
President and Publisher
IDG Books Worldwide, Inc.

**Eighth Annual
Computer Press
Awards ➢ 1992**

**Ninth Annual
Computer Press
Awards ➢ 1993**

**Tenth Annual
Computer Press
Awards ➢ 1994**

**Eleventh Annual
Computer Press
Awards ➢ 1995**

Dedication

To God in thanksgiving for my parents who raised me to know what's right and what's wrong; and the best wife, Colleen, and children — Kate, Peter, Ted, Mary, and Therese — imaginable.

Acknowledgments

None. I did it all myself. Just kidding. While I'm the one who got his name on the cover, this book wouldn't have been possible without the work of Tim Gallan, who somehow managed to put up with me while showing me how to write a *Dummies* book. Thanks to Kelly Ewing and Diane Giangrossi for fixing what I laughingly refer to as grammar, and thanks to Don Olson, Mac scripting guru, who hunted through my first draft prose finding my mistakes.

Publisher's Acknowledgments

We're proud of this book; please register your comments through our IDG Books Worldwide Online Registration Form located at http://my2cents.dummies.com.

Some of the people who helped bring this book to market include the following:

Acquisitions, Editorial, and Media Development

Project Editor: Tim Gallan
Acquisitions Assistant: Gareth Hancock
Copy Editors: Kelly Ewing, Diane L. Giangrossi
Technical Reviewer: Donald O. Olson
Editorial Managers: Kristin A. Cocks, Mary C. Corder
Editorial Executive Assistant: Richard Graves
Editorial Assistants: Constance Carlisle, Chris Collins, Stacey Holden Prince, Kevin Spencer

Production

Associate Project Coordinator: J. Tyler Connor
Layout and Graphics: Shawn Aylsworth, Brett Black, Angela F. Hunckler, Todd Klemme, Jill Lyttle, Jane Martin, Laura Puranen, Carla Radzikinas, Gina Scott, Michael Sullivan
Proofreaders: Mary C. Oby, Christine Meloy Beck, Gwenette Gaddis, Dwight Ramsey, Carl Saff
Indexer: Steve Rath

General and Administrative

IDG Books Worldwide, Inc.: John Kilcullen, CEO; Steven Berkowitz, President and Publisher

IDG Books Technology Publishing: Brenda McLaughlin, Senior Vice President and Group Publisher

Dummies Technology Press and Dummies Editorial: Diane Graves Steele, Vice President and Associate Publisher; Mary Bednarek, Director of Acquisitions and Product Development; Kristin A. Cocks, Editorial Director

Dummies Trade Press: Kathleen A. Welton, Vice President and Publisher; Kevin Thornton, Acquisitions Manager

IDG Books Production for Dummies Press: Michael R. Britton, Vice President of Production and Creative Services; Beth Jenkins Roberts, Production Director; Cindy L. Phipps, Manager of Project Coordination, Production Proofreading, and Indexing; Kathie S. Schutte, Supervisor of Page Layout; Shelley Lea, Supervisor of Graphics and Design; Debbie J. Gates, Production Systems Specialist; Robert Springer, Supervisor of Proofreading; Debbie Stailey, Special Projects Coordinator; Tony Augsburger, Supervisor of Reprints and Bluelines

Dummies Packaging and Book Design: Robin Seaman, Creative Director; Jocelyn Kelaita, Product Packaging Coordinator; Kavish + Kavish, Cover Design

◆

The publisher would like to give special thanks to Patrick J. McGovern, without whom this book would not have been possible.

◆

Contents at a Glance

Cartoons at a Glance

By Rich Tennant

page 356

page 1

page 55

page 226

page 7

page 363

page 153

page 290

page 297

page 374

Fax: 978-546-7747 • E-mail: the5wave@tiac.net

Table of Contents

Introduction

W hile the title of this book makes you think that it's about AppleScript, it's really about saving time. Only techno-nerds, several steps below dummies on the evolutionary scale, care about scripting or programming. If you're a techno-nerd, then you should pick up one of those other books. You know, the ones that you have to produce proof of a Ph.D. in rocket science before the bookstore will let you buy them. On the other hand, if you're a normal human being whose idea of fun doesn't consist of spending hours at the keyboard — games are excepted, as even normal folks sometimes get addicted to a good computer game — and you want to discover how to use AppleScript to save lots and lots of time, then this book is for you. You'll discover that with a minimal investment in time and the price of this book, you'll be able to get your Mac to do many useful things that you currently have to spend time doing. As you'll be seeing, AppleScript will let you automate your Mac activities, including automating scriptable applications such as Word and FileMaker Pro.

The 5th Wave   **By Rich Tennant**

IF BOB DYLAN HAD PURSUED A CAREER IN COMPUTERS.

"PUT HIM IN FRONT OF A TERMINAL AND HE'S A GENIUS, BUT OTHER-
WISE THE GUY IS SUCH A BROODING, GLOOMY GUS HE'LL NEVER
BREAK INTO MANAGEMENT."

You'll be able to perform tedious, time-consuming tasks with a single mouse click, or even better, with no mouse click at all!

The bottom line is that AppleScript is programming for the rest of us. Using AppleScript is much easier than using C, just as using a Mac is easier than using Windows 1895, or as using a tax program is easier than filling out the forms with a pen.

Why Should I Spend My Time Reading This Book?

It beats watching TV after all. Well, most of the time. In any case, the real reason is that learning AppleScript will end up saving you time — time you can use to watch even more TV or close that stock deal that'll make Bill Gates look like a pauper. Once you've mastered the relatively simple basics of AppleScript, you'll be able to automate lots of things you now do manually. Let's say you've been surfing the Internet and you've got 600 pages of messages about Albanian pasta-making techniques. Without AppleScript, you've got one option: Read the whole mess in order to find the few messages you want about the proper use of Spotted Owl feathers. With AppleScript, you can write a script that will find the messages of interest and move them to a file or database for you with a single mouse click, or, if you prefer, your script can automatically search the message files when they're created. Or suppose you're worried about getting a repetitive stress injury, and you want to be reminded to take a break every 30 minutes. No problem. A simple script — see Chapter 16 — will fill the bill. The bottom line is that you probably bought a Mac because it was efficient and easy to use. Working with AppleScript will let you improve the Mac in both those areas.

One of the reasons that using AppleScript will save you tons of time is that you can use it to control applications. For example, you can write a script that uses Word or WordPerfect to format a document to a certain style, or you can write a script that automatically loads a bunch of pictures into a FileMaker Pro database. You can write scripts that watch a folder, and when a new picture file shows up there, you can automatically import it into a Photoflash catalog or move it to a "Jobs to work on" folder on another disk. While not all applications are *scriptable,* you'll find that many of the ones you use every day, such as Microsoft Word, WordPerfect, FileMaker Pro, and Microsoft Excel, can be controlled from AppleScript. Take a look at the list of scriptable applications in Chapter 27 to see if the applications you use every day are scriptable. If they are, you'll probably be able to save yourself a lot of drudgery. If they aren't, there's still hope because you can use nonscriptable applications with AppleScript using the techniques shown in Chapters 25 and 26.

scriptable: This doesn't mean that an application would make a good movie. It just means that the application was designed so that you have at least some control over the application from inside an AppleScript script. The amount of control and its ease of use can vary widely among applications, so just knowing that an application is scriptable doesn't necessarily tell you how useful it'll be.

The Finder is also scriptable — all of the examples will assume you have System 7.5 although some earlier versions are scriptable, which means that you can do all sorts of useful things. How about a script that backs up selected files at an interval you can define, or would you prefer a script that tells you at a glance how much free space you have on all your hard disks? You'll be able to develop scripts like these by the time you've finished this book.

The bottom line is that AppleScript is a tool that makes it easier and more fun to use the Mac because you'll be able to have the Mac do more of the dull, uninteresting but necessary tasks while you can concentrate on what you do best: being creative.

How to Use This Book

Well, if you've got a stack of papers that tends to get blown around by the wind, you can put this book on top of them to keep them in place, or if you've got a door that just won't stay open, you can wedge this book under the door, or best of all, if you've always wanted to get in the *Guinness Book of World Records,* you can buy 13,000 copies of this book and build a house out of them.

On the other hand, if you want to be a bit staid, you can read Part I of this book to get a feel for what scripting is all about. Then skim through Part II to get a feel for how the language works. If you've programmed before, the concepts should be familiar. Even if you've never written as much as a HyperTalk script for HyperCard before, the fact that AppleScript reads a lot like English makes it easy to get a general understanding of how AppleScript works. The objective of Part II is to provide an understanding so that you know where to look for more information when you encounter the various example scripts.

With Part II under your belt, take a swim through Part III and concentrate on those applications that are of interest to you. This part will give you a feel for what you can and can't do with scripting. Armed with that knowledge, you should think of some task that you'd like to automate with a script. Start following the development approach you will read about in Chapter 3. As you go, you'll find you need to get more detail on some aspects of AppleScript. That's the time to go back and read the relevant chapters of Parts II and III in more detail.

My experience with scripting and a number of other programming languages is that when you start off, what's important is that you know what the language can do, not that you have every nuance of the language's syntax memorized. For example, it's important to know that in AppleScript if you want to do something multiple times, you use the **repeat** statement. It's not important that you remember off the top of your head all of the variations on the **repeat** statement *syntax*. As long as you know the name of the statement you need, you can look it up quickly — try the table of contents and then the index, as all commands are listed in one or both — and find out how to use it. After you've done this a time or two, you'll find that you remember the right way to use the feature and you won't have to jump back to the book anymore. The book is also structured to make it easy to use it as a reference to find obscure syntax information after you've become proficient.

syntax: This isn't a new tariff on beer. It's just the way things need to be said for AppleScript to understand them. If you don't use the proper syntax when writing instructions for your Mac, which is all scripting is, it won't understand what you want it to do.

Another way to become a proficient scripter is to enter the various sample scripts in Part II and run them. This approach will work, too, but you'll spend a lot more time before you get around to working on a script that you can actually use. In addition, because AppleScript has so many features, you'll probably find that you only use a small fraction of the stuff that's covered in Part II in any given script. As a result, you might find that you spend a lot of time working through examples of features you don't use.

You should take the path that best suits your learning style. If you're the type who likes to memorize things and then use them, feel free to do so. If your experience shows that you learn best by working hands-on as you read about things, then type in all of the examples and run them. The objective is to learn to script, not follow some arcane approach that isn't right for you. In any case, this book is structured so that you can quickly find details on pretty much everything in AppleScript in Part II. Use that section as your reference as you embark on your scripting journey.

What I Expect You Already Know and Have

You know how to use a Mac

You ought to know little things like how to launch an application (double-click), how to navigate through folders, how to open a control panel, how to pick a file from the Open dialog box, how to save a file using the Save dialog box, and how to patch the GetNextEvent trap in order to override the basic event-handling behavior. Just kidding on that last one. After all, you know that you should really patch WaitNextEvent. If you're not familiar with the basic stuff, you should get David Pogue's *Macs For Dummies* to get a quick, easy-to-understand course in the basics of the Mac world.

You're not a hacker

I refuse to be held legally liable if, after reading this book, you develop a script that destroys the financial records of all of the world's banks, which results in worldwide chaos, war, famine, and plague. On the other hand, if you develop a script that turns you into the ruler of the world, and Bill Gates is willing to relinquish the position without violence, I wouldn't mind a small fiefdom — say Asia.

You have AppleScript

AppleScript comes free with System 7.5. You may have gotten AppleScript some other way. AppleScript itself will work with System 7 or later. While you can read this book without having AppleScript, you'll get the most out of it if you either script along with the book (sorta like those old sing-alongs they had at the movies where you'd follow the bouncing ball) or start working on your own scripts after skimming through the book. Another very useful part of System 7.5 is the scriptable Finder, which lets you use AppleScript to control things the Finder does, such as set the color depth of monitors, move files, delete files, and that sort of stuff. You can read this book and learn about AppleScript without having the scriptable Finder, but you'll be missing a lot of really nifty capabilities that can save you time. I strongly recommend getting System 7.5 if you want to do a lot of scripting. It's possible to add some scripting support to Systems 7.1 and 7.1Pro, but I don't cover that stuff in this book.

You know what a path to a file looks like

You might not know about this stuff. Actually, unless you've programmed, you probably have never had any need to think about paths, but you can represent a file's location on your hard disk with some text. It looks like this:

```
disk name:folder name:another folder name:the file name
```

So if you've got a file called *letter,* which is inside a folder called *work,* which is in turn inside a folder called *important stuff,* which is inside a folder called *back this up every day,* which is on a hard disk called *Volcano,* then its path string would be

```
Volcano:back this up every day:important stuff:work:letter
```

Paths to folders always end with a colon, so the path to folder *important stuff* would be

```
Volcano:back this up every day:important stuff:
```

You need to know about paths because you'll often use path strings when you're working with files in AppleScript, especially if you're not using the scriptable Finder, which is discussed in Chapter 22. By the way, if you hold the Command key — the one with the Apple outline on it and a little pretzel — and hold the mouse button down on the name at the top of a folder's window, you'll see the full path for the folder as a list.

What the Silly Little Pictures Mean

This icon flags juicy bits of information, usually shortcuts and other tricks, that will save you time and make life easier.

When you see this icon, know that I am flagging something you ought to read and file away in your brain for future reference.

I use this icon to point out information that might be considered too technical for the average reader. You can skip over this stuff if you are so inclined.

This icon lets you know that I'll be defining some cryptic piece of jargon in ways that will make things easier for you to understand.

To indicate that there's danger afoot, I use this icon.

One Last Thing

When you see this thing `- ->` in a script, it indicates that the script line on the left-hand side of this symbol returns the value on the right-hand side of this symbol. Take a look at the following example:

```
round 3.1415 --> 3
```

In this case, applying the round command to the number 3.1415 results in the number 3. The `- ->` symbol isn't part of the script, but if you leave it in, the script will still work.

Part I
Getting Started

In this part . . .

*T*his part will introduce you to the wonderful world of
automation via AppleScript. You'll see some examples,
write your first script, and learn how to use the free Script
Editor that comes with AppleScript. You'll also discover a
process that will help you write efficient scripts that'll save
you time.

Chapter 1

A Cannonball Dive into the Scripting Pool

Writing Your First Script

Lots of things that seem tough aren't. Nonetheless, we tend to worry about how hard something is until we do it for the first time. So now I'll show you how to write your first script. Once you see how easy it is to write a script, you'll be better able to put the rest of the book in perspective. Remember, writing a script is just telling the computer what to do in writing rather than by using a mouse.

1. **Launch the Script Editor by double-clicking on its icon, which is shown in Figure 1-1.**

   If you don't have the Script Editor, check Chapter 28 to find out where you can get it.

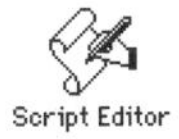

Figure 1-1:
The Script
Editor icon. Script Editor

2. Type what I'm about to tell you into the script window called "untitled."

Because this is your first script, let's make it nice and easy. Just type the following line into the lower window, as shown in Figure 1-2.

```
display dialog "Hello AppleScript Genius!"
```

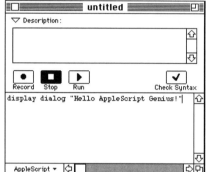

Figure 1-2:
Typing a
simple
script.

Even though you may have never used AppleScript before, I bet you've got a good idea of what this script is going to do, don't you? That's because AppleScript reads a lot like good old English, and I don't mean Shakespeare. So when you run into some complex script, just take a deep breath and say, "It's like English. It's like English." If you want to see how the script works in detail, just read the following discussion. By the way, if the fonts and sizes look different in your version, don't panic. They can be customized, as is discussed in Chapter 3.

The first, and in this case only, script line

```
display dialog "Hello AppleScript Genius!"
```

It turns out that **display dialog** is an AppleScript command that tells AppleScript to put up a fairly standard — albeit highly customizable, as you'll see in the next example — dialog box. The quote — called a string in AppleScript — that follows the display dialog command is the message that appears in the dialog. Figure 1-4 shows the dialog that results from AppleScript running this script line.

Once you've typed the script in, click the Check Syntax button, which *compiles* your script. In case you're worried, this doesn't mean you're voting to raise taxes on beer and wine. When you click on this button, AppleScript reads what

you typed and checks to make sure it understands it. If you made a mistake —
not that you the customer ever does, mind you — you'd get a little dialog telling
you that there was a problem. If you get such a message, just retype the script
from scratch.

When you get more experienced, you'll be able to figure out what part of a line
might be causing a problem, so you won't have to retype a whole line.

If AppleScript understands what you typed, it reformats the script slightly,
using a different font size, as shown in Figure 1-3.

Notice that the Check Syntax button is dimmed, which indicates that
AppleScript has read the script and understands it.

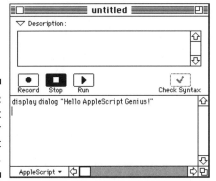

Figure 1-3:
Your script
after
AppleScript
reads it.

Just because AppleScript understands a script *doesn't mean* that the script will
do what you want it to. If you mistakenly tell the script to delete all of your files,
but you enter it correctly so that AppleScript understands it, then AppleScript
will acknowledge that it understands your script even though you told it the
wrong thing to do. AppleScript doesn't know what you want, only what you
typed.

All you have to do to run your script is to click on the Run button. AppleScript
will display the dialog shown in Figure 1-4.

Figure 1-4:
Welcome to
the world of
scripting.

> Hello AppleScript Genius!
>
> Cancel   OK

compile: This term doesn't refer to building an evidentiary base so that you can sue your neighbor for letting his dog eat your geraniums. When you click on the Check Syntax button, AppleScript compiles your script into something that the Mac can understand. Computers are nice, friendly creatures, but they're pretty deficient in the language arts. They understand 0s and 1s. In the early days of computers, people had to speak the computer's language in order for the computer to understand what the heck they wanted. That's why old programmers — those over 30 — like to speak in terms of hex numbers — base 16, not witchcraft — or binary numbers — 0 or 1. The closest most people get to that these days is Windows. Just kidding. Anyway, when AppleScript compiles your script, it makes a version of it, which you don't see, that's in a language your friendly but linguistically challenged Mac can handle. Unfortunately, AppleScript can't make the Mac understand what you meant when you typed something incorrectly just by raising the speaker volume.

You can display different messages by changing the text in your script that appears between the two quote marks. Pretty straightforward stuff, isn't it?

Writing a Second (and Even Better) Script

Now let's take on a fairly complex script. You'll see that because scripts look a lot like English, you can understand what they do. It'll take awhile, and reading the next part of this book, before you can write your own script, but you'll find that you don't need to be intimidated by scripts. With a little effort, you can understand what the script is doing even if you couldn't have written the script yourself.

One of the best ways to increase productivity is to start with a script someone else has done and modify it. You'll find that various computer services — see Chapter 24 for a list of resources — have example scripts online. In addition, System 7.5 comes with a bunch of scripts, called *Automated Tasks,* that are installed in the same folder as the Script Editor when you install System 7.5. You'll find that even if you're not 100 percent sure of why a script works in a certain way, you'll be able to understand enough to modify it to do what you want. This method of scripting saves you time and effort.

This next script is a slightly more sophisticated version of our first "Hello AppleScript" script. Follow the same procedure to enter it as you did before, making sure you press the Return key or put a ¬ character at the end of each line. When you're done, it should look like Figure 1-5 before you click on the Check Syntax button and like Figure 1-6 after you click that button. If you get an error message telling you that AppleScript doesn't understand something, compare what you've typed with the script shown below. One common mistake is to press Return rather than Option Return inside a script line. You can check for that mistake by making sure that the funny ¬ characters in your copy are in the same places as in the sample script.

The ¬ character, called a soft return in the trade, tells AppleScript to treat the stuff on the next line as though it were part of the current line. It's a carriage return for you but a nothing for AppleScript when it reads the line. You don't need to use the ¬ symbol; you can just use wide windows or the scroll bar. I'm using it in this book so that long script lines don't require a 15-inch page. You get the ¬ by holding down the Option key and pressing the Return key.

```
set user_stuff to display dialog ¬
    "My name is AppleScript. What's yours?" default answer ¬
    "Who Knows" buttons {"Buzz off", "Hi"} default button "Hi"
set button_name to button returned of user_stuff
if button_name is "Hi" then
    set your_name to text returned of user_stuff
    display dialog "Welcome to AppleScript, soon to be Dr. " & your_name & ¬
        ", expert AppleScript genius." buttons {"Howdy"} default button "Howdy"
else
    display dialog "Sorry you don't want to be friends." buttons {"For sure"} ¬
        default button "For sure"
end if
```

If you put a ¬ inside a quote, a *string* for you technical types, everything will work, but the ¬ will show up when the text is displayed, which probably isn't what you want. So avoid putting an ¬ inside a quote for aesthetic reasons.

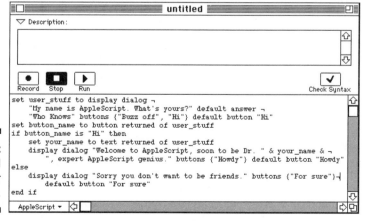

Figure 1-5:
Your second
script after
it's typed in.

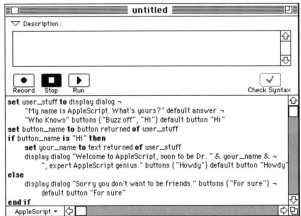

Figure 1-6:
Your script
after it's
been
compiled.

I bet by just reading through this script, you've got a fairly good idea of what it does. If you're not 100 percent sure, take a stroll through the following detailed, line-by-line description.

Line 1

```
set user_stuff to display dialog ¬
   "My name is AppleScript. What's yours?" default answer ¬
   "Who Knows" buttons {"Buzz off", "Hi"} default button "Hi"
```

The first thing to remember is that this is all one line as far as AppleScript is concerned because even though it is on three lines, the first two lines end with ¬, which AppleScript ignores. This line is just a slightly more complicated version of the **display dialog** command you saw in your first script. Ignore the "**set** user_stuff **to**" for a moment. The first item after the display dialog is a quote — "My name is AppleScript. What's yours?" — which will get displayed in the dialog just as the "Hello AppleScript Genius!" line was displayed in your first script.

The **default answer** phrase tells AppleScript that you want the user to be able to enter a response of some sort. The quote that follows **default answer**, "Who Knows," will be displayed to the user as the default value that will be used if the user doesn't enter anything.

The **buttons** word tells AppleScript to put two buttons in the dialog: one labeled "Buzz off" and the other labeled "Hi." Just as the **default answer** uses a quote as input, **buttons** uses a list —discussed in Chapter 4 — which is just two curly brackets with some items in the middle separated by commas. If you want to be creative, you can have three buttons by just adding another item to the list. The

default button phrase tells AppleScript to make the button labeled "Hi" the default button. In the Mac world, the default button is the one with the extra-wide border, as shown in Figure 1-7. A default button acts as though it was clicked if you press the Return or Enter key. If you want to see what the dialog box looks like, jump ahead to Figure 1-9.

Figure 1-7:
A default
button.

Bet you didn't forget about the "**set** user_stuff **to**" part, did you? Bet you thought I did, though. First thing to realize is that when AppleScript sees something like

```
set x to y
```

it sets the value of **x** to whatever the value of **y** is. So the line

```
set x to 2
```

will set the value of the variable **x** to 2. (See Chapter 5 for more information on variables.) Variables in AppleScript are just named places to store stuff such as numbers and words that you want to use later on in a script.

OK, so our script is trying to set the value of the variable **user_stuff**. But how do you stuff a dialog into a variable? The answer is that many AppleScript commands return a value. Here's the way it works:

1. AppleScript will display the dialog from Figure 1-9.

2. The user can enter a value and click on one of the buttons.

3. The **display dialog** command builds a value that it returns. Lets call it *the result.*

4. AppleScript puts that value into the script where the **display dialog** is, so the line looks like

```
set user_stuff to the_result
```

5. AppleScript sets the value of **user_stuff** to whatever **display dialog** returned.

The next question that's probably running, uncontrolled, through your mind is what in the heck does that dialog return? Well, stay tuned for the next thrilling episode . . . oops, wrong medium. The answer is that the **display dialog** returns a list of things that have to do with what the user did.

Actually, the **display dialog** returns a record. The difference is that the items in a record have names while those in a list don't. For more on the differences, take a gander at Chapter 4 or just read it if you don't have a goose.

If the user clicks on the button labeled "Hi," the record looks like this:

```
{text returned:"Who Knows", button returned:"Hi"}
```

Each item in this record is separated from the other by a comma. The record is bounded by those funny parentheses-like things — {}. A record item is made up of two pieces separated by a colon. The first piece is a name by which you can access the value, and the second piece is the value. The next line shows you how to access items in a record by name.

Line 2

```
set button_name to button returned of user_stuff
```

This line sets the value of the local variable called **button_name** to the value associated with the name *button returned* in the variable **user_stuff**. Remember that the value of **user_stuff** looks like this:

```
{text returned:"Who Knows", button returned:"Hi"}
```

So if the user clicked the "Hi" button, then AppleScript will do the following:

1. Figure out what value in **user_stuff** is associated with the label *button returned.*

2. Set the value of the variable called **button_name** to that value.

If there was no label *button returned,* or if I'd misspelled it when I typed it in, I'd get an error message and AppleScript would tell me there was a problem.

Line 3

```
if button_name is "Hi" then
```

This line introduces a couple of concepts. The first is fairly clear. The script is checking to see if the value of the variable **button_name** is "Hi." If it is, what then? Well, then the script will do something. But what? Figuring out what the script will do requires you to know the full form of an **if** statement. A full-blown, ultra spiffy **if** looks like this:

```
if something then
    some script lines (A)
else
    some other script lines (B)
end if
```

Before trying to go through this in detail, let's translate this into its English equivalent:

```
if something is true then execute the script lines labeled A.
if something is false then execute the script lines labeled B.
```

What is truth? While that's a toughie in real life, in AppleScript, it's fairly easy. Things like 2 < 5 — 2 is less than 5 — are true while things like 18 > 54 are false.

An **if** statement checks some value or expression and sees if it's true. If it is, then the **if** executes the script lines you've associated with that condition. If there's an **else** clause and the value or expression being tested is false, then the script lines associated with the **else** clause are executed. You use **if** statements in your scripts to make decisions based on user actions or other events that you can't predict when you write the script.

To recap: If the item right after the **if** evaluates to true, then the script lines between the **if** line and the **else** line are executed by AppleScript. If the item right after the **if** evaluates to false and there is an **else** statement, then the lines between the **else** statement and the **end if** statement are executed.

Line 4

```
set your_name to text returned of user_stuff
```

This line is only executed if the value of the variable called **button_name** is "Hi." If the user clicks on the "Hi" button, the script assumes that he or she has entered a name in the edit field replacing the default answer of "Who Knows." Not surprisingly, the value in that edit field is stored in an element of the record called "text returned" — as in "the text returned by this dialog." Line four just takes the value of the text that the user entered and puts it into the variable called **user_stuff**.

Give variables names you understand.

Even though it might result in a little bit more typing, you'll find that you save time if you give variables names that reflect their contents. Check out Chapter 5 for tons of info on naming variables, but trust me, I know what I'm doing when I say that variable names that mean something will save you time — time that you can use to earn money to buy my next book!

Line 5

```
display dialog "Welcome to AppleScript, soon to be Dr. " & your_name & ¬
    ", expert AppleScript genius." buttons {"Howdy"} default button "Howdy"
```

Like the fourth line, this line is only executed if the user clicks on the button labeled "Hi" because that's the only time that the variable **button_name** will have the value of "Hi." By now you're probably an expert on the **display dialog** command, so I won't go over the obvious things; however, you might be wondering about that funny **&** character. Is it a typo? Is it a printing error? Is it an alien being spying on you? The actual explanation is much more mundane. The **&** just appends one quote to another. For example, when AppleScript executes this line

```
set a_sentence to "This is the first " & " sentence here."
```

the value of the variable **a_sentence** is set to

```
"This is the first sentence here."
```

If either or both of the values on either side of the **&** are variables, AppleScript replaces the variable with its value and then appends it. So this script

```
set part_1 to "To be or not to be "
set part_2 to "that is the question."
set line_1 to part_1 & part_2
```

sets the value of **line_1** to "To be or not to be that is the question."

Using this character allows you to show the user a dialog personalized with his or her own name. Feel free to skip ahead for a second to look at Figure 1-9.

Line 6

```
else
```

This line just serves to separate the script lines that are executed if the value of **button_name** is "Hi" from the script lines that are only executed if the value of the variable **button_name** isn't "Hi."

Line 7

```
display dialog "Sorry you don't want to be friends." buttons {"For sure"} ¬
    default button "For sure"
```

Another fun-filled display dialog command. Nothing exciting here, but you should note that even if you've only got one button, it doesn't automatically become the default button. You've got to use the **default button** option to make one of the dialog buttons the default if you use the **buttons** option. If you don't do that, then the dialog won't have any default button.

Line 8

```
end if
```

This line just marks the end of the **if** statement and the end of the script lines that will be executed if the user doesn't click on the button labeled "Hi."

Now that you understand what the script is supposed to do, it's a good time to save the script.

Saving Your Work

AppleScript is a pretty stable tool. You have to work pretty hard to come up with a script that can crash your Mac and bring up the dreaded Bomb dialog box. However, it does happen, usually when you're working with other applications, so you should save your scripts once in awhile. It turns out that there are several options for saving a script, all of which are discussed in Chapter 3, but for right now, you can just use the Save command in the Script Editor's File menu. You'll get a fairly standard Mac Save dialog box, as shown in Figure 1-8.

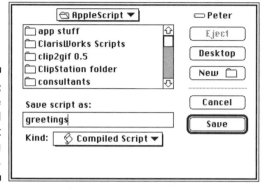

Figure 1-8:
The standard AppleScript Save dialog box.

You can just ignore the Kind pop-up menu at the bottom because the default selection is what you want. If your script has a problem, though (you get an error message when you click on the Check Syntax button), AppleScript can't save your script as a compiled script. To find out what to do when that happens, see Chapter 18. For right now, though, if you get an error, compare what you've typed to what's in Figure 1-5 and correct any differences, no matter how insignificant they may seem. Be especially sure that you've got those funny Option Return characters ¬ where they're supposed to be.

After you save your script, you're ready to run it.

Running Your Script

Running or executing a script just means that AppleScript follows the instructions you wrote down.

Once AppleScript says your script is A-OK, it's time to run the script by clicking on the Run button on the left side of the script window. The first thing you see is the window in Figure 1-9.

Figure 1-9:
Starting a conversation.

My name is AppleScript. What's yours?

Who Knows

Buzz off   Hi

Just because AppleScript understands, it doesn't mean it's right.

Never forget that computers don't think. They just follow instructions. So just because Apple-Script can understand what you type doesn't mean that a script will do what you want. If you have a script that's supposed to delete all files containing the word "old" but you accidentally type the string "new" into the script, AppleScript will understand what you typed and cheerfully delete all files containing the word "new," even though that script deletes ten years of work.

In addition, some types of errors don't show up until you actually try to run a script. Suppose your script is supposed to move files from one place to another, and you put in a nice way to pick the files to move. AppleScript has no way to determine that the files you'll pick in the future, when you run the script, will be available. As a result, you could run the script and get an error even though AppleScript "understood" what you said.

The bottom line is that just because you don't get an error message when you click on the Check Syntax button doesn't mean your script will do what you want.

Because there are two buttons in this dialog box, the script has to be able to deal with two possible user responses. That's why the **if** statement is in there. Of course, if you want the script to respond the same way to the user pushing either button, you can, but I'd be hard pressed to figure out a response that was equally appropriate for both "Hi" and "Buzz off." Because the script checks what button you click on when you click on the "Hi" button, you see the dialog box in Figure 1-10, while if you click on the "Buzz off" button, you get the dialog box in Figure 1-11.

Figure 1-10:
The script is friendly if you are.

> Welcome to AppleScript, soon to be Dr. Who Knows, expert AppleScript genius.
>
> [Howdy]

Figure 1-11:
You've hurt its feelings, you wretch!

> Sorry you don't want to be friends.
>
> [For sure]

I originally arranged it so that if you hit the "Buzz off" button, your Mac would explode, leveling a three-block radius, but IDG told me that would raise their insurance rates. I told them that the book told you that we weren't liable for anything the scripts do, but for some reason, the folks at IDG still weren't enthused. So my attempt to rid the world of unfriendly people was temporarily stymied.

While this script doesn't do very much, it does illustrate how easy it is to build a script whose behavior can be tailored to user inputs. Much more complex user input can be implemented by just asking the user more questions. But most of all, if you've entered the script, you now are halfway to being a proficient scripter because you know the basic mechanics of how to use Script Editor. You'll find a lot more detail in Chapter 3, but right now, you know enough to enter, save, and run scripts. All that's left is to learn a bit of the AppleScript language, which is a lot like English, and you'll be all set.

Oh yeah, one other thing: While I ran these scripts from inside the Script Editor, you can save scripts as applications that you can run by double-clicking on their icons, just like any other application. You'll see how to do that in Chapter 3.

Chapter 2

AppleScript Basics without Stomach Acid

What Is Scripting? What If Your Penmanship Is Poor?

A common question I hear is why is this AppleScript stuff called scripting? The answer is unclear, but my personal guess is that it was a marketing ploy to keep people from thinking about programming. While real people tend to think of programming as some arcane ritual, masterable only by nerds, it's really just a way to tell the computer what to do. Unfortunately, telling a computer what to do can be very, very complex. It requires lots of training due to the poor quality of tools available and the wide spectrum of capabilities that have to be controlled — everything from CD-ROMs to files. Fortunately, Apple has been at the forefront of developing technologies, first *HyperCard* and now AppleScript, that make it easier to tell computers what to do.

HyperCard is a nifty application that makes it fairly easy to develop applications without having to know much about programming. While it used to be bundled free with every Mac, you have to shell out $99 for it these days. While you could originally script HyperCard in, yes, you guessed it, HyperTalk, you can now also script it with AppleScript. See Chapter 26 for more info on how to use HyperCard with your scripts.

Think of your Mac as your servant, a very efficient, very fast, but not too bright aide-de-camp who really wants to make your life nicer. All you have to do is tell it what to do in a very simple language that it can understand: AppleScript.

The Mac is very nifty — way cool for those under 30 — but it can't yet read your mind. So you have to tell it what to do. Of course, you already do that. After all, what is clicking on menu items or dragging files around with the mouse but telling the Mac what to do? AppleScript makes life nicer by letting you tell the computer once, by writing a script, rather than by pointing and clicking with the mouse every time you want to do something.

That's really all there is to scripting — writing a set of instructions for the Mac. Imagine sending a friend a set of directions to your house or telling someone over the phone how to do something in MacWrite Pro. In order to write a script, you just set those same instructions down in AppleScript. After you've got the instructions down so that your Mac can understand them, you can have the Mac follow them any number of times. Think of scripts as add-on smarts for your Mac that let your Mac do the tasks that you want it to, when you want it to, and how you want it to.

AppleEvents Aren't Just Parties Anymore!

You may or may not have ever heard of AppleEvents, but they're critical to the success of AppleScript. The good news is that while the details of AppleEvents and the Object Model are fairly complex, Apple has succeeded in hiding all of that nasty stuff from you. In fact, you can spend your whole scripting life without ever once using either term. However, having at least a vague idea of what these terms mean will give you an understanding of how AppleScript works its magic.

AppleEvents are just messages that are sent from one Mac application to another.

Yep, that's all they are. The bad news is that just as you need to wire your house for cable, application developers have to work to make their programs support AppleEvents. If they don't spend the time, then their applications won't be able to send or respond to AppleEvents. Such applications aren't control-lable from AppleScript scripts — but see Chapter 25 for a high-tech note on how to work around this obstacle.

To make life more exciting, not all scriptable applications are the same. Some support only the four basic messages — Open, Print, Quit, and Run — which is essentially the same as not being scriptable because you don't have any real control over what the application does. Other applications are so scriptable that you can change their basic behavior through scripts.

Levels of Scripting

There are four officially — at least by the one person I talked to at Apple — recognized levels of AppleScript support:

- **Scriptable:** This term covers any program that has some level of support for AppleEvents.

- **Recordable:** These applications let AppleScript automatically build a script by watching you work. It performs this feat by watching the AppleEvents generated by your actions — selecting a menu item, using the keyboard, and so on — and translating them into AppleScript commands by using the applications dictionary.

- **Attachable:** These fine examples of advanced software engineering let you attach scripts to various items in the program. For example, Symantec C++ has a special script menu that contains scripts you put into a specified folder.

- **Tinkerable:** These applications are few and far between, but they go one step beyond attachable by letting you change the basic way the program behaves with a script. For example, if you don't like the way a certain menu command works in a tinkerable program, you can write a script that replaces the default action of that menu item with the action you want to perform. HyperCard 2.2 or higher and FaceSpan are examples of tinkerable programs.

Fortunately, it's easy to tell if an application is scriptable. In fact, in Chapter 22, you'll see a little script that will search out all the scriptable applications on your computer's hard disk. A less-automated approach is to use the Script Editor to look for applications with *dictionaries*. Just go to the File menu in Script Editor and select the Open Dictionary command. You'll get a standard file picking dialog box. Select the application you're interested in. If it's scriptable, a window will pop up with a bunch of dictionary entries, as shown in Figure 2-1. If the application isn't scriptable, you'll get a dialog box, shown in Figure 2-2, telling you so.

A *dictionary* is a description of the commands that a program responds to and the types of values, such as words or paragraphs, that it understands. Dictionaries are discussed in detail in Chapter 17. Webster's dictionary won't be covered here.

Just because an application is scriptable doesn't mean you'll be able to use it in your scripts. Some scriptable applications have so few scripting commands that they're not really very useful. If you need to work with an application that isn't scriptable or doesn't give you enough commands to be useful, check out Chapters 25 and 26 for ways to work around these limitations.

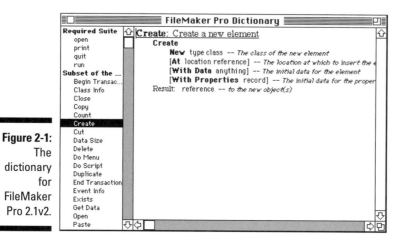

Figure 2-1:
The
dictionary
for
FileMaker
Pro 2.1v2.

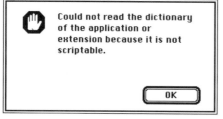

Figure 2-2:
This
application
isn't
scriptable.

Now that you know about scriptability and Apple Events, what about that *Object Model* I mentioned? Well first off, it's not some lawyer's ideal. No, the Object Model is a way to define information in a modular manner. You've probably used the Object Model many times in everyday life. That's right, even if you've never used a single script, you've probably used something very much like the Object Model. Let me give you an example: You've probably said something like, "Look at the second paragraph in that article" or "The second word in that paragraph is misspelled." Both of these statements represent information in a modular, container-oriented fashion. In the first example, an article — one type of object — contains paragraphs — another kind of object. In the second example, a paragraph contains words.

An application doesn't have to implement the Object Model in order to be scriptable, nor is the definition of the Object Model so precise that you can define a "correct" implementation of the Object Model for a given application. In fact, you'll find that you never really have to worry about the Object Model. What you will care about, and what is discussed more in Chapter 17, is whether an application defines enough information objects to let you script it effectively. A word processor without a word or paragraph object would be a bit tough to work with.

Object Model: This term is Apple's way of defining information in a modular manner to facilitate the interchange and manipulation of data. Applications can implement the Object Model by defining different information objects. Words, paragraphs, documents, cells, and records are all examples of typical objects that an application can define. Objects can contain other objects, as paragraphs contain words, and objects can have characteristics, called attributes, which can be read or set. For example, a paragraph may have an attribute for its style — bold, underlined, italic, and so on — which can be set from a script. A field object in a database might have an attribute called *editable,* which can be set to true (if the user can change the value in the field) or false (if the user can't edit the field).

What Can I Do with a Script?

Make a movie. Of course, if you don't have $120,000,000 lying around to finance a big-screen extravaganza, you can settle for saving time by automating things you currently do manually.

Writing a script is just telling your Mac what to do with words instead of by moving and clicking the mouse. You might tell a coworker what job needs to be done verbally — that's like using the mouse on your Mac — or you might write him or her a note — probably e-mail these days — and that's like using AppleScript. AppleScript is just a really simple language that your Mac can understand.

AppleScript itself is not very powerful. That's not a *bug;* it's a feature! AppleScript was designed to be the glue to control and integrate the activities of various Mac applications, including the Finder.

bug: This is computerese for a problem in a piece of software or a script.

This is one of the most forgotten Mac facts. The Finder is just another application, like Excel or Word 6.0 . . . well, like Word 6.0 if it'd been done right.

Because AppleScript lets you control applications, you can do all sorts of neat automation with very little AppleScript experience, as you'll see in Part III. But right now, you're just a beginner, so what can you do? Well, let's see: Selecting, sorting, and printing records in a FileMaker Pro database only takes six lines of AppleScript, which you can handle. Changing the number of colors your monitor is set to is also really easy if you have the scriptable Finder and takes only these three script lines:

```
tell application "Finder"
    set monitor depth 8
end tell
```

Pretty easy to read, right? Since the Finder is responsible for the Monitors control panel, you tell the Finder — which is an application just like Word or Excel — to set the monitor depth to 8 bits, which is 256 colors. If you wanted black and white instead, just switch the 8 to a 1. Chapter 22 will show you how to do lots of things like this with the Finder. One last simple example: You'll see in Chapter 16 that it's very easy to make a script that wakes up every 15 minutes and warns you to take a break so that you don't come down with repetitive stress injuries (RSI). Now you could spend $30–$50 for a commercial product, or you can spend 15 minutes writing yourself a script — less if you just copy it from Chapter 16.

The bottom line is that even with very little scripting experience, you'll be able to write scripts that will save you time and make your life a little bit better unless, of course, you like doing mindless and repetitive tasks on the Mac.

What Can a Real Expert — You with a Few Months' Experience — Do with a Script?

Just about anything. Well, almost. You can write a script that uses SITcomm to download interesting news files from an information service such as GEnie or CompuServe, use MacWrite Pro to find articles with interesting text, copy those articles to a FileMaker Pro database and/or a QuarkXPress document, which will print a personal newspaper for you. If you want, you can set up this procedure as a self-running script that runs every morning when you boot your computer, or at a specified time if you leave your computer on. If you're interested in the Internet, you can write a script that automatically gets your mail and indexes all of the various mail. At work, you can write scripts to check to see if new images have shown up in certain folders, and if they have, you could add them to a PhotoFlash image directory. You can write an automatic backup program that finds files you've created or modified each day and copies them to a server when you shut down your computer.

As you can see, scripting can become very complex and extremely powerful. But even then, scripting is a zillion times easier than writing C code. The more experienced you become, the more useful and powerful your scripts can be.

Chapter 3

How to Write a Script without Ink

In This Chapter

▶ A seven-step process for writing scripts

▶ The Script Editor, Apple's free scripting application

▶ An example of how easy it is to control applications with AppleScript

The Path toward a Script

Just like anything else you do in life, it helps to have a plan for developing a script. When you're cooking a meal you follow a recipe. When you write a script, you follow a similar set of steps. It's a lot like writing a letter — or in this day and age, sending a fax or an e-mail. The process has a beginning in which you decide what you want to write, a middle where you actually write and edit the message, and an end in which you send the missive off. In both the scripting and cooking cases, when you first start out, you find it beneficial to follow the plan fairly closely. However, as you become more proficient, you start taking shortcuts and developing your own style. For simple scripts, the plan is easy enough to do on the fly, but for complex scripts, you'll discover that spending a little time thinking about what you're going to do is beneficial.

So what plan — called a *software development methodology* by software aficionados — is best for AppleScript? To be honest, neither I nor anyone else knows. Every 27 seconds, some professor somewhere comes up with a new way to develop software. These ideas range from the obvious to the obviously obtuse, and they're all the best for someone — often only the professor who thought them up, however.

As a result of the lack of a good way to define "best," I'm going to show you how I write scripts. The process I use works well, it's fairly general, it's in synch with the lessons folks have discovered over the last 30 years about writing software, and, perhaps most important, it's fairly commonsensical. But because my process is not mathematically proven to be optimal, guaranteed to prevent all problems, certified by the AMA, approved by nine out of eight scripters, and endorsed by a recipient of the Nobel prize for software kinda thing, you should feel free to modify it to fit your style as you become more proficient with scripting.

The plan has seven steps — which probably take more time to describe than to actually do — but bear with me for a moment in order to save a ton of time later. The steps are, in a very particular order:

1. **Figure out what you want to do.**
2. **Decide if it's doable.**
3. **Figure out how you're going to do it.**
4. **Write the script.**
5. **Test the script.**
6. **Fix the script.**
7. **Document the script.**

Let's take a quick tour of how this works. Let's start at the first step — a novel concept — and figure out what you want the script to do.

Step 1: Figure out what you want to do

This step usually starts out as a problem in your Mac life. Something you want to do on the Mac is too boring or too time-consuming, so you think, "Perhaps I can improve my life, get a date with the woman/man of my dreams, get rich, take over the company, be elected president, and win the Nobel peace prize if I only had the time I now waste on this dull, boring, and repetitious task." At this point, you've defined a problem and your not-overly ambitious objectives. For the sake of this little walk-through, I'm assuming that you've got a bunch of text files and you want to extract from them the parts that are of interest to you. The files can be downloads from Internet newsgroups, corporate reports, or an online Bible — it really doesn't matter (in terms of the script, that is). You can manually read page after page of text looking for the stuff that interests you, or you can write a script that finds what you want and transfers just that stuff to a new file that you can read in a fraction of the time.

Given this, what should the script do? It should be able to read files of the type you care about — they can be in Word, WordPerfect, Nissus, text, MacWrite Pro, or whatever — and find and move things you're interested in to another file with some format. Sounds good, doesn't it? But wait, what is a "thing?" Wait again, what does "interesting" mean? When you're writing a script, you have to be fairly concrete. Computers, even your Mac, are very dumb. You have to spell everything out for them in perfect detail, or they either don't do what you want or they do nothing at all.

Spending the time up front to define what you want your script to do — rather than just starting to script and figuring out what you want as you go — saves you mucho time. When you become a really proficient scripter, you'll be able to define what you want your script to do so fast you'll think you're skipping that step. Even then, complex scripts benefit from a little thinking before typing.

In this example, a thing is the unit of information that concerns you. For example, if the text file is full of messages from the Internet, a thing is probably a message. How you tell whether a message is interesting can be very complex. But since this is just a simple script, not a lifelong attempt to develop a computer with common sense and the ability to really understand a message, assume a message is interesting if it contains some special words, called *keywords*. Imagine that you're looking for information about your Cleveland branch office. In that case, you may want to pick Cleveland as a keyword. But if you're looking for information on using AppleScript to control MacWrite Pro, you may pick "AppleScript" and "MacWrite Pro."

Now you've got enough definition to go to the next step.

Step 2: To script or not to script: That is the question

Not everything is worth scripting. Although AppleScript is really powerful, it can't do everything, even when it's used in combination with scriptable applications, and clearly, if you can't script a task, you can't script it. Law of nature kind of thing. How do you decide what's doable? Well, that's a bit tougher. In some cases, it's obvious. For example, say you want to automate something you do with an application. If that application isn't scriptable, then you're out of luck unless you buy a macro utility such as Tempo II or QuicKeys. In other cases, you won't discover that you can't do something until you've tried using that script. As you discover more about scripting, you'll find it easier to make this call. For right now, you're fairly safe in assuming that pretty much anything is possible but some things take a heck of a great deal of effort and expense to get working, which leads me to the second key point.

Is it worth it to script this task? That may sound a little heretical, but considering this question really makes sense. You can always write a script if you think it's fun. More often, though, you should think about what the script can do for you. You want the script to save you more time than it took you to write it, for example. Imagine that you do some monthly task — such as deleting all the files that contain the name Fred because he stole your high school sweetheart — and this task takes six minutes of your time. If it takes you 10 hours (600 minutes) to write a script to automate this task — it won't, but just suppose — it'll be 100 months or (quickly using my graphing calculator under the Apple menu) 8.333 years before you save any time. Heck, by then you won't even remember your high school sweetheart's name. On the other hand, if you do some job daily, such as searching through 400K of Internet message texts, and it takes 2 hours each day and it takes you a full week — 40 hours — to write the script, you start saving time in a measly 20 days. Within a year, you'll have saved (365 -20)*2 = 690 hours. Enough to impress even the most time inefficient among us.

In most cases, you won't even think of scripting an infrequent task that doesn't take very long to do, but do keep an eye out for scripting possibilities. You're most likely to run into a case where the script takes more time than it's worth to develop when it requires using a nonscriptable application or one that's only marginally scriptable — these are unfortunately all too common. Even a fairly scriptable application may lack the specific types of controls that your script needs. When this is the case, it can take a mighty long time to develop a script.

As you've probably guessed by now, these two issues force you to do a little thinking about how you plan to do your script. Although that decision is the next step in this process, don't worry if you blend together the steps of deciding whether or not to do a script and doing the initial design.

Before diving into writing a script, spend a few seconds to make sure the job you want to do is doable and that it's worth the time it'll take to write the script.

Step 3: Define how the script will work

If you didn't skip over step 2, you've probably got a good idea of what you do in this step. Basically, you build the script in your head and visualize how it will work. This is when you decide which applications, if any, your script will use. At this point, you don't really decide line by line what your script will look like but rather get a general feel for its structure. Think of this as the outlining step. For example, say you want to write a script to find all of the scriptable applications on your hard disk. You may come up with an outline that looks like this:

```
1) Look at every file on the disk
   1a) Check and see if the file is scriptable — Need Scriptable Finder
      1a1) If it's scriptable make an alias of it
       1a1a) Have I made a destination folder for the aliases?
        1a1a1) If not make a destination folder
       1a1b) Move the alias to the new folder
```

You haven't figured out the details of the script, but you've decided the basic structure. In the process, you've thought a bit about how you're going to do each step, just enough to feel comfortable that each of the steps is doable. You've also decided that you need the scriptable Finder in order for the script to work. As you get more experienced, this step will get easier and easier, and you'll be less likely to think that something is doable and then discover, in the next step, that it isn't.

Step 4: Write the script

Finally, you get to write some AppleScript. In this step, you take your outline and flesh it out. You can use Script Editor or any of the commercial tools described in Chapter 28 — or any new ones that have come out since this book went to press. At this point, you may find that you can't do something you thought you could. Perhaps one of the applications you're using doesn't let you do what you want, or AppleScript itself is lacking some capability. Either way, you don't have to give up. The most common thing to do is review the design step to see if you can change the script design so that you don't need the capability that is lacking. If reviewing the design step doesn't work, you can try using a different application, or you can see if there's a third-party scripting addition around that does what you want.

After you've got a few scripts under your belt, you'll need a larger pants size or a good diet, but you'll be less likely to start a script that turns out to be unworkable. But you should keep an eye out for cases where the script is doable, but too much effort is necessary to make up for the time and boredom the script will save you.

Step 5: Test the script

Now you run your script. Odds are, it'll have some problem. But be of good cheer. Even longtime scripters, and even longtime programmers, rarely write a script that's even a few lines long without discovering that it doesn't work right the first time. On the other hand, if your script does work the first time, you deserve a hearty slap on the back. If your script doesn't work, it just means that you've found out about another scripting lesson. You'll find that as you get more experience, the probability that a simple script will work right the first time will increase. Even more important, you'll find that the total time to write, test, and fix the script will decrease dramatically.

scripting addition: This doesn't allow you to add two scripts in order to get one that's twice as good. The AppleScript design team made AppleScript extensible. Apple and third parties can develop extensions to the AppleScript language — new commands and functions — that increase its power. Chapter 19 talks about some of the freeware and shareware scripting additions you can find. To use a scripting addition, just put it in the Scripting Additions folder you'll find inside the Extensions folder, which is in turn inside your System folder.

As you test the script, make sure you test the unusual cases. For example, if your script asks the user for some input, what happens if the user doesn't enter anything but says he did? This scenario can happen in a dialog box — see Chapter 9 — when there's no default answer but the user, without looking, hits the Return key, which causes the default OK button to be clicked. It's important to make sure that your script can handle any mistakes the user — which could be you, remember — can dish out without causing problems. A script that is easy for the user to understand how to use and that deals patiently with his or her mistakes is called *user friendly* for obvious reasons.

user-friendly scripts: This doesn't mean that your script will buy you lunch — if you figure out how to do this, though, give me a call ASAP. This means that first off, using the script will be easy — a user can figure out what to do without talking to you — and secondly, no matter what the user does, no matter how stupid, the script doesn't break.

If you should find a mistake, or a user action that can break your script, the next step is to figure out what caused the problem and how it should be fixed.

Step 6: Find and fix the problems

This step is called *debugging* in programming parlance but unfortunately, DDT doesn't do any good. Chapter 18 gives you some tips on how to debug a script. The bottom line is that you try to find where in the script an error happens and then, armed with that information, figure out what in your script caused the problem. Having discovered the cause, you can then work on a cure.

Step 7: Document the script

This step is the one most often skipped by beginners and professionals alike. After all, after you write the script, you fully understand everything it does, so why bother to document it? The answer is that when you come back to the script in seven months in order to update it to deal with a slightly different set of circumstances, you'll save a great deal of time if the script is well documented. By reading the documentation, you'll quickly remember why the script looks the way it does and why you did certain things. Of course, if you're only going to use the script once, you can dispense with documentation, but it's unlikely that any script you'd only use once is worth writing in the first place.

document: This isn't a piece of paper. In most cases, it's a set of comments embedded in your script. These comments describe what your script does in combination with the text in the script description box that you'll find at the top of the script windows in all of the various script-editing tools — see the next section for documentation options in the Script Editor.

debugging: This isn't removing illegal listening devices from your office. It's tracking down and fixing script problems, which are referred to as bugs. While the term is exotic, the objective is simple: Make sure the script does what it's supposed to. Even the best scripters' scripts will usually have some bugs, so don't be upset if yours does too. The difference between a good scripter and a bad one is how many bugs are left after the testing is done. A good scripter will have few, if any, bugs left after he or she is done with a script.

Figure 3-1 shows the overall flow for this process.

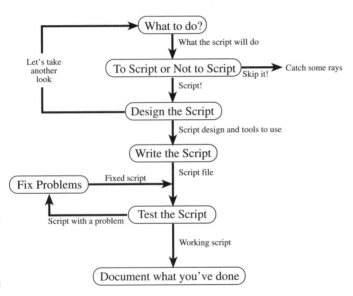

Figure 3-1:
Developing
a script.

Take a minute to look over Figure 3-1. Developing a script is really pretty commonsensical. You figure out what you want to do, you see if it's doable, you figure out how to do it, you test your solution, you fix problems, and you finish by documenting what you've done.

The bottom line is that if you take a bit of time as you develop your script and don't just jump in and hack some script lines, you'll save time overall. As you get more and more experienced, you'll find that you can race through these steps in minimal time.

Script Editor: Free and Worth a Lot More

After you upgrade to System 7.5 — you can get 7.5 from any place that sells Mac software — you get the Script Editor for free. In general, no matter how you get AppleScript, you'll get the Script Editor with it. As you saw after you wrote your first script in Chapter 1, the Script Editor is the tool that lets you write the instructions, the script, that you want the Mac to follow. Other spiffier tools do this — see Chapter 28 — but I'm going to primarily use Script Editor in this book because

  ✔ It's free.

  ✔ The other tools are pretty similar, as far as the basics go. Their advantages lie in the extra features they have that are more useful, in general, for developing complex scripts. If you start spending a great deal of time scripting, say an hour or more a week, it's probably a good idea to plunk down the doubloons for one of the commercial tools described in Chapter 28.

Figure 3-2 shows the Script Editor interface. As with most Mac applications, the Script Editor interface has a menu bar and some windows. The window shown is a standard script window. The **A** label points to an area where you can type in a description of your script. The **B** label points to where you type in your script.

As with all Mac applications, just click the mouse in either area and the cursor changes to a vertical bar and whatever you type appears at the location of the vertical bar. All of the normal text-editing functions are available, so writing a description or a script is just like writing a document in MacWrite Pro, SimpleText, Teach Text, Microsoft Word, or WordPerfect. You can use the Command-C and Command-V key combinations, as well as the menu items from the Edit menu discussed later, to copy and paste pieces of a script.

System 7.5

System 7.5 is the latest major release of the software that runs your Mac. It's got lots of nifty features, but unlike earlier versions of the Mac operating system software — prior to 7.1 — it's not free. You've got to shell out good money to get it, or buy a new computer, which is even more bucks. Fortunately, System 7.5 is worth it. In addition to Script Editor and the scriptable Finder — see Chapter 22 for details — you get lots of other nice features. If you're planning on doing much in the way of scripting, you really have to get System 7.5.

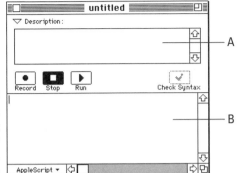

Figure 3-2:
The Script
Editor
interface.

I'll skip over the Apple menu, because it's the same as in all other Mac applications, except there are two About menu items. One is for the Script Editor, and it just tells you the version that you're using and developer credits. The second item, About AppleScript..., brings up the version and credits for the version of AppleScript that you're using.

The File menu

The first really interesting menu is the File menu. As with all Mac applications, the File menu contains commands that relate to opening, closing, creating, and saving files. Figure 3-3 shows the File menu.

Figure 3-3:
The Script
Editor File
menu.

Most of these commands are ones you've seen in a billion Mac apps, so I'll run through them really quickly in the following sections.

New Script

Makes a new, untitled script window.

Open Script

Gives you the standard file dialog for selecting an existing script file to open.

Open Dictionary

Every application that you can tell what to do with AppleScript has a built-in dictionary that shows what AppleScript commands it responds to. This menu item gives you the standard Mac file dialog box for selecting a file. After you select the file, the Script Editor opens a new window, which displays the application's dictionary. See Chapter 17 for more information on dictionaries.

Close

This command closes the frontmost script window. If you've made changes, you'll be asked if you want to save or discard the changes.

Save

This command saves the frontmost script window. If you haven't saved that script, this command will be dimmed as in this figure. The default way to save a file is as a compiled script. As a result, after you choose the Save command, AppleScript will try to compile your script — just as though you'd used the Check Syntax button. If AppleScript doesn't understand your script, it'll generate an error to tell you that you can only save the script as text file. Don't worry, you won't lose any work if you save the script in a text file. When you get a chance, you should try to fix the problem so that you can save the script as a compiled script. In any case, until you fix those sorts of problems, you won't be able to run the script.

Save As

This command lets you save the script to a different file name or as a different type of file. The types of script files — application, compiled script, text — are explained a bit later in this chapter.

Save As Run-Only

This command lets you save a script so that others can run it without seeing the actual script. This command is useful when you've spent a bunch of time writing a really fantastic script that you want to sell.

Revert

This command reverts your script to the way it was the last time it was saved. This command comes in handy when you've been mucking around with a script and have made a bunch of changes and the script no longer works, but you're not entirely sure what changes you made. By reverting to the saved version — assuming you didn't save the script after you started making changes — you can eliminate all the changes that were causing problems. This command will be dimmed until you make changes to a script.

Page Setup

This is the standard dialog box that you've seen in a million or more Mac applications for setting print parameters. Nothing new here.

Print

This command lets you get a hard copy of your script.

Set Default Window Size

You'll get a dialog that asks you if you want to use the size of the frontmost script window as the default size for all new script windows. This means that before you use this menu item, you should adjust the size of the front script window to what you consider the ideal window size for new scripts.

Quit

If, for some strange reason, you don't plan to be scripting 24 hours a day, 7 days a week, 365.25 days a year, you can use this command to exit the program.

The Edit menu

The Edit menu contains commands that relate to editing the script, or the script description, you're working on. Figure 3-4 shows the Edit menu. Once again, the commands are mostly ones you've seen before in most Mac applications. However, some are specific to Script Editor, so don't skip over the following descriptions.

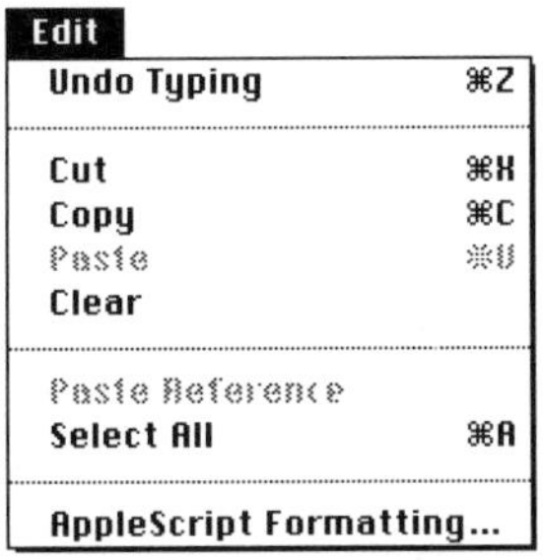

Figure 3-4:
The Script Editor's Edit menu.

Edit	
Undo Typing	⌘Z
Cut	⌘X
Copy	⌘C
Paste	⌘V
Clear	
Paste Reference	
Select All	⌘A
AppleScript Formatting...	

Undo Typing

This command undoes the last thing you did, including cuts and pastes. If you're recording a script, this command undoes the last line in the recording — more on recording in Chapter 17 and in the upcoming discussion of the Controls menu.

Cut

Removes whatever is currently selected and puts it into the clipboard so that you can paste it somewhere else.

Copy

Leaves the currently selected text while copying it to the clipboard so that you can paste it somewhere. Really complex, right?

Paste

Puts the current content of the clipboard wherever the flashing vertical cursor is. This command works with text, including text from word processors, but not with things such as QuickTime movies or pictures.

Clear

This command deletes whatever text is currently selected without saving it to the clipboard. Use this command if you've copied or pasted something and want to delete something else without getting rid of what's stored in the clipboard.

Paste Reference

This is a really exotic item that I've never used. The command only works with a few applications, such as the Scriptable Text Editor. To use this command, you copy a word from a document in the Scriptable Text Editor. Then in Script Editor, you use Paste Reference rather than Paste. Instead of getting the word you put on the clipboard, you get a reference — see Chapter 7 — such as "word 2 of document 1." If you've got the scriptable Finder, this command is a nice way to get a path to a file. Just select the file and then use the copy command in the Finder's Edit menu, and then use this menu command in Script Editor. Script Editor will paste in a reference to the file you selected.

Select All

Selects everything in the area where the cursor is located.

AppleScript Formatting

Lets you change your script's appearance. Figure 3-5 shows the dialog box you get after you pick this menu option. After this dialog box is displayed, the Font and Style menus, which are normally dimmed and unusable, can be used. As the instructions at the top of the dialog box say, you can use those menus to change how various elements of your script are displayed. While this doesn't have any impact at all on how your script works, this command does let you customize your work environment.

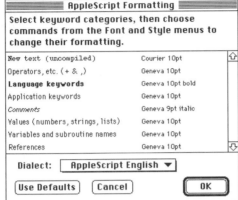

If you've got a color monitor, use Style to change the color of keywords to something that stands out, such as blue or red.

The Controls menu

The Controls menu (shown in Figure 3-6) contains some very important AppleScript-specific commands, which you'll find useful. Unfortunately, you don't know, unless you've skipped ahead to Chapters 17 and 18, about the aspects of AppleScript these menu items control, so you may want to skip this section and come back later or maybe take a quick peek at Chapters 17 and 18 to get a top-level understanding of recording and the event log. But, hey, I promise if you wait 'til later to read these descriptions, the page won't turn blank. Unless, of course, the check you used to pay for the book bounces.

Figure 3-6:
The Controls
Menu.
There is no
CHAOS
menu.

Controls	
Record	⌘D
Run	⌘R
Stop	⌘.
Show Result	⌘L
Open Event Log	⌘E

Record

This command lets you cut your own CD. Just kidding. This puts the Script
Editor into record mode. When Script Editor is in this mode, a little tape
cassette icon alternates with the apple in the Apple menu, as shown in Figure 3-7.
While recording, Script Editor automatically builds up a script that duplicates
whatever you do with the mouse and keyboard if, and this is a really big if, the
applications you use are recordable. Because few applications are recordable
and because when you record you can't include loops or **ifs,** this feature is not
the magic solution it first appears to be. Check out Chapter 17 for more detail
on recording.

Figure 3-7:
The
recording
icon.

Run

This command checks the frontmost script window to see if AppleScript
understands (which is the same as clicking on the Check Syntax button in the
script window) and then runs the script.

Stop

This command stops the currently running script or stops recording.

Show Result

This displays the result window that will contain the result of the last script line
executed. For example, if you enter the script

```
1 + 1
```

and click the Run button, the result window will contain 2.

Open Event Log

This displays the Event Log window. Bet that surprises you. This window
will display all of the AppleEvents sent while your script runs, as well as the
values returned by those AppleEvents. The Open Event Log is the most
powerful debugging tool you've got in the Script Editor, so make sure you
read Chapter 18 for an example of how to use it.

The rest of the menus

The Font and Style menus contain the usual options for picking a font and setting the font size and style that you've seen in just about every word-processing application that runs on a Mac. The Font and Style menus seem to be dimmed most of the time, so you may wonder why these menus are there. If you read about the AppleScript Formatting command in the Edit menu, you know that you can use the Font and Style menus and that command to change the way your script looks. You can also use the Font and Style menus when you're typing in the description box. As soon as the insertion cursor — the vertical bar — is in the description field of a script window, the Font and Style menus undim and become available for use.

The Windows menu is another semistandard Mac menu. As you open a window, the name of the window is added to this menu. Therefore, when your screen is a cluttered mess of 35 windows, you can still easily bring the one you're interested in to the front by selecting its name.

After you've written a script, you'll want to save it to disk so that it doesn't disappear in case your Mac crashes.

Save early and save often. While AppleScript is pretty safe to use and unlikely to crash, you'll find that not all applications' implementation of AppleScript support is that well done. If the Mac should crash while you're testing a script and you haven't saved it, then you'll have to reenter the script, assuming you remember it. The best bet is to save the script fairly often as you develop it.

Figure 3-8 shows the Script Editor's Save dialog box.

Figure 3-8:
Saving a
script.

🗂 scripts under construction ▼	💾 Mary
📄 aol in script debugger	Eject
📄 AOL launch logon send mail	Desktop
📄 bossing apps demo	New 📁
📄 choose application example	
📄 CW import word & save	
Save script as:	Cancel
Take a break script	Save
Kind: 📄 Compiled Script ▼	

You saw this dialog before, and I told you to ignore the pop-up menu labeled Kind. It turns out that pop-up menu is there because you can save a script in three different ways (five if you count the run-only versions). The three main formats are as follows:

 ✔ **Application:** This produces a standard double-clickable application that executes the script.

 ✔ **Compiled Script:** This is an executable script, but when you double-click on it, you open Script Editor to edit the script.

 ✔ **Text:** This is mainly useful for when your script has a problem and AppleScript reports an error when you click on the Check Syntax button. If AppleScript doesn't understand the script, the script can only be saved as a text file.

Figure 3-9 shows the icons for these three formats.

Figure 3-9:
Icons of
a script
application,
compiled
script, and
script as
text files.

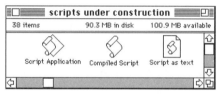

You'll find you essentially never use the text format unless you want to save a script that AppleScript can't understand. That can happen if you're in the middle of writing a script and have to go to dinner.

During your script's development, you'll probably save the script as a compiled script. By doing so, you can easily open your script in the Script Editor by double-clicking on its icon. You're also able to run the script without checking syntax again.

If you want your script to act just like a Mac application, you can save it using the dialog box shown in Figure 3-10.

Figure 3-10:
Saving a
script as an
application.

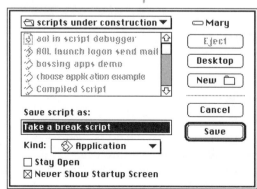

The two new check boxes at the bottom of the dialog box appear when you set the Kind pop-up to Application. The first check box, Stay Open, is used when you develop scripting agents, discussed in Chapter 16. When the Stay Open box is checked, the script stays open and keeps running after you double-click it. In general, stay-open scripts are awoken periodically by AppleScript each time running the *on idle... end idle* handler (also discussed in Chapter 16), which does some job.

The second check box, Never Show Startup Screen, lets you control what happens when the user first clicks on the application. If this box is unchecked, the user sees a dialog box similar to that shown in Figure 3-11, where the text in the Description box of the script window is displayed. While that's fine for most scripts, if you plan to automatically launch a script by putting it in the Startup or Shutdown Items folder in your System folder, you probably don't want the user to have to make a selection in this dialog box. In cases like that, you should check the second check box so the user won't have to interact with the Startup dialog box in order for the script to run.

Figure 3-11:
A script
application
startup
screen.

Wetting Your Whistle by Bossing Around a High-Paid Hacker's Code

Microsoft spends millions to pay its team of software gurus to develop its applications (not that you can tell from Word 6.0, though), Apple's got 500 people working on Copland (System 8), and Claris has tons of people working to bring you software products that are used by millions. All of these people, no matter what company they're with, are experienced programmers proficient with all of those "power" languages you hear about, such as Smalltalk and C++ (appropriate that that language gets only a passing grade). They're the best in the world at programming.

But now it's your turn to make those complex applications do what you want. That's right. Without knowing a single thing about programming, without any knowledge whatsoever about the syntax of C++, without your hands ever leaving your wrists, you can take complete control of lots of high-powered applications. You do this not by buying Microsoft, but by using AppleScript. AppleScript was designed to make it easy for you to control applications.

How easy? Well, suppose you're a highly paid PR person who's got to send out press releases to a bunch of reporters about a new product. You want to send the releases to the reporters in your database who work at publications that have more than a certain number of readers (no wasting time on riffraff after all), and whose interests indicate that they'd want to hear about your new wonder product. Wouldn't it be nice if you could automate this task, especially since it's something you do on a regular basis? Well, with AppleScript, technological wonder of the 20th, nay, 21st century, you can.

The script will find the relevant reporter records in a FileMaker Pro database and then start custom letters for those lucky few in MacWrite Pro. Sounds fairly useful. It's also quite easy. The entire script is shown here:

```
--let the user select which database to use
set database_to_use to choose file with prompt "Select Reporter database" of type {"FMPR"}
--tell FileMaker Pro what to do
tell application "FileMaker Pro"
    -- open the database you want to use
    Open database_to_use
    -- Get the reporters names in alphabetical order
    Sort Layout 1 By Field "Name" In Order Ascending
    -- select those reporters who're interested in scripting and who are read by
    -- more than 1000 people
    Show (Records where Cell "interests" contains "scripting" and Cell "circulation" > 1000)
    -- find out how many reporters meet these criteria
    set number_of_matches to Count Records
    -- If any reporters with acceptable credentials exist then
    if number_of_matches > 0 then
        -- process each matching record in the database
        repeat with i from 1 to number_of_matches
            -- get the reporters name
            set reporter_name to Cell "name" of Record i
            -- start pushing MacWrite Pro around
            tell Application "MacWrite Pro for Power Mac"
            -- make a new document
            new document
                -- Start off the letter with a friendly salutation
                put chars "Dear " & reporter_name & ":" & return
```

```
            -- save the letter to await filling it in
            save document as "letter for " & reporter_name
        end tell
    end repeat
  else
      -- warn the user if no matches were found
      display dialog box "No reporters met the criteria" buttons {"Ok"} default button "Ok"
  end if
end tell
```

This script is only 19 lines long if you don't count the *comments*, which aren't really part of the script after all.

comments: While this is what you'll get at parties when you casually mention that you're a scripting guru, in this case comments refers to descriptive text you put into your script to make it easier to understand how the script works. AppleScript ignores anything you type after two dashes " -- ." You can comment out multiple lines by using (* and *). AppleScript will ignore everything after the (* until it sees a *), even if the text is on multiple lines. When you check the syntax on a script, AppleScript changes the comment lines style to italic, as shown in Figure 3-12.

Figure 3-12:
Comments
in
AppleScript.

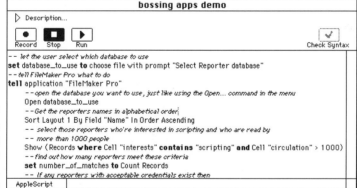

Just in case you don't find the script intuitively obvious, I'll walk through it line by line.

Line 1

```
set database_to_use to choose file with prompt "Select Reporter database" of type {"FMPR"}
```

This line uses the **choose file** command, see Chapter 9, to give the user a standard Mac file selection dialog, shown in Figure 3-13, to select which database file should be used. The value of the variable (a variable is just a named place to store some information — more in Chapter 5), called **database_to_use,** is set to a reference to the file that can be used later in the script to tell FileMaker Pro which file to work with. The **of type** option tells AppleScript to only show FileMaker Pro databases in the dialog — folders are always shown.

Figure 3-13: A standard Mac file selection dialog box accessed via the Choose File command.

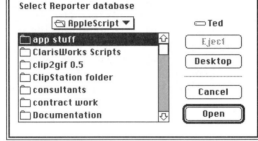

Line 2

```
tell application "FileMaker Pro"
```

The **tell** statement tells AppleScript to send FileMaker Pro commands that lie between the **tell** and **end tell** lines that AppleScript doesn't understand. Those commands, such as **open** on the next line, are defined by FileMaker Pro and show up in FileMaker Pro's dictionary (see Chapter 17). You can look at the dictionary by using the Open Dictionary command in Script Editor's File menu. A **tell** statement applies to all script lines that lie between the **tell** and **end tell** lines.

Line 3

```
Open database_to_use
```

This line just uses the FileMaker **open** command to open up the database file you selected in line 1. It's just like using the Open menu command in FileMaker Pro's File menu.

Line 4

```
Sort Layout 1 By Field "Name" In Order Ascending
```

This line uses FileMaker's **sort** command to sort the database by the value of the field labeled Name. If you wanted the entries in reverse order, you can type **in order descending** instead of **in order ascending**.

Line 5

```
Show (Records where Cell "interests" contains "scripting" and Cell
     "circulation" > 1000)
```

This line uses FileMaker Pro's **show** command to select which records will be processed. Only reporters who pass the test because their interests include scripting and who work for a publication with a circulation of more than 1,000 will receive letters.

cell: While it's true your body is made up of billions of cells (unless you're an alien space monster, that is), in this case, cell is a particular entry in a particular record. In FileMaker, a database has a bunch of fields with different labels. In this example, interests and circulation are fields. Each record has a cell that corresponds to one of those fields. So to access the data from a particular record, you use the term cell. To change something about that field in every record, you use the term field. See Chapter 24 for more details.

Line 6

```
set number_of_matches to Count Records
```

The **count records** command from FileMaker returns the number of selected records (in this case the number of records that met the criteria in line five's **show** command). This line puts the number of records into the variable **number_of_matches** for use later.

Line 7

```
if number_of_matches > 0 then
```

This line checks to see if there are any reporters in the database who meet the criteria. If there aren't (the number of selected records is 0), then you may as well just stop. The **if** statement, see Chapter 10, looks at the expression that follows to see if it's true. In this case, the expression is

```
number_of_matches > 0
```

which translates to English as "is the value of the variable **number_of_matches** greater than 0?" If that statement is true, then lines 8 through 15 will be run. If not, then the lines after the **else** statement in line 16 will be run. Scripts use the **if** statement to change their behavior based on the data the script finds while it's running.

Line 8

```
repeat with i from 1 to number_of_matches
```

The **repeat** statement executes lines 9 to 14 once for each value of **i** from 1 to the value of the variable **number_of_matches.** This value happens to be the number of reporters you want to send press releases to. The **repeat** statement (see Chapter 11) is your main tool in AppleScript for doing something repeatedly. In this case, you're using the **repeat** statement to process each and every one of the reporters who matched our criteria. The first time the **repeat** executes the value of **i** is 1, the second it's 2, the third it's 3, all the way up until its final value, which is the number of reporters who matched the criteria up in line 5.

Line 9

```
set reporter_name to Cell "name" of Record i
```

This line gets the name of the reporter from record number **i** in the selected set. It then puts that value into the variable **reporter_name**.

Line 10

```
tell Application "MacWrite Pro for Power Mac"
```

Now that you've got the data from a record in FileMaker Pro, you need to make a new MacWrite Pro document to serve as the template for your release. In order to work with MacWrite Pro, you have to tell AppleScript to look to MacWrite Pro to handle commands, such as the **new document** command in line 11, which are defined by MacWrite Pro.

Line 11

```
        new document
```

This line, surprise, surprise, makes an new, untitled document in MacWrite Pro.

Line 12

```
        put chars "Dear " & reporter_name & ":" & return
```

Put chars is a MacWrite Pro command that puts the text that follows it into the frontmost MacWrite Pro document at the current location of the insertion point. In this case, the text is

```
"Dear " & reporter_name & ":" & return
```

which, if the reporter's name is Joe, turns out to be

```
Dear Joe:
```

The **&** is the append operator, which adds one piece of text to another. Return is an AppleScript constant that represents a carriage return.

In order to keep this script simple, I've only put in this short salutation. However, you could have gotten the reporter's address from the database along with a boilerplate letter body, which you could customize later. You could even have gotten both the full name and the name he or she likes to be called, such as Judy for Judith. The basic concept is the same.

Line 13

```
        save document as "letter for " & reporter_name
```

This line uses MacWrite Pro's **save document** command to save the file with the name "letter for Joe" if the name of the reporter is Joe.

Line 14

```
end tell
```

This just tells AppleScript to stop looking to MacWrite Pro for the meaning of commands it doesn't understand.

Line 15

```
end repeat
```

This ends the **repeat** statement. Only the lines between the **repeat** and **end repeat** statements are executed each time the value of the variable **i** is changed.

Line 16

```
else
```

Remember line 7 with the **if** statement? This is the middle of that **if**. The **else** divides the script lines that fall between the **if** .... **then** and the **end if** line, which is line 18, into two groups. The lines between the **if** and the **else** are executed if the expression in the **if** statement is true. The ones between the **else** and the **end if** statements are executed if the expression up in the **if** statement is false. In this case, if the expression in line 7 is false, it means that no reporters had been found that matched the search criteria. So you wouldn't want to make any template files, but you would want to let the user know that they'd been too picky in selecting reporters.

Line 17

```
display dialog box "No reporters met the criteria" buttons ("Ok") default button "Ok"
```

This just puts up the dialog box, as shown in Figure 3-14, to let the user know that no reporters in the database matched the criteria you specified. If you want to get fancier, you can add the search criteria to the message in the dialog box so that the user can see the criteria used.

expression: While it's true we've got freedom of expression in the USA, in AppleScript, an expression is some set of AppleScript elements that turns into a value — a number, true, false, or a string, for example — when your script is run. Expressions can be simple

```
1 + 1
```

which turns into 2 when AppleScript comes across it when it runs the script, or complex

```
the second paragraph of document 3 ¬
    doesn't contain "stupid" and x ≥ 32
```

which will turn into either true or false depending upon whether the author put "stupid" into that infamous second paragraph and what in the heck the value of **x** is.

For contrast, you've already seen things that aren't expressions, such as

```
repeat with i from 1 to 5
```

which doesn't get turned into a value when AppleScript comes across it in a script.

Evaluate: This term is used to describe AppleScript's turning an expression into a value. When AppleScript encounters an expression while executing the lines in your script, it replaces the variable names with their current values — see Chapter 5 for the details about variables — and then executes the operators, such as **+**, **-**, **and**, **<**, and **≥**, to compute the final value of an expression. Yes, **and** is an operator. Check out Chapter 6 for the full scoop on operators. Here's a quick example of how AppleScript evaluates an expression.

```
set z to 4
set y to 1
set w to 39.87
set test_string to "A Test"
(z - y) < w and test_string contains
    "test"
```

First, AppleScript replaces the variables — **z,y,w** and **test_string** — with their values, which are defined by the 4 set statement, so the first step is

```
(4 - 1) < 39.87 and "A Test" contains
    "test"
```

Next, it executes the operator in the parentheses:

```
3 < 39.87 and "A Test" contains "test"
```

Next, the operator on the left is evaluated:

```
true and "A Test" contains "test"
```

The comparison operators, such as **<**, **>**, and **=**, evaluate to true if the comparison is valid — 3 is less than 39.87 — and false if it isn't. The **and** operator evaluates to true if the expression on the left-hand side of it and the expression on the right-hand side of it both evaluate to true. If the left-hand side doesn't evaluate to true, AppleScript doesn't waste time with the right-hand side. In this case, though, the left-hand side is true, so until AppleScript evaluates the right-hand side, it won't know if the overall value returned by the whole expression is true or false. The right-hand side also evaluates to true, because the quote does contain the word **"test."** So the expression is now

```
true and true
```

which evaluates to true.

No reporters met the criteria

Ok

Line 18

```
end if
```

This just marks the end of the **if** statement started way back up in line 7.

Line 19

```
end tell
```

This ends the **tell** statement directed at FileMaker Pro that started back up in line 2.

Now that wasn't that bad, was it? While you shouldn't expect that you could have figured out the whole script without reading through this description, I bet you did find many parts of the script fairly easy to understand because they read a lot like English. I bet you figured out what the **sort** command did right away, for example. And the **if** statement. What's more natural than saying, "If this, then do this, or if not, do that?"

You may be thinking that creating a bunch of new files with just Dear Joe in them isn't that big of a deal. Well, it does save some time, but you're right that it would be nice to do more. The good news is that it's easy to extend this script. Instead of just putting in the salutation, you can put in the recipient's address, your name and address at the end, and any product-related description, and then all you have to do is add a personalized introductory paragraph to finish the job.

If that's not enough, you can also use AppleScript to print all the letters, and, if your printer supports it, the envelopes too. Of course, if you're a hardened veteran of e-mail, you can just e-mail your messages to their destination with a script as well.

Part II

All You Ever Needed to Know about AppleScript You Learned in Part II

The 5th Wave   By Rich Tennant

Re·al Pro´gram·mers

OH WOW!

MONDO-TECH

Real Programmers do their best work between 1 and 5 a.m.

In this part . . .

Repeat after me: "Scripting is easy." Now say that a
hundred times, take two aspirin, and call me in the
morning. Just kidding. Actually it's very important to realize
that scripting isn't that hard. If you've ever written a recipe
or directions to your house, you've already done something
very much like writing a script. The only difference is that
when you're writing instructions for a human being, or even
someone like me, you can rely on the person's common
sense. If you accidentally say to add a cup of garlic to a
cupcake recipe, the average person would, unless he or she
is from Gilroy, the garlic capital of America, do a double take
and try to figure out what you really meant. The Mac, on the
other hand, has no common sense. If you're writing a script
to save all of your important accounting files the night
before the big IRS audit and you write a script with a small
boo-boo that tells the Mac to delete all of your files and send
the IRS a note confessing to being the mastermind behind
the S&L disaster, it'll do it. It'll even have a smile on its face
when it starts up the next time! The moral is that
AppleScript will do exactly what you tell it to, so you should
make sure that what you're telling it to do is really clear, and
even more important, exactly what you want it to do. Sound
challenging? Not to worry. With a little practice, you'll see
that it's pretty easy to do the right thing.

The best approach is to work your way through the chapters in the order they're in. But you don't have to memorize
every bit of detail. In fact, you might want to skim through
the chapters to get the basic concepts and glance at the
samples. Then when you run across something you're not
sure about in a script, just jump back to the relevant chapter
and read about it in more detail.

Chapter 4

Values: Different
Types of Information

For most people, values are things such as believing in God, serving your country, and helping the poor — that sort of thing. In the fun-filled world of computing, *values* are strange names assigned to everyday ways of presenting information. For example, "this is a sample string" is known in real life as a bunch of words or a quote, but in scripting, these words are called a string. Before you go through the following list values types, I want you to know that when you actually write a script, you'll never — well, almost never — have to worry about which types of values you'll be using. So don't worry about memorizing the different types of values.

You can find out more about the object model in Chapter 17, but for now, all you need to know is that value classes — remember, that's just AppleScript's name for types of information — can have properties and elements. For example, strings have a property called length, which is the number of characters, including spaces, in the string. Therefore, the length of "this is a string" is 16. Elements, on the other hand, are objects that are inside other objects. For example, strings have words as elements. This means that you can access words inside strings by writing

```
get the seventh word of "this is a fairly long string so that it has a¬
        seventh word."
```

Throughout the book, especially in Chapter 7, you see how to use both properties and elements. For the time being, just glance over the properties of the data types shown on the next few pages so that you have a general idea of what they are.

> **value class:** This isn't a course in values. Value class is how AppleScript refers to different types of data. Data in AppleScript is organized in an object-oriented manner, and in object-oriented systems, data structures are called classes. See Chapter 17 for more information on the object model.
>
> **data structure:** No, this isn't a house built from punched computer cards. A data structure is a fancy way of talking about the grouping of one or more pieces of information. Your address can be a data structure with your name as one element, your street number as another, the city as another, and so on.

You may notice that every value has a property called **class**. That's because AppleScript is one classy language. Actually, the class property just lets you find out an item's type of value. You discover variables in Chapter 5, but suppose you've got a variable called **x** where your script has stored some information. Later on in the script, it may be important to know if the variable contains a string or an integer. You can determine that with the following script line

```
set x to 3
get the class of x
```

This script line returns the name of the class of the value stored in the variable **x**— integer in this case.

In order to make life easier for you, AppleScript allows you to *coerce* one type of value into another. Actually, coercing values is fairly simple; you just use the **as** operator, discussed in Chapter 6, as shown in these examples.

```
3 as string        --> "3"
"3.1415" as real   --> 3.1415
```

The first example converts the integer value 3 to a string, while the second converts a string to a real value — a number with a decimal point.

coerce: This involves hitting a value with a sap — a cloth full of buckshot, not your boss — until it tells you where the secret rebel base is. Whoops, wrong book. Actually, coercing a value just means converting it to another type. For example, suppose you have the integer 3. It may be nice to put that number in a dialog so that the user can read it. In order to do that, you have to coerce the number to a string. Not all types of values can be coerced into all other types. After all, it's pretty unclear how you coerce a list into an integer, so take a look at each value type to see what other types it can be coerced to.

My teaching approach

When learning a language, two different approaches exist. The first approach teaches students all the details of the language and then asks them to understand sentences. The second approach tosses students into an immersive environment from the very beginning. In this book, I'm going to take an intermediate path, sort of like slowly inching your way into a cold ocean rather than cannonballing in like the second approach. What that means is that sometimes I'll use example scripts with stuff in them you don't know about. I did that back in Chapter 1 when you saw how to work with the Script Editor. In general, the stuff you haven't seen will be fairly straightforward (after all, it didn't shock you that the command **display dialog** causes a Mac dialog box to be displayed) and somewhat tangential to the topic I'll be discussing. Whenever items that haven't been covered turn up, I give you a reference to the place in the book where they're covered.

AppleScript Values

You shouldn't worry about the operators listed in these entries until you've looked at Chapter 6, where operators are described. The operators and reference forms that work with the various value types are listed here so that you can use the following list as a quick reference.

Integer

Example: 1 2 3 237 985

Integers are just numbers with no fractional part.

Properties: Class

Elements: None

Coercible to: List, Real, String

Operators that work with this value type: +, -, /, *, Div, Mod, ^, =, , >, , <,

Reference forms: None Applicable

Integers larger than ±536,870,911 are automatically converted to real numbers.

Real

Example: 1.2 2.0 3.141516

Reals are just numbers that have a decimal point.

Properties: Class

Elements: None

Coercible to: List, String, Integer (only if the value has no fractional part, such as 3.0, not 3.1415)

Operators that work with this value type: +, -, /, *, Div, Mod, ^, =, , >, , <,

Reference forms: None Applicable

String or Text

Example: "a" "this is a string" "What?"

A string is just a bunch of letters, numbers, and other characters, such as $, #, _, and %, contained between quotes.

Properties: Class, Length

Elements: Character, Paragraph, Text, Word

Coercible to: Integer, Number, Real, List

Operators that work with this value type: &, =, >, <, , , Starts With, Ends With, Contains, Is Contained By, As

Reference forms: Property, Index, Middle, Arbitrary, Every Element, Range

Paragraphs are groups of characters separated by carriage returns — if there is no carriage return, then the entire string is one paragraph. Text is just all of the characters in the string. The definition of words varies depending upon the language you use, but the basic rule is that what you'd consider a word is a word. For example, "nonfunctional" is a word, while "none functional" is two words. Other chunks of characters can also be words if there are spaces before and after them, such as " $67.89." You can insert quotes into a string by using the backslash character. For example, if you want to display "This is a "test"" you can write it as "This is a \"test\"." To put a \ in, you need to use \\. You can put in special characters such as tab, \t, and return, \r, as well.

Note that this next section on text item delimiters uses many concepts that haven't been defined yet. You may want to skip this stuff until you've read up to Chapter 7.

AppleScript's text item delimiters are the characters that define separations between text items in a string. For example, this script

```
set first_text_item to the first text item of "Disk:Some folder:some file"
```

sets the value of the variable **first_text_item** to "D" because the default text item delimiters are {""}.

You can change these delimiters with a script such as this:

```
set old_delimiters to AppleScript's text item delimiters
set AppleScript's text item delimiters to {":"}
set first_text_item to the first text item of "Disk:Some folder:some file"
set AppleScript's text item delimiters to old_delimiters
```

This script sets the value of the variable **first_text_item** to "Disk" because it tells AppleScript to define text items as things separated by a colon (:). If you used a space instead, as in this script,

```
set old_delimiters to AppleScript's text item delimiters
set AppleScript's text item delimiters to {" "}
set first_text_item to the first text item of "Disk:Some folder:some file"
set AppleScript's text item delimiters to old_delimiters
```

you get "Disk:Some" as the value of the variable **first_text_item** because AppleScript has been told to define text items as chunks of characters separated by spaces. I walk through this script in detail.

Line 1

```
set old_delimiters to AppleScript's text item delimiters
```

Save the current value of the AppleScript text item delimiters so that you can restore it when you're done.

Line 2

```
set AppleScript's text item delimiters to {":"}
```

Change the value of the text item delimiters. It has to be a list with at least one entry, but while you can specify more entries, only the first item in the list is used by AppleScript.

Line 3

```
set first_text_item to the first text item of "Disk:Some folder:some file"
```

Get the first text item using the new text item delimiters.

Line 4

```
set AppleScript's text item delimiters to old_delimiters
```

Restore the former value of the text item delimiters. This step is important because AppleScript's text item delimiter is a global property that is used by all scripts until you quit and restart the Script Editor or quit and restart your computer. That means that if one script changes this property and doesn't restore it, all subsequently run scripts use the new version, which can lead to scripts producing the wrong results. An error such as this can be very hard to track down. Be aware that if your script crashes prior to resetting the old values of the text item delimiter property, the new values stay in effect. Unlike most things, the new values don't go away when the script stops running. If you have a problem like this, you can fix it by executing the next line, assuming that you want the default value.

```
set AppleScript's text item delimiters to {}
```

You use the AppleScript text item delimiters property mostly to parse things such as path names. For example, if you *parse* "Disk:some folder:some file," you're breaking it into useful items, such as the disk name, the folder name, and the file name. It's also useful if you have the user enter a list of comma-separated items into a **display dialog** command-generated dialog — see Chapter 9.

parsing: This basically means to break something down to its components. So if you parse the string "Mike Lifka," you get a first name "Mike" and a last name "Lifka." You may also have to parse an address string to get separate strings for street address, state, city, and ZIP code.

List

Example: {1,4,7} {"a","b","c"} {"a",1,"d",3.54,{"a",3}}

A list is just a group of values stuck between { and } and separated by commas. Entries in a list can be of any type of value, and you can mix values in a list, including using lists within lists.

Properties: Class, Length, Rest, Reverse

Elements: Item

Coercible to: String, various — single-item lists can be coerced to the value of the single item, for example {"3.1415"} can be coerced to the real value 3.1415 but {"this is a test"} can't be coerced to an integer.

Operators that work with this value type: &, =, , Starts With, Ends With, Contains, Is Contained By

Reference forms: Property, Index, Middle, Arbitrary, Every Element, Range

For a list, the **length** is the number of items. **Rest** is another list with every item except the first one, so

```
rest of {1,2,3,4}
```

is {1,2,3,4}. **Reverse** gives you the list in backward order so that

```
reverse of {1,2,3,4}
```

is {4,3,2,1}.

An **item** is just an entry in the list so that

```
item 2 of {1,"this is a string",3,4}
```

is "this is a string."

Record

Example: {name: "Fred," age: 397} {check: 345 amount:34}

A record is like a list, but each entry has a label. A labeled entry is called a property. In the first example, the value "Fred" is associated with the label **name**. You can access items in a record by using the item's label. Here's an example.

```
set x to the name of {name:"Melvin", age:396}
```

This script sets the value of the variable **x** — variables are discussed in Chapter 5 — to the string "Melvin."

Properties: Class, Length

Elements: None

Coercible to: List

Operators that work with this value type: &, =, , Starts With, Ends With, Contains, Is Contained By

Reference forms: Property

When you get the class property of a record you've created, you just get **record**. Some applications have specialized records that aren't read only. A text editor can use such a record for the text style of text objects. If you encounter such a record, the class property returns a record rather than just the constant identifier **record.**

When you coerce a record to a list, you lose all of the property labels.

Boolean

Example: true

Booleans are just values that are either true or false. For example, when AppleScript evaluates the comparison

```
5 is greater than 6
```

it returns the Boolean value false.

Properties: Class

Elements: None

Coercible to: List

Operators that work with this value type: and, or, not, &, =,

Reference forms: None Applicable

Reference

Example: Word 2 of paragraph 1 file "hard disk:a folder: a file"

A reference is just a description of a data object, such as the tenth word in a paragraph. A reference isn't the object but a pointer to the object. It's like an address. When you give people your address, they don't get your house, just a pointer to where to find it. When you give AppleScript a reference, it can track down the thing the reference points toward. You use these a great deal, but you find you don't really ever think about it. After all, word 3 of the second paragraph of document 1 is a reference, it's fairly intuitive, and it doesn't involve using the word "reference."

Properties: Class, Contents

Elements: None

Coercible to: List

Operators that work with this value: and, or, not, &, =,

Reference Forms: None Applicable

The **contents** property returns the value of the object that's being referenced. For example, if the reference is

```
word 3 of paragraph 1 of document 10
```

and paragraph 1 is

```
"Now's the time for all great men to come to the aid of their country"
```

the **contents** would be "time." You can assign reference values to variables using the **a Reference to** operator discussed in Chapter 6.

Date

Example: date "Tuesday, September 5, 1995 14:07:56"

The date value is the standard way to represent time. Even though it's called date, it contains timing information accurate to the nearest second — assuming your Mac's clock is that accurate — and you can use it for precision timing. When you type in dates, you can use a variety of formats. AppleScript converts them to its standard format, as shown in these examples:

```
date "5 sept 95"    -->   date "Tuesday, September 5, 1995 00:00:00"
date "11:45"        -->   date "Tuesday, September 5, 1995 11:45:00" ( on 9/5/95)
date "9/5/95"       -->   date "Tuesday, September 5, 1995 00:00:00"
```

Properties: Class, Weekday, Month, Year, Time, Date String, Time String, Date

Elements: None

Coercible to: List

Operators that work with this value: &, +, -, =, , >, <, , , comes before, comes after, as

Reference Forms: Property

The day property returns an integer corresponding to the day of the month.

```
day of date "Monday, September 18, 1995 16:34:00" --> 17
```

The **weekday** property returns the constant that is the name of the day of the week, such as Monday. The **month** property returns the constant corresponding to the name of the month, such as January. The **year** property returns the year as an integer, such as 1995. The **time** returns the number of seconds since midnight of the day specified in the date. So the **time** property of date "Tuesday, September 5, 1995 01:00:00" would be 3600. The **date string** property returns the date as a string

```
date string of date "Monday, September 18, 1995 16:34:00"  -->
        "Monday, September 18, 1995"
```

while the **time string** property returns a string containing the time portion of the date as in

```
time string of date "Monday, September 18, 1995 16:34:00"  --> "16:34:00"
```

How to use the math operators with dates is described in Chapter 6, while the use of dates with logical operators, such as = or >, is described in Chapter 10.

Other values

Other types of values that you won't use much but may be of interest to experienced programmers exist. I've listed them here:

Number

This is just a synonym that can be used instead of *real* or *integer*.

Data

Information that AppleScript doesn't understand but can be stored in a variable. For example, you can read in a MacPaint picture using a **read** command and store it in a value of type data.

Constant

This is a reserved word defined by an application or by AppleScript. You can't define constants in your script. Examples of constants are *true* and *false*.

Class

This describes the type of data something is; for example, a strings class is **string**, a records class is **record**, and so on.

Properties: Class

Elements: None

Styled Text

This is a string that has style (bold, italic, underlined, and so on) and font (Geneva, Chicago, Bookmark, and so on) information in it.

You'll discover as you script that you rarely have to worry about data types. Your scripts tend to use numbers and strings with an occasional date, list, or record. The most common reason for working with records and lists is that various AppleScript commands, discussed in Chapter 8, return them as their result. As you look at the subsequent chapters, you'll see data types being used all the time. If you come across a script line where you don't understand how a value type is being used, take a quick hop back here to refresh yourself on the details of the relevant value type.

Chapter 5
Variables: Data Cupboards

. . . .

In This Chapter

▶ Storing values in variables

▶ Naming variables intelligently

▶ Using variables with the **set** and **copy** commands

. . . .

Remember high school algebra? You used to have to find out what **x** was. Well, scripting makes it easy because you get to tell your script what value **x** should have. In fact, a variable is just a named place to store some value. You might put in a string such as, "This is a string" or a number like 3.141516 or even a path to a file such as, "My Hard Disk:Some folder:Some folder inside Some folder:a file" into a variable. Any variable can hold any type of data value.

Unlike most programming languages — such as C — in AppleScript, a variable can have any type of value associated with it. You can even store different types of values in a variable at different points in your script. For example, **x** might start out with a value of 0.2 and later on be set to "I want to quit this script." Also, unlike many languages, AppleScript doesn't require that you declare a variable before you use it. All in all, AppleScript makes using variables as easy as possible.

Rules for Naming Variables

Because the Mac lacks common sense, there are rules that define what a variable can be called. Variable names . . .

> ✔ Consist of the letters of the alphabet (both uppercase and lowercase), the numerals 0 through 9, and the underscore character(_)

> ✔ Can't have spaces

> ✔ Can't start with a number

> ✔ Can't be the same as reserved words

You get the underscore character by holding down the Shift key and typing the - (minus sign or dash) key.

In general, if you accidentally give a variable a name that is a reserved word, AppleScript gives you an error message. The bad news is that the error message won't say something intelligible, like `set is a reserved word`. Instead, you'll get something like Figure 5-1.

Figure 5-1:
An error
message
you can get
when you
misuse a
reserved
word.

The good news is that once you get a little practice under your belt — and you read Chapter 17, which talks about dictionaries — you'll find that avoiding reserved words is no big deal. For now, just tuck this particular fact into the sidebar space of your mind.

Table 5-1 shows some examples of acceptable and unacceptable variable names.

Table 5-1	Sample Variable Names
Variable	*Acceptability*
fred	OK
x7zxc_45tre_aaffef	OK, but pretty hard to understand
this is a variable	Uh-uh: breaks rule 2 (no spaces allowed)
this_is_a_variable	A-OK
NumberOfCars	Fine: You can mix and match uppercase and lowercase letters in a variable name
ThisIs_a_percent	Fine
ThisIs_a_%	No way: % isn't an allowed character
repeat	No, no, no! This is a reserved word

reserved word: These words aren't shy; they're just words that AppleScript assumes mean something special. For example, as you find out in this chapter, you set the value of a variable by writing

```
set some_variable to 3
```

AppleScript can figure out what this line means because it knows that **set** and **to** have specific meanings. AppleScript reserves these words for its own use — that's why they're called *reserved words* — so you can't use them as variable names. In general, any word found in the system or application dictionaries — see Chapter 17 — are reserved. Reserved words include command names, such as *display* and *dialog* — because of the **display dialog** command — and the soon-to-be-ubiquitous **set**.

If you really, really, really want to use a variable name with spaces or some other strange characters, you can make use of the | (vertical bar). If you enclose a nonstandard variable name in vertical bars, AppleScript understands and lets you get away with it. For example

| this is a variable name | Fine because of the vertical bars

| This_is_a_% | Another name rescued by the |

I recommend against using the vertical bar because it'll tend to be confusing.

You don't have to worry about mixing uppercase and lowercase letters in a variable name because AppleScript isn't case sensitive. On the other hand, if you define two variables as **The_Boss** and **the_boss**, even though they look different to you, AppleScript will treat them as being the same, which may cause problems in your script if you're thinking that they're different.

case sensitive: This term has nothing to do with emotional lawyers. A case-sensitive language is one that distinguishes variables and other items, such as file names, based upon whether or not letters are capitalized. AppleScript isn't case sensitive, so **the_variable, The_Variable,** and **tHE_vaRiable** are all the same. In a case-sensitive language, such as C++, those three variable names would be treated as being different, with each being able to store a different value. I don't like case-sensitive languages because it's usually enough effort to remember the name of a variable without having to remember which letters are capitalized. Fortunately, AppleScript took the smart path and is case insensitive.

All right, you know what you can name variables. Here are some suggestions as to what style to use when picking variable names.

Pick names that mean something

While **xxzs435** works just the same as **The_Last_Cashed_Check_Number**, it's a heck of a lot easier to understand what's going on in a script that uses comprehensible variable names.

Mark the start of words

I tend to use the underscore to separate words in a variable name, as in **Check_amount.** Other people like to use capital letters, as in **CheckAmount.** Neither is intrinsically better, but you should pick some scheme that works for you because you'll find that a name like **checkamount** is harder to read as you quickly skim through a script than one that somehow marks the start of words.

Don't worry too much about the rules

Sometimes you'll be in a hurry, or you'll use a variable to hold a value for only a line or two in a script. In cases like those, feel free to use a shorter variable name, such as **x**, **y**, or **temp**, instead of a longer but clearer name, like **width_of_window**, **height_of_window**, or **temporary_holding_spot**, in order to save time and typing. Remember, unless you're doing this professionally — in which case you probably know more than I do, so you shouldn't be wasting your time reading this book — you're the boss. No one but you has to be happy with your scripting style.

In Chapter 13, you discover the wonders of global variables. They're variables that are usable in multiple functions — you also find out about functions in Chapter 13. It's generally a good idea to use a special variable-naming convention for them so you realize that they're global. A common approach is to begin the name with a **g** or **g_**. For example, if you want to call your global variable **time_of_day**, use **gtime_of_day** or **g_time_of_day** instead.

Now that you know how to name a variable, what do you do with one?

Using Variables

Whenever AppleScript comes across a variable name in a script line that it's executing, it replaces that variable name with the *current value* of the variable — the last thing that you stored in the variable with either the **set** or **copy** command.

Here's a simple script that lets you display a custom message:

```
set the_string to "My customized message!"
display dialog the_string
```

The first line of this script stores the string "My customized message!" in the variable called **the_string**. That script is identical to this script

```
display dialog "My customized message!"
```

because in the first script, when AppleScript gets to the second line, it replaces the variable **the_string** with its current value, which is the string "My customized message!"

After you enter the two-line script and click on the Run button in the Script Editor window, you get the dialog box shown in Figure 5-2.

Figure 5-2:
Your customizable message dialog.

```
My customized message!

                       [ Cancel ]  [[   OK   ]]
```

The full syntax for the **set** command is

```
set some_variable to some_expression_or_variable
some_expression returning some_variable
```

Some_variable is any legal variable name you want to use.

Some_expression_or_variable is a legal variable name or an expression.

Chapter 6 covers expressions, but these examples should give you an idea of what they are:

```
set x to 3
set some_name to "this is a test"
set some_name to "Melvin"
set x to y + 2
7 + 3 returning z
set z to 7 + 3
```

To be honest, I've never used the version of **set** that uses **returning**. It doesn't seem too intuitive to me. But just so you know, the last two script lines in this example are identical, and in both cases, **z** ends up having a value of 10. To help you remember how **set** works, you might think of it as being

```
set the value of some_variable to the value of some_other_variable_or_expression
```

You should take a second to remember how to use the **set** command because it's one of the most, if not *the* most, commonly used commands in AppleScript. You'll probably use it more than any other AppleScript command.

As you read through the scripts in this book, you'll be seeing variables every-where. They're pretty easy to use. In general, you use them when you want to store a value or use it in more than one place. The two things to remember are

✔ Give a variable a value by using **set**.

✔ AppleScript automatically replaces the variable name with the current value of the variable when you run your script.

When to Use Set and When to Use Copy

In order to save memory when you set a variable (**x**) to the value of another variable (**y**) that is a list, record, or script object, AppleScript effectively makes an alias of the list, record, or script object and puts that alias in **x**. In the following example, the final value of item 2 of **list_2** is 3.141516, not 3, because both **list_1** and **list_2** refer to the same thing, just as an alias on the desktop and the actual file refer to the same thing in the Finder.

```
set list_1 to {"a", "b", "c", "d"}
set list_2 to list_1
set item 2 of list_2 to 3
set item 2 of list_1 to 3.141516
```

Using the drawer analogy, instead of making a new copy of the list, record, or script object that's in **list_1**'s drawer and putting it in **list_2**'s drawer, AppleScript puts a note in **list_2**'s drawer that tells it to go to **list_1**'s drawer to find the value of **list_2**. You can avoid this problem by using the **copy** com-mand. The syntax of **copy** is

```
copy some_expression_or_variable to some_other_variable
put some_expression_or_variable into some_other_variable
```

Copy will always make a new copy of a list, record, or script object so that changing line 2 of the first script in this section to

```
copy list_1 to list_2
```

will insure that the final value of item 2 of **list_2** is 3. When working with lists, records, and script objects, it's always a good idea to use **copy** because the errors that can result from using **set** are often hard to track down. On the other hand, don't worry too much because I don't think I've ever had a problem with this stuff. Just use **copy** with lists, records, and script objects.

Chapter 6

Operators: Math without Mistakes

. . . .

In This Chapter

▶ Working with AppleScript operators: +, –, /, *****, **^**, **mod**, **div**

▶ Using other operators: **&**, **as**, **a reference to**

▶ Controlling the order of operations using parentheses

▶ Understanding date arithmetic

▶ Changing values with operators

. . . .

*O*perators are just a way to tell AppleScript to modify a value or create a new one. For example, if you want to add two numbers, you use the addition operator — the plus sign, to us normal folk — as in this example:

```
1 + 1
```

Just type this into the Script Editor window, as shown in Figure 6-1. Then make sure the result window is showing — choose the Show command from the Controls menu — and click on the Run button in the script window. Amazingly enough, 2 shows up in the result window.

In addition to the math operators you've all run across in school, AppleScript has a bunch of other operators that come in handy when working with text or other types of values. For example, you can add strings by using the **&** operator. Enter this script into a new script window and click the Run button:

```
"My name is " & "Melvin."
```

Notice that you need to put a space after the *is;* otherwise, you end up with

```
"My name isMelvin."
```

instead of

```
"My name is Melvin."
```

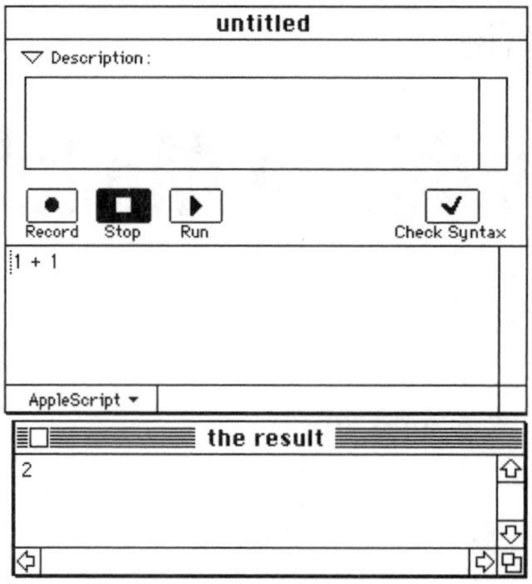

Figure 6-1:
Using the
addition
operator.

You'll find that you tend to use operators with variables. Here's a long script that shows you how to use the ***** (multiplication) operator.

```
set x to 4
set y to 5
set z to x * y
```

As you probably guessed, when you run this script — by clicking on the Run button — the result window will contain 20.

Math Operators

Math-related operators should be fairly familiar to you — you've seen most of them in high school math. For each operator, I'll tell you what it is, show you an example of how to use it, and tell you what types of values the operator works with. For example, the + operator works with numbers but not strings. If you're not sure that you understand what the operator does, just enter the sample script and play around with different numbers and see what results you get. Don't worry about memorizing all of these operators right now. Just get a feel for what operators there are, and then, when you're writing a script, you can refresh your memory by checking this list for the details.

The addition operator: +

```
set x to 1 + 1
```

This operator sets the value of **x** to 2. You can use the addition operator with date, integer, or real values. See the "Date arithmetic" section of this chapter to find out about using dates with math operators.

The subtraction operator: –

```
set x to 453 - 32
```

This operator sets the value of the variable **x** to 421. You can use integer, real, or date values with the subtraction operator.

The division operator: /

```
set x to 7 / 2
```

This operator sets the value of the variable **x** to 3.5. You can use real or integer values when you ask AppleScript to divide.

If you want to use the ÷ character instead of /, you can get it by holding down the Option key — found to the left of the Apple key — and then clicking the / key.

The multiplication operator: *

You can't use **x** as the multiplication operator because it's a legal variable name.

```
set x to 3 * 4.5
```

This operator sets the value of **x** to 13.5. You can use real or integer values with the multiplication operator.

The exponent operator: ^

You use this operator to raise a number to a power, as in $2^2 = 4$ or $3^2 = 9$.

```
set x to 3
set y to 2
set z to x ^ y
```

This operator sets the value of **z** to 9.0.

Other math operators

Two other less commonly used math operators are **div** and **mod**.

div

This operator does integral division where any fractional part is dropped. For example, 5 / 2 is 2.5, but 5 **div** 2 is 2.

```
set x to 9 div 4
```

This operator sets the value of **x** to 2.

mod

This is the remainder operator. For example, 9 **mod** 4 returns 1 because 4 goes into 9 twice with 1 left over. Similarly, 14 **mod** 3 returns 2 because 3 goes into 14 four times with 2 left over.

```
set z to 18 mod 7
```

This sets the value of **z** to 4.

Date arithmetic

No, date arithmetic isn't trying to figure out how much of a tip will impress your date. AppleScript lets you use the + and − operators with dates. For example, if you want to find out what time it will be in nine hours, you can use the following script:

```
set x to (current date) + 9 * 60 * 60
```

If the current date is

```
date "Friday, September 8, 1995 14:16:27"
```

then the value of **x** will be

```
date "Friday, September 8, 1995 23:16:27"
```

This script works because there are [9 hours * 60 minutes/hour * 60 seconds/minute] seconds in 9 hours, and when the addition operator adds an integer to a date, it assumes that the integer is a number of seconds (unless you use one of the reserved words that I'll describe in a moment).

The command **current date** — described in Chapter 8 — returns the time and date on your Mac's clock. The + operator treats the other argument as a number of seconds so that 9 * 60 * 60 is 9 hours * 60 minutes/hour * 60 seconds/minute. You can make this type of script simpler by using four reserved words: *minutes, hours, days,* and *weeks.* So you can redo the example as

```
set x to (current date) + 9 * hours
```

If you want to get the current time plus 3 weeks, 2 days, 7 hours, 12 minutes, and 30 seconds, you can write

```
set x to (current date) + 3 * weeks + 2 * days + 7 * hours + 12 * minutes + 30
```

Subtraction works pretty much the same. You can subtract two dates from each other and get the time between them in seconds as in this example:

```
set x to date "Saturday, June 17, 1995 00:00:00"
set y to date "Monday, June 17, 1996 00:00:00"
set z to y - x
```

This script sets **z** to 31,622,400 — which is within 0.7% of $\pi * 10^7$. You can convert the value of **z** from seconds into more usable units by using the **div** operator, as in the following example:

```
set x to date "Saturday, June 17, 1995 00:00:00"
set y to date "Tuesday, June 18, 1996 00:00:00"
set z to y - x
set weeks_different to z div weeks
set z to z - weeks_different * weeks
set days_different to z / days
set message to "Difference is " & weeks_different & " weeks " & ¬
    days_different & " days"
```

The result window will show the value of the variable **message,** which is "Difference is 52 weeks 3.0 days."

Logical and Comparison Operators

Enough math operators. AppleScript has got bunches of other operators. The largest group consists of those that are used to generate Boolean values (true or false). These are the **comparison operators**, such as **greater than** and **less**

than, as well as operators such as **contains** and **begins with**. Because these operators are almost always used with the **if** statement, I cover them in Chapter 10.

Miscellaneous Operators

But there's more to life than comparison operators, so here are some other nonmathematical, noncomparative (is that a word?) operators.

&

The concatenation operator is very useful. You can use it to combine strings and to add to lists or records. The general syntax for the concatenation operator is

```
something & something_else
```

How this operator works depends on what types of values *something* and *something_else* are. If *something* is a string, then the result will be a string. So

```
set z to "abcd" & "efg"
```

will end with the variable **z** having the value "abcdefg." If *something* is a string and *something_else* isn't a string, it will be coerced to a string so that

```
set z to "Highway " & 987
```

will result in the value of the variable **z** being "Highway 987." If *something* is a list, then *something_else* is added to the list, as in these examples:

```
set z to {1, 2, 3} & "a"
```

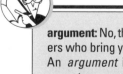

argument: No, this isn't what you have with waiters who bring you sushi instead of shish kebab. An *argument* is an input to something. An operator operates on its arguments to produce its result. Some operators take one input, while others take two. So in this example,

```
1 + 2
```

1 and 2 are the arguments to the + operator. Chapter 13 covers *handlers,* but for now just remember that the input parameters to a handler can also be called arguments.

This script sets the value of **z** to {1,2,3,"a"}, while

```
set z to {1, 2, 3} & {7, 8, 10}
```

sets **z** to {1,2,3,7,8,10}.

You'll probably find that you use the **&** operator most often with strings and variables in order to create messages for the user. For example, if you've got a script that backs up files, you may want to tell the user when the script is done how many files were backed up and if there were any problems. You can do that with a script like this:

```
set status_message to "Backed up " & number_of_files_backed_up & " files." & return
set status_message to status_message & "There were " & number_of_problems
display dialog status_message
```

The first two lines can be combined into one very long line, if you like.

as

as is the *coercion* operator. It is used to turn one type of value into another. The general syntax is

```
some_value as some_value_class
```

where *some_value* is some variable or expression, such as "3" or 78.3 / 98, and *some_value_class* is a value type such as integer or string.

Some typical examples of using **as** are

```
set z to "3" as integer          --> sets z to 3
set k to {"a", "b", "c"} as string   --> sets k to "abc"
set u to 3 as real               --> sets u to 3.0
```

Most of the time, you don't have to worry about using **as** because AppleScript automatically coerces values as necessary. For example, in these cases AppleScript takes care of the coercion:

```
set z to "There were " & 89.7 & "% of the people opposed."
set sum to 3.89 + "3.1415"
```

In the first example, the real number 89.7 is coerced to a string, "89.7;" in the second, the string "3.1415" is coerced to a number, 3.1415. If you're not sure that AppleScript will automatically coerce a value, feel free to use the coercion operator. If it's unnecessary, it won't cause any problems.

One thing to be careful of is that not all value classes can be coerced into every other value class. While changing a list into a string makes some sense, converting a list to an integer is something that not even AppleScript will try to tackle. See the entries for the various value classes in Chapter 4 to find out which coercions are possible for the various value types.

a reference to

This operator creates a reference to an object rather than the object itself. See Chapter 7 for more information on references. The full syntax is

```
[a] ref [to] | reference to some_reference
```

where *some_reference* is a reference of some sort. Some examples are

```
set main_document to a reference to document "Test case" of application "Microsoft Excel"
set last_word to a reference to the last word of document "Papers" of application ¬
"Scriptable Text Editor"
set application_ref to a reference to application "Finder"
```

You can use a reference value wherever you'd use a reference. So you can use

```
set last_word to a reference to the last word of document "Papers" of application ¬
 "Scriptable Text Editor"
set last_phrase to last_word & " is the final word."
```

instead of

```
set last_phrase to the last word of document "Working Papers" of application ¬
"Scriptable Text Editor" & " is the final word."
```

You may be wondering why you'd use a reference to something. One reason is that a reference is always up-to-date. For example, if you put the last word in a document in a variable with **set** and then your script adds some more words at the end of the document, the value in the variable is no longer the last word. But if you use a reference, you can be sure that no matter what has happened, when you use the reference you'll get the current value of the item that the reference points to. You can find out more about references in Chapter 7.

Precedence: When to Use Parentheses

Whenever you've got more than one operator in an expression, you need to know what the rules of precedence are.

precedence: This isn't what you want Santa to bring you, or the guy in the White House. In the wacky world of AppleScript, and in any other more suitish programming language, *operator precedence* is a fancy way of saying the order in which AppleScript executes operators in an expression.

To understand why operator precedence makes a difference, look at this expression:

```
3 + 4 * 5
```

If AppleScript executes the *(multiplication) operator first, which it does, then you get

```
3 + 20
```

which (where did I put that calculator?) is 23. On the other hand, if AppleScript were to execute addition operators first, which it doesn't, then you'd get

```
7 * 5
```

which is 35. Clearly, the order in which AppleScript executes operators in an expression can make a difference. The order in which AppleScript evaluates expressions is shown in Table 6-1. The middle column tells you what sequencing rule AppleScript follows in evaluating a type of operator when there's more than one of that particular type of operator in an expression.

Table 6-1	How AppleScript Evaluates Expressions	
Operator	**When There's More than One**	**Description**
()	Innermost to outermost	Parentheses for grouping
+ or −	Nearest item	Not addition or subtraction but the sign of a number (−23)

(continued)

Table 6-1 *(continued)*

Operator	When There's More than One	Description
^	Right to left	Exponent — 3^3 is 27, for example
*	Left to right	Division and multiplication
/	Left to right	Division and multiplication
div	Left to right	Division and multiplication
mod	Left to right	Division and multiplication
+	Left to right	Addition and subtraction
−	Left to right	Addition and subtraction
as	Left to right	Coercion — ve haf ways to make you talk!
<	None	Comparison
	None	Comparison
>	None	Comparison
	None	Comparison
=	None	Equal and not equal
	None	Equal and not equal
not	Nearest item	Not true is false, and not false is true
and	Left to right	and operator (see Chapter 10)
or	Left to right	or operator (see Chapter 10)

You might be wondering why parentheses are an operator. It's a grouping operator; everything inside it is treated as being a subexpression by AppleScript. It turns out that you can tell AppleScript how to evaluate an expression. All you have to do is use parentheses.

The rule is that everything inside parentheses is evaluated before it's combined with anything else.

Chapter 7

References: Being Picky about Data

*W*hat do you do when you want to select a word of a paragraph? Well, in English you say something like "select the second word of the third paragraph." AppleScript supports references that do just that.

What Is a Reference?

A reference is a pointer to some piece of information. In order to understand references, you need to have a bit of a handle on how AppleScript views information. In AppleScript, pieces of information are called objects. Think of an object as a chunk of information that AppleScript can work with. Objects have properties — some editable, some not — which contain information about the object. While you may have heard all of the hoopla about object-oriented programming and C++, you don't need to worry; objects in AppleScript aren't complex. In general, AppleScript objects are both simple and commonsensical. Objects tend to be things that you'd think about anyway — things such as words, database records, documents, and so on. Properties are similarly straightforward. You can find the properties of an application object by looking in the dictionary of the application that defines the object, as explained in Chapter 17.

You may be wondering how these object classes relate to the value classes in Chapter 4. The answer is that in terms of structure, object and value classes are very similar. The difference is that object classes are defined in various applications and reside, in a logical sense, in those applications, while value classes are part of AppleScript and are available in every script line.

reference: What employers want? Yes, if they're looking for AppleScript gurus. For the rest of us, a reference is a pointer to some information, such as the third paragraph in a document. A reference is different from the data itself. For example, if the third paragraph of a document changes, a reference gets the new third paragraph, not the old one. Another way to think of a reference is as a street address. You could give someone your address. You might put an addition on your house, or even completely replace it, but the address would still point to that same place on the street.

object: No, this isn't a lawyer's favorite term. An object is a type of information, such as a word or a database record, that can have properties (the length of the word in characters, for example), and that may contain other objects, such as cells inside a database record. AppleScript defines some objects, such as words, while applications define others, such as database records. Every object belongs to some class, which defines the structure and characteristics of the object. In C++, an object is referred to as an instance of a class.

class: Something I've never been accused of having. In AppleScript, a class is a blueprint for a type of information. I discuss the built-in value

classes in Chapter 4. An object class defines the properties and commands a given object responds to. Think of actual objects as being manufactured based on the blueprint defined by the object class definition. So the class of string has certain properties, such as length, and contains certain elements, such as words and characters. When you create a string in your script, AppleScript makes an object that has those properties and fills in the properties and contained elements with the values that are appropriate for the specific string you're using.

properties: While this is what you want on Boardwalk, it's also the name for characteristics of objects. Objects can have properties that describe them. For example, a word has a length property whose value is the number of characters in the word. Application objects — those objects defined by applications as described in Chapter 17 — can have properties. The Finder defines an object, called a **file**, that AppleScript can manipulate. File objects have a number of properties, including **locked** (if the file is locked), and **version** (the version string you'd see in the Get Info dialog box). In FileMaker Pro, each record entry is a **cell**, which has a **name** property among others. By the way, sometimes properties are called *attributes*.

Alright, so you've got a bunch of objects floating around and you want to use a specific object or group of objects, what do you do? Well, not surprisingly given the title of this chapter, you use a reference. Remember: A reference is a *pointer* to something while an object *is* something.

For example, if a string is "This is a test," I can ask for the third word by using a reference as shown in this script

```
set some_string to "This is a test"
set some_word to the third word of some_string
```

which will leave the variable **some_word** with the value "a." But the reference, "the third word of **some_string**," isn't the word "a" but rather a pointer to a specific subitem in the variable **some_string**. If we change the value of **some_string** as in

```
set some_string to "Yet another test"
set some_word to the third word of some_string
```

the value of **some_word** changes even though the reference doesn't. This behavior of references is really useful because you don't have to alter your script when the data changes. For example, say I want to write a script to look at how many extensions I have in my System folder. I can use a reference to the startup disk. If I did that, then even if I changed the startup disk by using the Startup Disk control panel, my script always accesses the current startup disk. If I just put the name of the disk in the script without using a reference, then my script looks at the wrong System folder, if there is one, on the wrong disk.

Another advantage of references is that they're easy to read in a script. But the most important advantage of all is that references let you pull apart complex data structures, such as text documents or databases, to get at the data you need — the value of the name field of all database records where the value of the net worth field is greater than 100,000,000, for example — with very simple scripts.

References have three components:

- ✔ The type of object you're looking for (word, paragraph, record, and so on)
- ✔ Where you should look for the object (a string, a document)
- ✔ How to distinguish the object(s) you want from others of the same type (the third word, the last paragraph)

The normal sequence, although this isn't always true, is to put the type of object, followed by the distinguishing characteristics, finished off by the *container* to look in.

---

container: This isn't a backpack. A container is any object, such as a string, that can contain other objects. A string can contain words and characters. A document can contain paragraphs. A database contains records, and records contain cells. Containers can potentially contain multiple types of objects, and the objects being contained can themselves be containers.

Objects inside of a container are called element objects.

elements: Also known as element objects, these are objects that are contained inside other objects. Elements can be containers themselves. For example, a paragraph, which contains words, can be an element of a document, which also contains words.

Following are some typical references:

```
word 7 of paragraph 3 of document "fred"
characters 2 through 9 of "This is an example of a range reference"
tell application "FileMaker Pro"
    the third Record of Database "science books"
    the Record after the Current Record of Database "library books"
    every Record where Cell "name" contains "Yuri"
end tell
```

The **tell** and **end tell** lines, discussed in detail in Chapter 17, tell AppleScript to use FileMaker's objects when interpreting the various database references. Those lines are necessary because AppleScript itself doesn't understand **records, cells,** or **databases**.

Just to confuse things, a reference can be complete or partial. A complete reference is one that has all the information needed to uniquely specify the objects of interest. A partial reference, such as

```
word 10 of paragraph 3
```

doesn't have enough information for AppleScript to figure out what objects you want. The reason this example is partial is that I haven't told AppleScript where to find paragraph 3. Is it in the Scriptable Text Editor? Is it in Word? Is it in MacWrite Pro? But even if I specify the application, I've also got to specify which document to use. If AppleScript gave you paragraph 3 from the contract for 14,000 pairs of Bolivian sneakers instead of the third paragraph from a legal brief on the upcoming corporate merger, you probably wouldn't be too terribly happy. You can make a complete reference several ways. The simplest is to just write it all out, as in

```
word 10 of paragraph 3 of the frontmost document of application "MacWrite Pro"
```

Another way is to use the fun-filled **tell** statement, described in much more detail in Chapter 17. An example of using **tell** is

```
tell application "WordPerfect"
    set z to word 10 of paragraph 3 of front document
end tell
```

When AppleScript tries to execute script lines that occur between a **tell** and an **end tell,** it directs those lines to the item which is being told — application "WordPerfect" in this case. In the preceding example, the reference can be expanded to

```
set z to word 10 of paragraph 3 of the front document of application
        "WordPerfect"
```

when AppleScript executes the line. You can nest **tell** statements so that
the following

```
tell application "WordPerfect"
   tell document 1
      set z to word 10 of paragraph 3
   end tell
end tell
```

is equivalent to

```
set z to word 10 of paragraph 3 of the front document of application
        "WordPerfect"
```

One thing to be careful of is that not all scriptable applications support containers in the same way. Check out Chapter 17 and the chapters on the various
applications to find out how to tell what types of containers an application
supports.

nesting: Something the descendants of dinosaurs do in your backyard trees.
Actually, nesting is when one control structure — such as **try**, **if**, or **repeat** — is
inside another control structure.

One of the reasons references are so useful is the wide spectrum of reference
forms that you can use to define which objects you want in AppleScript. You've
seen the index reference form, word 3 of *some_string,* but other *reference forms*
are very useful as well. Table 7-1 shows the full complement.

reference form: This is not another piece of bureaucratic nonsense. It's a rule
for how to write a phrase, "word 3 of *some_string*" for example, that identifies
one or more objects.

Table 7-1	Reference Forms
Reference	*Description*
Arbitrary	AppleScript picks an object at random from the specified container.
Every	AppleScript returns all objects of a certain type from the specified container.
Filter	AppleScript picks all objects that meet a set of tests you specify, such as those words that start with "z."

(continued)

Table 7-1 *(continued)*

Reference	Description
ID	AppleScript picks the objects based on their ID property — not used very often.
Index	AppleScript picks the item based on its position with respect to the first item in the specified container, such as word 9 of paragraph 2.
Middle	AppleScript picks the middle item in the specified container.
Name	AppleScript picks the item based on the item's name property.
Property	AppleScript picks the items based on the value of a property you specify.
Range	AppleScript picks a contiguous range of items, such as characters 2 to 9.
Relative	AppleScript picks an object based on its position relative to another object, such as the word after word 3.

While this table talks about AppleScript picking objects, that's only true if the reference is to an AppleScript object; if the reference is to an application object, say a cell in a FileMaker Pro record, then the application will execute the reference form. Not all applications support all reference forms, nor will they always behave in exactly the same way as shown here. The application dictionary, described in nauseating detail in Chapter 17, shows you which types of reference forms can be used with which types of application-defined objects. The reference forms that are usable with AppleScript value classes, such as strings, are listed in Chapter 4.

Different Kinds of Reference Forms

So now that you know everything about reference forms . . . What? You'd like examples? More information? Well, if that's what you want, then take a look at the next several pages where I describe several different reference forms.

Arbitrary

This reference picks in a random or arbitrary fashion one item out of a container.

Syntax

```
some name_of_some_class
```

Examples

```
some word of paragraph 3
some word of document 3 whose style contains bold
some item of {1, 2, 67, 81.2, -23}
```

Description

This form arbitrarily picks an object that belongs to the class you specify and that also meets any other criteria you specify, such as having a certain style, shown in the second example. If you're working with AppleScript, the container is a value, such as a list, and then the object is randomly selected using a random number generator from the group of all objects that meet your criteria. If you're working with a container defined by the application, as in the second example, it's up to the application to pick an object. The application can use a random approach or any approach it decides to. So applications could return a nonrandom selection if they so choose. This form is one I've never had to use, but it could be used as a randomizing function.

Every

This reference returns every object in the specified container that belongs to the given class.

Syntax

```
every name_of_some_class
plural_name_of_some_class
```

Examples

```
set z to every word in paragraph 3 of document 1
set z to words in paragraph 3 of document 1
```

Description

This form returns a list of all objects of a given class in a container. So that this script line

```
set z to every word of "this is a test"
```

sets the value of the variable **z** to

```
{"this", "is","a","test"}
```

The plural syntax, "words of paragraph 3," is not supported by all types of objects. You can check in an applications dictionary — see Chapter 17 — to see which object types support the use of the plural format. If there are no objects of the specified class in the container, the empty list {} is returned.

You can use this form to get lists of the values of object properties as well. This script line

```
set z to the length of every word of "this is a test"
```

sets **z** to

```
{4,2,1,4}
```

which is a list of the values of the length property of the words in the string. This reference can be used with any object property.

Filter (called a *whose clause* by those in the know)

This reference lets you define a test, and all objects which past the test are returned.

Syntax

```
reference to one or more objects whose¬
        some_expression_that_evaluates_to_true_or_false
reference_to_one_or_more_objects where¬
        some_expression_that_evaluates_to_true_or_false
```

Examples

```
every word in paragraph 3 whose first character is "z"
first word whose style contains underline
(words 1 through 500 whose first character is "1") of paragraph 35
tell application "FileMaker Pro"
    every Record where Cell "Name" contains "Jonah"
end tell
tell document 1 of application "Scriptable Text Editor"
    paragraphs where it contains "American"
end tell
```

Description

The filter form works by examining all objects of the specified class — word in the first three examples, record in the fourth, and paragraph in the last — to see which ones meet the test criteria — for example, the test expression evaluates to true. You may be wondering what sort of expressions evaluate to true or false. That's probably because you haven't read Chapter 10 yet. You can either skip ahead and skim that chapter or settle for this abbreviated description. Essentially, any expression that you look at and say yes to evaluates to true, while all others evaluate to false. For example, if someone said, "Is the first letter in zoom a z?" you'd say yes. In the filter form, you say first character is "z." That expression is applied by the filter form in the first example to all words in paragraph 3. For each word, AppleScript acts as though it was executing something like this:

```
if first character of this_word is "z" then
    add it to the list of accepted objects
else
    it's out of luck
end if
```

So AppleScript replaces **this_word** with the value of each word in the paragraph. At the end, it makes a list with an entry of each word which passed the test.

The third example shows that you have to use parentheses if you want to put the container specifier after the filter test. The last example shows the use of the **it** value. In a filter form, **it** is replaced by the value of each of the potentially matching objects. So in this example,

```
tell application "Finder"
    set z to files of startup disk where the name of it contains "activity"
end tell
```

z is set to a list of references to the files on the startup disk whose names contain the word "activity."

ID

This reference lets you pick objects based on their ID property.

Syntax

```
some_class_name id some_ID_value
```

Examples

```
document id 9878
window ID 890
```

Description

The ID property may be supported by some applications. It's just a unique integer value that is assigned to each item of each class inside a container, say all documents in the application. You'll have to check the documentation for the application you want to script to see whether it supports IDs. In general, ID is a very infrequently, if ever, used reference form, so if you've got to forget something, this is it.

Index

This reference lets you specify an object based on its position with respect to the first object in a container.

Syntax

When you see something like a | b | c, it means you can use either a or b or c at that point in the command.

```
some_class_name index some_integer
some_class_name some_integer
some_integer st | nd | rd| th some_class_name
first | second | third | fourth | fifth | sixth | seventh | eighth | ninth | tenth¬
        some_class_name
last | front | back some_class_name
```

Examples

```
word index 2
word 2
8th word
seventh word
first word
last word
```

Description

The basic idea of this form is that you can select an item based on its position relative to the beginning of objects of its class in the container. So the first object that belongs to a certain class inside some container, such as a paragraph, is numbered 1, the second one is numbered 2, and so on. Following is an example of how things work when there are multiple classes contained in a container:

```
set test_container to {"a", 1, "a test", 124.5, 17, "oops"}
set x to the first integer in test_container
set y to the second string in test_container
set z to the first real in test_container
set final_list to {x, y, z}
```

The value of the variable **final_list** is

```
{1, "a test", 124.5}
```

Even though the first integer in the list is the second item, it gets returned because items are numbered within their class so that the numbering of the items in the variable **test_container** is

```
{first string, first integer, second string, first real, second integer, third
        string}
```

You can phrase an index reference form in AppleScript in a wide variety of ways, as you saw in the previous syntax and examples. In general, phrasing an index reference form is pretty straightforward, and you should just pick the phrasing that's most readable for you.

You can actually use negative values to count back from the end of the container object as well. For example, these two script lines refer to the last and second to the last word in paragraph 3

```
set z to word -1 of paragraph 3
set z to word -2 of paragraph 3
```

The beginning, front, back, and end terms refer to places where you can insert new objects. For example, in this script

```
set test_list to {1, 2, 3}
copy -1 to the beginning of test_list
copy 4 to the end of test_list
```

the final value of the variable **test_list** is

```
{-1, 1, 2, 3, 4}
```

Be aware that **front** and **back** do not work with lists, but their synonyms, **beginning** and **end**, do. Don't bother pondering that, but do keep in mind that adding items to a list using **end** is much more efficient than using the concatenation operator (**&**). That means that you should use

```
set test_list to {1, 2, 3, 4}
set the end of test_list to 5
```

to set **test_list** to {1,2,3,4,5} rather than using

```
set test_list to {1, 2, 3, 4}
set test_list to test_list & 5
```

Middle

This reference picks the middle item in the container.

Syntax

```
middle some_class
```

Examples

```
middle word of "this is a test"
middle item of {1, 2, 3, 4, 5, 6}
```

Description

This is a little-used utility reference that lets you pick the middle item. If an odd number of entries aren't in the container, then this form rounds down. So, if seven words are in a string, the middle word is fourth, and if six words are in a string, the middle word is third.

Name

This picks an item by name.

Syntax

```
some_class_name [ named ] name_string
```

Examples

```
window named "Melvin"
document "fred"
```

Description

Not all objects have names, but those that do can be referenced with this form. This is a good form to use because it's easy to read. For example,

```
document "books"
```

is a great deal easier to read than

```
document 1
```

and is also less likely to lead to problems because the document numbered 1 can change the next time you open your program. However, the document that is called "books" changes only if you rename it.

Property

This reference accesses the value of a property of an object.

Syntax

```
property_name some_object
```

Examples

```
set z to length of "this is a test"              --> result is 14
name of {name:"Igor", job:"mad scientist"}       --> result is "Igor"
```

Description

Properties are named characteristics of some types of information. Chapter 17 shows how to find out what properties various types of information, such as documents in a word processor or a file in the Finder, have. Chapter 4 shows what properties the various value classes, such as strings, have. Think of properties as variables hidden inside information objects, such as strings. This reference form allows you to get the value of those properties. If the property is read only, such as the **length** of a string, you can't change it. Some properties can be changed, though, as in this example

```
set test_case to {name:"Mlvin", job:"Used Nuclear Weapons Salesman"}
set name of test_case to "Melvin"
return test_case
```

which fixes up poor Melvin's name.

Many of the objects that you come across in scriptable applications have properties that you can set. For example, in WordPerfect, a chunk of text has a **font** property. By changing the **font** property, you can change the font of that text. Chapter 17 talks about working with applications.

Range

This reference selects a contiguous group of items belonging to a class out of a container.

Syntax

```
every some_class_name from start_reference to end_reference
plural_class_name from start_reference to end_reference
some_class_name start_index thru | through stop_index
plural_class_name start_index thru | through stop_index
```

Examples

```
characters 1 thru 5 of "this is a test" --> {"t", "h", "i", "s", " "}
characters 1 thru 7 of "this is a test" --> {"t", "h", "i", "s", " ", "i", "s"}
characters 1 thru 2 of "this is a test" --> {"t", "h"}
characters 1 through 5 of "this is a test" --> {"t", "h", "i", "s", " "}
integers 2 through 4 of {"a", 2, "f", 3, 4.45, 7, 9, 25} --> {3, 7, 9}
```

Description

This reference form lets you pick a series of objects of the same type from a container. Sounds like something out of a government document, doesn't it? In plain English, it means you can pick a set of similar items, such as words or database records, out of some containing object, such as a string or a document. You'll find this especially useful when parsing strings. One thing to remember is that the items that are pointed at by this reference form are returned as items in a list. So if you ask for the 3 thru 5 characters of a string, you get a list {"a","b","c"}, not "abc." If you're dealing with strings, you can avoid getting this list by coercing the list to a string as in this example:

```
set temp to characters 1 thru 3 of "abcdefg"
set temp to temp as string
```

In this case, the final value of the variable **temp** is "abc."

The other thing to remember is that if a container has a mixed set of objects, the items are numbered sequentially in each class so that the second item in the list may be the first integer and the second integer may be the eighth item in the list. For example,

```
set test_list to {1, 3.2, 192, 3, 4, "a", 3.1415, "x", 2.3, 2.5, 3.9, 1}
set z to reals 2 through 4 of test_list
set y to integers 1 through 3 of test_list
```

sets the value of the variable **z** to

```
{3.1415,2.3,2.5}
```

and the value of **y** to

```
{1,192,3}
```

Relative

This reference lets you specify an object by its position relative to some other object.

Syntax

```
[some_class_name] before | [in] front of the_base_reference
[some_class_name] after | [in] back of | behind the_base_reference
```

Examples

```
tell application "Finder"
    set y to disk before disk 2 of disks
    set z to file after file 3 of startup disk
end tell
```

Description

This lets you specify items that are before or after some other item. All applications that support this referencing form let you use this when *some_class_name* is the same type as *the_base_reference*. Applications may allow you to use this reference with different classes, as in

```
set x to file after disk 2 of some_container
```

Referencing Files

You'll find that a great deal of your scripts involve working with files, so you need to know how to refer to a file. Basically, you can use two different approaches:

You can refer to a file, as in

```
file "Hard Disk:some folder:another folder:the file"
```

Or you can use an alias, as in

```
alias "Hard Disk:some folder:another folder:the file"
```

Both of these forms work just fine wherever you need to refer to a file. The difference has to do with how AppleScript deals with these two items. When you use the **file** version, AppleScript doesn't look for the file until the script is run. In addition, if you want to put the file reference in a variable, you need to use the **a reference to** operator as in this example:

```
set file_ref to a reference to file "system:format errors"
tell application "WordPerfect"
   open {file_ref}
end tell
```

When you use **alias**, AppleScript makes an alias when you compile the script that will always find the file no matter where it's located. You also don't need to use the **a reference to** operator to put an alias into a variable. The one reason not to use **alias** is that if you're working with remote computers, the process of finding the file every time you compile the script can be a bit bothersome. By the way, you refer to folders the same way you refer to files. The only difference is that the strings representing a folder end with a colon.

If you haven't gotten enough examples of references by now, just keep on reading. Just about any AppleScript script contains several references. You might think of your search as one of those stupid car games you get your kids to play — you know, spot all license plates that start with *z* or that sort of thing. Keep track of all of the references you spot and see what the total is when you've finished the book.

Chapter 8

Commands: Ordering AppleScript Around

In This Chapter
▶ What commands are
▶ The basic AppleScript commands

Commands are just orders you give to AppleScript to tell it what to do. Commands can do a wide variety of things, from choosing a file (**choose file**) to getting a listing of all of your hard disks (**list disks**). You can even use commands to control scriptable applications, which leads us to a key point.

The AppleScript language is extensible. By adding scripting additions (see Chapter 19), you can increase the number of commands that are available. In addition, each scriptable application has its own set of commands (see Chapter 17). Fortunately, all the commands are fairly easy to understand because they are based on the American you speak every day.

This chapter shows you the standard commands that come with AppleScript version 1.1. Everyone who's got AppleScript has access to these commands. Each entry describes what the command does, how to use it, and what values, if any, the command returns. You can use a returned value in an **if** statement (see Chapter 10):

```
if some command > 0 then
```

Or you can set a variable to the value returned as in

```
set x to choose application
```

where **x** is set to a reference to an application because that's what the **choose application** command returns.

Basic Commands

A great deal of stuff in this chapter is really more of a reference than an exercise in industrial-strength fun. I'd recommend just skimming through this chapter to get a quick idea of what the commands do. When you come to the various sample scripts later in the book, just hop back here and read the description of the commands you come across in more detail. I think you'll find that when you write scripts, as long as you've got a vague idea that a command out there does what you want, you'll be able to find the commands that you want in a jiffy. Bottom line: Don't try to memorize all of the detail that's here — just get a nodding acquaintance with the commands, and things will work out just fine.

I don't cover all of the commands that come with AppleScript 1.1 in this chapter. I cover the commands that relate to reading and writing data from files in Chapter 14. The ones that deal with the event log window are discussed in Chapter 18. Finally, I cover the ones that let you communicate with the computer in Chapter 9.

In the syntax portion of each command description, where I show all the variations on the command, anything in [] is optional. If you see two words separated by a |, that means that either of the two words can be used; they're synonyms that mean the same thing to AppleScript.

Activate

Launches an application, if it's not running, and brings it to the front.

Syntax

```
activate application some_application_name
```

Variables as parameters

AppleScript replaces a variable used as a parameter with the value of the variable before executing the command. In fact, AppleScript evaluates any expression prior to executing the command, so

```
set number_of_beeps to 9
```

```
beep number_of_beeps
```
is identical to
```
beep 9
```
which is identical to
```
beep 5 + 4
```

Parameters

some_application_name: This is a path to an application, or just the name of the application if it's in the same folder as the script. If the application is on another Mac, the application must be running. You also must use the application's name as it's shown in the application menu, accompanied by the zone and name of the Mac the application is running on.

Example

```
activate application "Some disk:some folder:Filemaker Pro"
```

This either launches FileMaker Pro and brings it to the front or brings an already-running FileMaker Pro to the front.

Description

This command brings the relevant application to the front and launches it, if necessary. An application running on another Mac must be running before this command is issued.

This command often brings up a standard file dialog that asks the user to find the application if it isn't running. If this occurs in a script that's running when no one is around, it can be a problem.

Value returned

Nothing.

Copy

This makes a copy of a value and places it into a new location, such as a variable.

Syntax

```
( copy | put ) some_expression ( to | into) some_variable
( copy | put ) some_expression ( to | into) some_reference
```

Parameters

some_expression: Any expression such as 1 + 1.

some_variable: Any legal variable name, list of variables, or record of variables.

some_reference: A reference to where to place the value of the expression. If nothing is specified, the value is placed in the clipboard as though you had used the Copy command in the Edit menu.

Example

```
copy "Melvin" to name_string
tell application "Finder"
    copy position of front window to {x, y}
    copy the name of the first file in startup disk to x
end tell
```

Description

The **copy** command is part of AppleScript and many scriptable applications' dictionaries. The first syntax example is applicable to AppleScript, while the second can be used when dealing with scriptable applications. **Copy** makes a new copy of lists, records, and script objects that take up more memory. **Copy** avoids a problem that can occur when you use the **set** command to set the value of a variable to a list, record, or script object (see Chapter 5 for details).

Value returned

The new value of the variable.

Count

This command counts the number of items of a certain class (such as strings) in some container (a list, for example).

Syntax

```
count [ [each | every] some_class ( in | of ) ] compound_value
number of [ plural_class_name ( in | of) ] compound_value
```

Parameters

some_class: The type of items to count, such as strings, integers, or Booleans.

compound_value: This is an item of some class that has countable items. The allowable AppleScript value classes are list, record, reference, or string.

plural_class_name: This is the type of item to be counted but with an *s* at the end, such as words, integers, strings.

Example

```
count words of "this is a test" --> 4
count each string in {"a", 1, 2, 3, "b", "this is a test"} --> 3
number of reals in {name:"Melvin", age:34, IQ:-30.3} -->1
count {1, 2, 3, 3.1415, "abcdefg", 2.2} --> 6
```

Description

This command lets you count the number of items of a certain class inside a value or object that has multiple elements. If you don't specify what type of objects to count, the command returns the total number of elements of all classes.

Value returned

The number of items that meet the criteria that are in the target compound value.

Current Date

This returns the time, day, and date, as determined by the Mac's clock.

Syntax

```
current date
```

Parameters

None.

Example

```
current date
```

Description

This returns a date and time, which can be used in a variety of ways, including comparisons such as

```
if (current date) comes after date "Friday, January 13, 1995 00:00:00" then
    display dialog "Later than I thought"
end if
```

which displays the dialog if the current date is later than 1/13/95. By the way, I typed in "Jan 13 1995" but AppleScript changed it to "Friday, January 13, 1995 0:00:00" when I checked the syntax of the script.

Value returned

If all goes well, a date value of the form day of week, month, day, year, and time is returned. You can access parts of the value returned by using the properties of the date value class described back in Chapter 4. Several possible errors range from -108 (out of memory) to -1718 (reply has not yet arrived).

Get

Puts the value of an expression into the special variable called **result**.

Syntax

```
[get] some_expression [as value_class]
```

Parameters

some_expression: Any legal expression.

value_class: The name of any value class that the result of **some_expression** can be coerced to.

Example

```
set y to 3
get y
set z to result + 3 --> z is now 6
get 7 + 3 as string
```

Description

This command is a bit superfluous. It's mainly there to make things easier to read. I rarely use it.

Value returned

The value of the expression, coerced to the specified class type if the **as** option is used.

Info For

This returns a record full of information about files and folders.

Syntax

```
info for some_file_reference
```

Parameters

some_file_reference: This is a reference to a file or folder of the form file "disk:file name" or alias "disk:file name."

Example

```
info for file "Applications:About "
```

returns the following record, which indicates it's a folder — the folder property (folder:true) has the value true.

```
{name:"About ", creation date:date "Sunday, May 29, 1994 17:12:16", modification
      date:date "Sunday, May 29, 1994 21:08:11", icon position:{-1, -1},
      visible:true, size:109373, folder:true, alias:false, folder window:{0,
      0, 0, 0}}
```

This example

```
info for file "Kate:New York Gold Price Hist"
```

returns these values for this file containing a chart, created by DeltaGraph Pro 3.5, of the price of New York gold.

```
{name:"New York Gold Price Hist", creation date:date "Sunday, January 8, 1995
      8:43:22", modification date:date "Sunday, April 2, 1995 14:09:06", icon
      position:{0, 52}, visible:true, size:65288, folder:false, alias:false,
      locked:false, file creator:"ttxt", file type:"PICT", short version:"",
      long version:"", default application:alias "Peter the man:SimpleText"}
```

Description

This command works even if you don't have the scriptable Finder installed — see Chapter 22 for tons of information on that wonder of the modern world — so it's a sure way to get useful information about folders and files. Most of the elements in the records are fairly obvious. The file's creator and type are discussed in Chapter 9. Long and short version are the version information strings that appear in the info box when you use the Get Info command in the File menu. The default application alias is a reference to the application that is launched if you double-click on the file. This command is very useful in obtaining the information you need to select a subset of files based on a variety of criteria, such as creation date, modification date, file creator, file type, and/or size, which is given in bytes.

Value returned

If everything works right, you get a record with the entries shown in Table 8-1.

Table 8-1   Values Returned Using the Info For Command

Value	Description
name	The file name. What did you expect?
creation date	The date the file was first made.
modification date	The last time the file was changed.
icon position	This is a list with the location of the icon specified as a two-element list: {horizontal position in pixels, vertical position in pixels}. If you manually move an icon, this value doesn't update until you close the window the icon is in. Furthermore, if you coerce the file description to an alias, the value never changes.
visible	True if the item is visible; false if it's invisible.
size	Size of the item in bytes — divide by 1,024 to get Kbytes.
folder	If the value of this is true, the item is a folder.
alias	If the value of this is true, the item is an alias.
folder window	This is only returned if the item is a folder. The returned value is a four-item list — {horizontal position of upper left, vertical position of upper left, horizontal position of lower right, vertical position of lower right} — all in pixels.
locked	True if the item is locked and undeletable.
file creator	The four-character creator code that identifies the application that created the file. This is only returned for files.
file type	The four-character type code that tells what type of file this is. This is only returned for files.
short version	This is the short version string that you see in a file's Get Info window. This is only returned for files.
long version	This is the director's cut of the version string.
default application	This is an alias reference to the application that the Finder launches if you double-click on this file. This only shows up for nonapplication files.

A bunch of possible errors are associated with this command, but the most interesting ones are shown in Table 8-2.

Table 8-2   Errors Associated with the Info For Command

Error	Description
-35	Disk wasn't found
-37	Bad name for the file
-43	File wasn't found
-120	Folder wasn't found

The Info For command is useful primarily if you don't have the scriptable Finder — see Chapter 22. With the scriptable Finder, you can get the same information from the properties of the file object.

List Disks

This returns a list of the names of the disks currently mounted on your desktop.

Syntax

```
list disks
```

Parameters

None.

Example

```
set disk_names to list disks
```

This sets the value of the variable **disk_names** to something like

```
{"Peter the man", "ted the man", "Kate the lady", "kate", "tiny", "Peter", "Ted",
    "Mary", "therese", "Archive", "Games", "Programming", "Source Code",
    "Applications", "Text archives", "Telecom", "Who knows", "multimedia",
    "Newton"}
```

on my Mac.

Description

If you don't have the scriptable Finder, this command gives you a way to find the names of all of the disks on the Mac. You can use these disk names to build up file paths. In combination with the **list folder** command, you can generate paths to all of the files on all of your disks. For example, this line will put the names of all of the files and folders in the top level of the first hard disk on a Mac into the variable **file_list**.

```
set file_list to list folder item 1 of (list disks) & ":"
```

You need to add the : because the list returned by **list disks** doesn't have a colon after the disk name and the **list folder** command needs to have folders — which a disk is — terminated with a colon. You need to put the parentheses around **list disks** in order to ensure it is evaluated first. Without the parentheses, AppleScript gives you an error when you try to check the syntax of the script.

If you've got the scriptable Finder and you want references to disks, not their names as strings, you can just use

```
tell application "Finder"
    set disk_list to disks
end tell
```

and **disk_list** contains a list of references to the disks that are currently available on your Mac.

Value returned

If all goes well, this command returns a list containing the names, as strings, of all of the disks on your Mac. These are just strings, not references to disks.

List Folder

This command returns a list of the names, as strings, of all of the items in the folder it gets as a parameter.

Syntax

```
list folder reference_to_a_folder_or_disk
```

Parameters

reference_to_a_folder_or_disk: This is a reference to a file or disk, such as

```
folder "Peter the man:system folder:extensions:"
folder "Peter the man:"
```

Example

```
set folder_to_list to "Mary:"
set list_of_items to list folder folder_to_list
```

This sets the value of **list_of_items** to

```
{" INIT Tracker","AppleShare PDS","book related stuff","Books text","c8 ad","cat/
    tops for article","Christmas Card Letter, '93","ClarisImpact 2.0
    Folder","Desktop","Desktop DB","Desktop DF","Desktop Folder",excelSupergun
    article","Files","Folder for Project about","Hard Disk","Latest Genie messages
    h","misc backups 3/25/95","Monitor","Norton FS Comment","Norton FS
    Data","Norton FS Index","Norton FS Volume","Norton FS Volume 2","Programs for
    Book","ProNet Regis, 9/9/93","PubUtils DeleteInfo","PubUtils VolInfo","Read
    Me","Read Me First (Latest Notes)","Resumes need updating","Saxon's Math
    K","SBIG ST4","SpaceSaver Temporary Items","start on 89 taxes","stuff for
    grandpa","Supergun article","Taxes","Temporary Items","test","things to
    do","THINK Reference f","Trash","turn the hearts","TV shows","untitled
    folder","untitled folder 2","wide margins","Word Print File","[DiskExpress
    Activity Log]}
```

The result on your disks will be different, of course, unless you've broken into my house and stolen my disk. Notice that even invisible files such as the Desktop DB and Desktop DF show up. Some of these items are folders, but you can't tell that from this list.

Description

If you've got the scriptable Finder, this command can be replaced by

```
tell application "Finder"
    set reference_to_folder to folder "Mary:files:"
    set item_list to items of reference_to_folder
end tell
```

which sets the value of the variable **item_list** to a list of references to the items, files, and folders visible or invisible, that are contained in the folder pointed to by the parameter supplied to the command.

When working with the scriptable Finder, you can't say

```
folder "Mary:"
```

when Mary: is a disk. In that case, you need to use

```
tell application "Finder"
    set reference_to_folder to disk "Mary:"
    set item_list to items of reference_to_folder
end tell
```

You can convert the value returned by the **list folder** command to paths using the following script sample:

```
set folder_ref to "tiny:"
set item_list to list folder folder_ref
set path_list to {}
repeat with t_item in item_list
   set temp_path to folder_ref & t_item
   if folder of (info for file temp_path) then
      set temp_path to temp_path & ":"
   end if
   set path_list to path_list & temp_path
end repeat
```

That script sets the value of the variable **path_list** to a list containing path strings of the form "disk:folder:folder:." The **if** statement (see Chapter 10) inside the loop decides if the item is a folder by using the **info for** command. You need to determine if an item is a folder in order to decide if the text version of the path should end in a colon. Fortunately, the **info for** command works if you tack **file** in front of the path string, even if the item is actually a folder. The **repeat** statement, described in Chapter 11, repeats the script lines between the **repeat** and **end repeat** lines once for each file or folder in **item_list**.

Value returned

If things work well, then the command returns a list of strings containing the names of the items found in the folder. Interesting error codes are shown in Table 8-3.

Table 8-3   Errors Associated with the List Folder Command

Error	Description
-35	Disk wasn't found
-37	Bad name for the file
-43	File wasn't found
-120	Folder wasn't found

Offset

This command tells you the location of one string inside another string. Offset won't work with an application that has offset as a property, such as the Scriptable Text Editor.

Syntax

```
offset of string_to_look_for in string_to_search_in
```

Parameters

string_to_look_for: This is the string you're trying to find.

string_to_search_in: This is the string that you're trying to find something in.

Example

```
set string_to_look_for to "Mary"
set list_of_disks to list disks
set i to 0
repeat with t_disk in list_of_disks
    set i to i + 1
    set t_offset to (offset of string_to_look_for in t_disk)
    if t_offset is greater than 0 then
        display dialog "Found " & string_to_look_for & ¬
          " in the " & i & "th disk name at location " & t_offset
        return i
    end if
end repeat
```

This script looks for the first disk whose name contains the string "Mary." The script determines that it's found a disk name that contains "Mary" when the offset is larger than 0.

Description

This is a very useful function when you're working with strings. Make sure you remember that the comparison used in this command is always case sensitive: "Mary" and "mary" do not match the same things.

If you don't care where the string you're looking for is in the string being searched, you can use the **contains** operator (see Chapter 10) instead, as in

```
if t_disk contains string_to_look_for then
```

which works just the same as

```
if (offset of string_to_look_for in t_disk) is greater than 0 then
```

Value returned

If things work, then **offset** returns an integer that defines the location of the searched-for string in the searched string. If the searched-for string isn't in the searched string, the command returns 0. Table 8-4 shows some examples of how the **offset** command works.

Table 8-4	Values Returned by the Offset Command	
String to Search	*String to Look For*	*Offset*
Mary:folder:	Mary	1
This is a test of the	t of	14
An apple a day	apple	4

Path to

This command lets you find the path, as an alias or a string, to a number of standard items, such as the startup disk and the active System folder.

Syntax

```
path to selected_item [as className]
```

Parameters

selected_item: This is one of the constants shown in Table 8-5.

Table 8-5	Parameters of the Path to Command
Selected Item	*Description*
Apple menu	Path to Apple Menu Items folder in System folder
Apple Menu Items	Same as Apple menu
Control Panels	Path to Control Panels folder in System folder
Desktop	Path to Desktop folder
Extensions	Path to Extensions folder in System folder
Preferences	Path to Preferences folder in System folder
PrintMonitor	Path to PrintMonitor Documents folder
PrintMonitor documents	Same as PrintMonitor

Selected Item	Description
Trash	Path to Trash folder
Start-up Items	Path to Startup Items folder in System folder
System folder	Path to currently active System folder
Temporary Items	Path to Temporary Items folder
Start-up disk	Path to Startup disk
Frontmost application	Path to frontmost application file

className: This has to be a string. If you omit it, then the command returns aliases. If it's present, then it returns the paths as strings.

Example

```
set constant_list to {apple menu items folder, apple menu items folder, control¬
       panels folder, desktop, ¬
    extensions folder, preferences folder, printmonitor documents, printmonitor¬
       documents, trash, ¬
    startup items folder, system folder, temporary items folder, startup disk,¬
       frontmost application}
set paths to {}
repeat with t in constant_list
    set paths to paths & (path to t)
end repeat
return paths
```

This script sets the value of the variable **paths** to a list containing the paths to each of the constants that the **path to** command can use. You may notice that the first two items in the **constant_list** seem to be the same. When I typed them in, it looked like

```
{apple menu, apple menu item...
```

When I checked the syntax of the script, AppleScript added the folder after several of the items and replaced the two cases — printmonitor and apple menu — where two different constants represent the same thing, with one of the options.

Description

You'll often want to write a script that doesn't contain *hardwired* references to a specific disk name or file path.

hardwired: This has nothing to do with stealing cars or the use of titanium for wiring your house. A hardwired reference to a file contains the filename as in "Peter the man:system folder:." That's fine if you're sure that you'll never change the folder's name and your script will never run on another computer. Something is hardwired in a script if you have to edit and recompile the script in order to change the value.

The **path to** command lets you write scripts that continue to work on machines other than your own. The command also allows you to change the name of your hard disks and/or files and folders without having to edit and recompile the script. For example, if your script is looking for all of the extensions in your currently active system folder, you can write a script like this:

```
set extensions_folder to alias "Peter the Man:System Folder:Extensions:"
set extension_items to list folder extensions_folder
set number_of_extensions to the count items in extension_items
```

This script doesn't count the number of extensions that are active because it counts folders as well as files. Some extensions, such as After Dark and AppleScript itself, put folders in the Extensions folder. You can use the sample script, shown in the **list folder** command description, to figure out how to tell if the items are files or folders and only count the files.

This script counts the items in the extension folder in an exemplary manner, but it only works on my machine if I use "Peter the man" — named after my son — as my startup disk. I can't give the script to anyone else because it wouldn't work on their Mac unless they renamed their startup disk. On the other hand, this script

```
set extensions_folder to path to extensions folder
set extension_items to list folder extensions_folder
set number_of_extensions to the count items in extension_items
```

works on any machine no matter which disk is used for startup. That type of portability is often very useful when you're developing scripts that you'll want to use over a long period of time, say a year, or that are to be distributed to a number of users.

Value returned

If the **as string** parameter is not present, the command returns an alias to the item specified by the first parameter of the command. If the **as string** parameter is present, then a string path of the form "Disk:folder:folder:folder:file" is returned.

Random Number

This command lets you generate a random number.

Syntax

```
random number [upper_limit_for_value] [from start_number to end_number]¬
       [with seed seed_number]
```

Parameters

upper_limit_for_value: This specifies the largest random number that can be returned. If it's a real number (it has a decimal point), then the value that the **random number** command returns is a real. If it's an integer, then the value returned is an integer. If you don't use this optional parameter, then a random number between 0 and 1 is returned.

start_number: This defines the smallest possible value the **random number** command can return. If it is a real number, then the value returned by the command is real.

end_number: This is the maximum value the command can return. If it's real, then the value returned is real.

seed_number: This specifies the seed value to be used in generating the random number. By specifying a seed value, you fix the sequence of random numbers that is generated so that you can repeat sequences of "random" numbers when testing your scripts. The sequence is random, and the correlation between items in the sequence is minimized, even when you specify the seed number; it's just that you can replicate it. You can rerandomize the sequence by setting the seed to 0.

Example

```
random number
random number 10 with seed 3
random number from 1 to 10
```

Description

This command lets you generate random numbers. If you're not a mathematician, just think of this command as a big die that can have any number of sides you want. Each time you call **random number**, the die generates a random — actually pseudorandom because computers can't generate truly random numbers, but unless you're a fanatic, the difference is irrelevant — number just as though you'd rolled a die. If you need to repeat a sequence of random numbers — to test a script, for example — you can specify the seed of the random number sequence. When the seed is specified, the sequence of random numbers is determined, but no correlation between the values in the sequence exists.

Value returned

This command returns an integer or a real, depending upon the values of the parameters. If no optional values are specified, then the default return is a real number between 0 and 1.

Round

This lets you round real numbers to integers.

Syntax

```
round some_number [ rounding ( up | down | toward zero | to nearest ) ]
```

Parameters

some_number: This is some number which you want to round off.

Example

```
round -3.1415                           --> -3
round 3.1415                            --> 3
round 3.1415 rounding up               --> 4
round 3.1415 rounding down             --> 3
round 3.1415 rounding toward zero      --> 3
round -3.1415 rounding toward zero     --> -3
round 3.1415 rounding to nearest       --> 3
```

Description

You use this command to convert real numbers (those with decimal points) to integers.

Value returned

An integer.

Set

This command sets the value of a variable or parameter.

Syntax

```
set some_variable to some_expression
some_expression returning some_variable
```

Parameters

some_variable: This is some variable, a list full of variables, or a record full of variables.

some_expression: Some expression such as 3, x - 7, z/(w-32), or the second word of paragraph 2

Example

```
set y to 3
set x to y - 32
3 returning x
tell application "Finder"
    set {x, y} to position of window 1
end tell
```

Description

This is the basic command for changing the value of a variable. You can safely ignore the **returning** version; I've never used it, and I haven't seen any scripts that use it either. In general, the syntax is simple. Keep in mind that when you set a variable's value to a record or list, you're not copying that record or list; you're merely giving it another name, an alias. If, in the Finder, you set up multiple aliases to a file and then change the contents of the file, all aliases point to the new changed file. In AppleScript, if you use **set** to change the value of a variable to a large data structure, such as a list, any changes to the value of the list show up in the variable, as in this example:

```
set x to {1, 2}
set y to x
set item 1 of x to 3
```

In this case, the final value of y is {3,2}. This is discussed in more detail in Chapter 5. You can avoid this problem by using the **copy** command.

The only other interesting thing about **set** is its ability to set multiple variables with a single line, as shown in the last example in the examples section. The position of any item, such as a window, on the Mac's screen is defined by two numbers. One number specifies how far away an item is from the top of the screen, while the other specifies how far an item is from the left-hand side of the screen. In the last example, the value of the variable **x** is set to the distance from the left-hand side of the screen, while the variable **y** is set to the distance from the top of the screen. You can use variables set in this way, as shown in this example.

```
tell application "Finder"
    set {x, y} to position of window 1
    set x to x - 3
end tell
```

The final value of **x** is the horizontal coordinate of the window 1 minus 3.

Value returned

The value returned is the new value of the variable.

Time to GMT

This returns the difference, in seconds, between the clock on your computer and Greenwich Mean Time (GMT).

Syntax

```
time to GMT
```

Parameters

None.

Example

```
time to GMT --> 0
time to GMT --> -28800
```

Description

If you've been a good boy or girl and told your Mac where it is (other than the center of your universe) by using the Map control panel, then this command returns the time difference in seconds between your Mac's clock — which is usually off by a reasonable amount unless you set it pretty often — and the current time in Greenwich, England. The fact that everyone measures time from some obscure village in England is one of the last vestiges of when England ruled the world, Pax Britanica. If you've not bothered to tell your Mac where it is by using the Map control panel, then this function returns to 0. If you live in Pacific Standard Time, you get -28800.

Value returned

Time difference in seconds between where your Mac thinks it is and Greenwich, England.

Advanced Commands

Some commands are mainly of interest to more advanced scripters or program-mers who are learning scripting. The actual commands are fairly simple, but you need to know a bit about programming to understand why you'd use them. I briefly cover the relevant concepts, just in case you're interested.

ASCII character

Returns the character that corresponds to an integer.

Syntax

```
ASCII character some_integer
```

Parameters

some_integer: An integer or an expression that evaluates to an integer between 1 and 255.

Example

```
ASCII character 100    --> "d"
ASCII character 68     --> "D"
```

Description

This lets you convert an integer between 1 and 255 into a character. ASCII stands for American Standard Code for Information Interchange and is just a way to let computers, which only work with numbers, have a platform-independent definition of text. The fact that most machines use ASCII is why you can read pure text files from just about any platform on just about any other platform. The limit of 255 is because the ASCII standard reserves 1 byte, 8 bits, for each character, and 1 byte has 255 possible values.

If you're curious as to which characters correspond to which numbers, you can run this little script and look at the result.

```
set result_string to "i Character" & return
repeat with i from 1 to 255
   set temp to ASCII character i
   set result_string to result_string & i & " " & temp & return
end repeat
```

Basically, the script defines a header line for the result and then repeats 255 times each time **i** takes on a new value one larger than it was the last time. The **ASCII character** command converts the value of **i** into a character which, along with the value of **i**, is placed into the string. The final result looks like Table 8-6, where I've taken a chunk out of the middle of the final result string.

Table 8-6	ASCII Character Commands
Number	*Character*
33	!
34	\"
35	#
36	$
37	%
38	&
39	'
40	(
41	)
42	*
43	+
44	,
45	-
46	.

Number	Character
47	/
48	0
49	1
50	2
51	3
52	4
53	5
54	6
55	7
56	8
57	9
58	:
59	;
60	<
61	=
62	>
63	?
64	@
65	A
66	B
67	C
68	D
69	E
70	F
71	G

Value returned

A one-character string.

ASCII number

This converts a character into an integer.

Syntax

```
ASCII number some_one_character_string
```

Parameters

some_one_character_string: A one-character string, such as "a" or "Z."

Example

```
ASCII number "a"  --> 97
ASCII number "A"  --> 65
ASCII number "0"  --> 48
```

Description

This is the inverse of the **ASCII character** command. It takes a character and returns the integer that corresponds to it.

Value returned

Integer between 1 and 255 corresponding to the character supplied as an argument.

Chapter 9

I/O (I Owe) without Credit Cards

I/O Commands

I/O is computerese for input/output. Life would be a lot duller if you couldn't input information to the computer or it couldn't output information to you. Imagine life with no bomb dialogs. Talk about dull. In general, I/O refers to any input or output, but in the context of AppleScript, it's most reasonable to talk about *inputs from* people and *outputs to* people.

The bad news is that AppleScript isn't exactly brimming with spiffy I/O options. The good news is that it's got enough options to meet the needs of most scripts. Table 9-1 shows the main I/O commands.

Table 9-1	The Main I/O Commands
Command	*Description*
beep	Makes a sound using the standard Mac beep.
display dialog	Uses a standard Mac dialog box with up to 255 characters of text.
choose file	Uses the standard Mac file selection dialog box.
choose folder	Uses the standard Mac folder selection dialog box.
choose application	Lets the user select a running application on any computer in the network.

beep is useful for catching users' attention. While their eyes may not be on the monitor, they'll hear a beep if they're in the same room.

display dialog is the primary way of telling the user things and getting text input.

The last three commands in the table — **choose file**, **choose folder**, and **choose application** — allow the user to specify files, folders, and applications in a manner that AppleScript can understand.

You'll find that you use **display dialog** the most, so you should spend a bit of time understanding how it works. It's not all that obtuse, as you can see in the examples in earlier chapters. Most of the time, you won't use most of its options. You should skim over the other commands just so you know what they do. When you need to use them, you can come back and read through their definitions in detail. You can also see them being used in a number of the example scripts elsewhere in the book.

display dialog

This command lets you create a typical Mac alert/message dialog box as well as one that lets the user enter a string, such as a file name.

Syntax

```
display dialog some_message_string ¬
   [ default answer default_answer_string] ¬
   [buttons a_list_of_button_names] ¬
   [default button name_of_default_button] ¬
   [with icon some_name_or_integer]
```

Parameters

some_message_string: A string that appears in the dialog box. It can be up to 255 characters long. Characters beyond 255 are not shown.

default_answer_string: The text that appears in the text field so that the user can edit it. If this value isn't supplied, the dialog box won't have an editable text field. Use "" for this parameter if you want an editable text field with no default content.

a_list_of_button_names: A list of strings, each of which will be used as the name of a button. AppleScript displays 1, 2, or 3 buttons. If this parameter is skipped, AppleScript uses the Cancel and OK buttons.

name_of_default_button: Specifies which button will be activated if the user presses the Return key. You can specify either the button's name in a string (for example, "OK") or an integer that indicates the position of the button in the button list — that is, 1, 2, or 3. If you use the default buttons and don't specify a value for this parameter, the OK button is shown as the default button, with a thick, black border. If you don't use the custom buttons and you don't use this option, the dialog box will have no default button.

some_name_or_integer: Specifies which icon should be displayed in the dialog box. If this value is a string, it's interpreted as the name of an 'ICON' *resource.* If it's an integer, it's interpreted as the number of the resource. AppleScript comes with three predefined icons: Stop, Note, and Caution, which have numbers 0, 1, and 2, respectively.

resource: One of the many innovations of the Mac was its use of two files to represent one file that you see in the Finder. One of these two files contains *resources* — things such as icons, pictures, code, windows, and menus — while the other contains data, such as the text in a word-processing document. Every resource has a four-character name. An 'ICON' resource is just an icon, a 32 x 32 pixel picture. Every resource can have a name, which can be more than four characters long, and an identifying integer number.

Examples

```
display dialog "This is a simple dialog"
```

See Figure 9-1.

Figure 9-1:
A simple
dialog box.

```
This is a simple dialog

                              Cancel    OK
```

```
display dialog "This is a dialog with 3 custom buttons " buttons {"oops!",¬
"Forget it!", "Sounds Great!"}
```

See Figure 9-2.

Figure 9-2:
A dialog box
with the
maximum
three
buttons.

This is a dialog with 3 custom buttons

oops!   Forget it!   Sounds Great!

```
display dialog ¬
    "This is a dialog with 3 custom buttons — last is default " buttons{"oops!".¬
    "Forget it!", "Sounds Great!"}
    default button "Sounds Great!"
```

See Figure 9-3.

Figure 9-3:
A default
button.

```
display dialog ¬
    "This is a dialog with 3 custom buttons — middle is default " buttons¬
    {"oops!", "Forget it!", "Sounds Great!"}
    default button 2
```

See Figure 9-4.

Figure 9-4:
A middle
button
default.

This is a dialog with 3 custom buttons--middle is
default

oops!   Forget it!   Sounds Great!

```
display dialog "Please enter your name" default answer ""
```

See Figure 9-5.

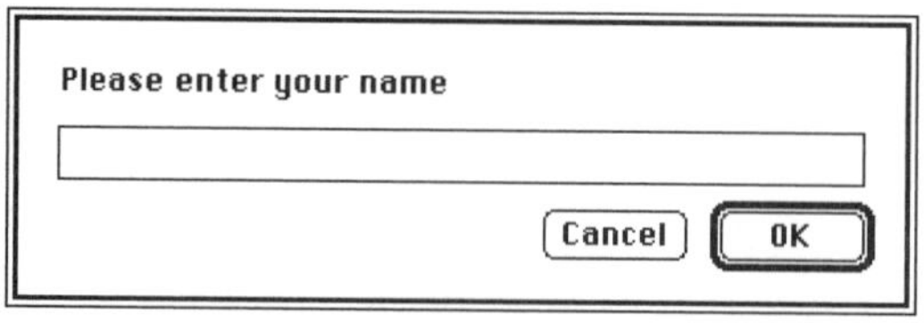

Figure 9-5:
Letting the
user enter
some text.

Please enter your name

Cancel   OK

```
display dialog "Please enter your citizenship." default answer "American"
```

See Figure 9-6.

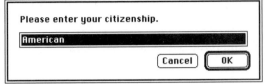

Figure 9-6:
A default
answer.

```
display dialog "This is the stop icon" with icon stop
```

See Figure 9-7.

Figure 9-7:
Adding a
stop icon.

```
display dialog "This is the Note icon" with icon note
```

See Figure 9-8.

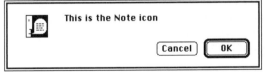

Figure 9-8:
Adding a
Note icon.

```
display dialog "This is the Caution icon" with icon 2
```

See Figure 9-9.

Figure 9-9:
Adding a
Caution icon.

Description

display dialog is the general workhorse I/O command. You can generate a wide spectrum of dialog boxes, but you're limited to three buttons, one icon, and one text entry field. In general, if you want anything more complex than that, you should look into using FaceSpan or HyperCard (see Chapter 26) to build a user interface for AppleScript.

The **display dialog** command returns a record that looks like

```
{text returned:"Melvin Smith, 35", button returned:"OK"}
```

The record has two properties: **text returned**, which is the value of the text in the text edit field — if present — and **button returned**, which is the name of the button the user clicked on. If the user presses Return, the name of the default button is returned. You can access the properties of a record by using a script like this one:

```
set temp to display dialog "Please enter your name" default answer ""
set text_the_user_entered to text returned of temp
```

Remember that although the data returned by the **display dialog** command is a string, you can coerce that string to another type — say, an integer, as in this example:

```
set temp to display dialog "Enter your age in years" default answer "17"
set text_entered to text returned of temp
set text_entered to text_entered as integer
```

This script assumes that the user will enter something that can be coerced to a number. If a user enters "none of your business," AppleScript generates an error. In a real script, you should put a **try** statement (see Chapter 12) around these script lines to catch this sort of problem and keep your script from crashing.

If the user clicks the Cancel button, your script ends right there. To avoid this situation, rename the Cancel button by using the **buttons** option to add a space to Cancel. That is, make it "Cancel " or " Cancel" rather than "Cancel." You can also use a **try** statement to catch the error generated when the user clicks on Cancel, as in this script:

```
try
    display dialog "Test of error catching"
on error
    some script lines that handle the case that the user hit cancel
end try
```

The **try** statement is covered in detail in Chapter 12.

If you really want the user to be able to enter multiple values, you can use a trick like this:

```
set temp to display dialog "Enter your name and age" default answer¬
"Melvin Smith, 35"
set text_user_entered to the text returned of temp
set old_delimiters to AppleScript's text item delimiters
set AppleScript's text item delimiters to {","}
set user_name to the first text item of text_user_entered
set user_age to (the second text item of text_user_entered) as integer
set AppleScript's text item delimiters to old_delimiters
```

This script generates the dialog box shown in Figure 9-10. It uses the AppleScript's text item delimiter property, discussed in Chapter 4, to pick out the two pieces of the user's answer, which are separated by a comma. It then resets the delimiters to what they were when the script started. You could use this same approach on any number of input values, but the chances of the user not entering data the way you want is high. If you're the only one who's going to use the script, this approach might be acceptable.

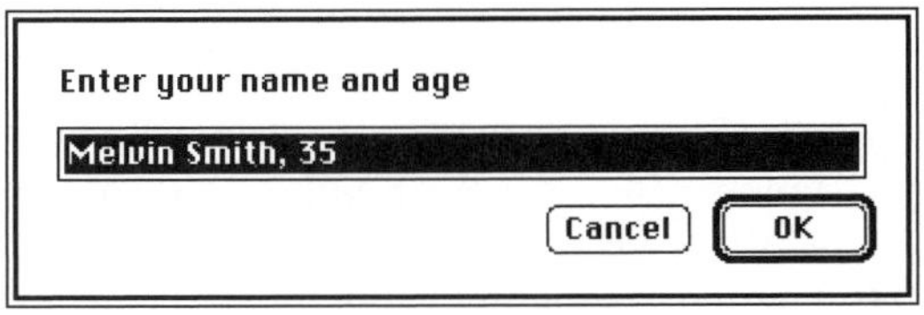

Figure 9-10:
Letting the user input multiple values from a single dialog box.

```
Enter your name and age

Melvin Smith, 35

            Cancel     OK
```

Value returned

The display dialog command returns a record of the form

```
{button returned:name_of_button_selected}
```

if the **default answer** option isn't used and

```
{text returned:string_in_text_field, button returned:name_of_button_selected}
```

if the **default answer** option is used.

beep

Plays the system alert sound.

Syntax

```
beep number_of_times_to_beep
```

Parameters

number_of_times_to_beep: An integer that specifies how many times the command should play the system beep sound.

Example

```
beep 10
```

Description

The example causes the system alert sound to be played ten times. You can have it play any number of times (as long as the number is an integer). Be warned that too many beeps will drive you crazy. You can set what the system alert beep sounds like by using the Sound control panel.

Value returned

None.

Adding icons

If you want to add your own spiffy, color icons, you need to use a resource-moving utility such as ResEdit to copy an icon resource from wherever you made it into the script file. You can access the icon by its resource number.

choose application

This command displays a dialog box that lets the user pick an application currently running on the local Mac or on any Mac on the same network.

Syntax

```
choose application [ with prompt some_prompt_string] [application label some_label]
```

Parameters

some_prompt_string: A piece of text up to 255 characters long that will be placed in the dialog box. Unfortunately, only the first 50 or so characters will be displayed. If you don't use this optional prompt, AppleScript automatically puts in "Choose a program to link to:"

some_label: Customizes the dialog box by changing the title of the scrolling field that contains the list of running applications on the selected Mac. It defaults to "Programs."

Example

```
set label_string to "Running Applications"
choose application with prompt ¬
    "Pick a program any program" application label label_string
```

This script generates the selection dialog box shown in Figure 9-11. If you're hooked into a network, the right-hand side is split in two, with the top list showing the local Macintoshes and the lower list showing the available AppleTalk zones.

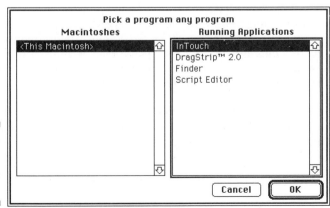

Figure 9-11:
Picking a running application.

Description

You use this command to let the user pick a running application. The command returns a reference to the application that you can use to direct commands to the application. Read Chapter 17, which explains how to work with applications, for more information on how to use the application reference.

Value returned

If the user chooses an application and clicks on the OK button, the command returns a reference to the application. If the user clicks on the Cancel button, an error -128 is issued; if you want the script to continue, you must use the **try** handler, which is described in Chapter 12.

choose file

This command displays a dialog box that lets the user pick a file.

Syntax

```
choose file [with prompt some_prompt_string] ③
    [of type some_list_of_types]
```

Parameters

some_prompt_string: This is just a string of which the first 40 characters will show up in the standard Mac file dialog box that this command creates.

some_list_of_types: Every file on the Mac has a *type* and a *creator,* which help the Finder figure out what kind of information it contains and which applications can use it.

file type: This has nothing to do with the psychological profile of a file. It does describe something about the format of the file. For example, common types are TEXT for all text files and PICT for the default Mac graphics format. All types are exactly four characters long — spaces do count — and they are case sensitive, meaning that TEXT works while text doesn't.

file creator: This is another four-character string that describes which application created a given file. The file creator is how the Mac knows which application to launch when you double-click on a file.

Example

```
choose file with prompt "Pick a file" of type {"TEXT", "PICT"}
```

This script generates the dialog box shown in Figure 9-12. It may not be obvious, but only files with type TEXT or PICT and folders are shown. You can't pick a folder (use the **choose folder** command for that); the folders are there so you can navigate around to find the file you want.

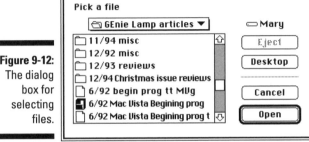

Figure 9-12:
The dialog
box for
selecting
files.

Description

Often your script will need to use a different file every time the script is run. The **choose file** command lets the user select the file to use. By restricting the types of files that are presented, you can make sure that the user doesn't select a file that the script can't work with. For example, if the script is designed to use Microsoft Word to look for keywords in a document, you don't want the user selecting a type of file — say, a Photoshop picture — that Microsoft Word can't work with.

Value returned

If the user clicks on the Open button, the command returns a reference to the selected file, which you can then use in the rest of the script. If the user clicks on the Cancel button, then error -128 is generated so that you have to use the **try** statement — described in Chapter 12 — if you want your script to continue executing. If you get a -108 error, then AppleScript ran out of memory.

Self-destructive scripts

Often, if the user is supposed to select a file, application, or folder but doesn't, the best thing for the script to do is quit. The **choose application, choose file**, and **choose folder** commands are all designed to stop the script if the user decides not to make a choice. This feature means that your script will automatically do what you want unless the script can work even without user input. If it doesn't need user input, use the **try** statement (see Chapter 12) to handle the error and allow your script to continue executing.

choose folder

This command lets the user select a folder.

Syntax

```
choose folder [with prompt some_prompt_string]
```

Parameters

some_prompt_string: This string, or at least the first 80 or so characters of it, will show up at the top of the selection dialog box. If you don't supply a value for this prompt, AppleScript uses "Choose a folder."

Example

```
set folder_ref to choose folder with prompt "Pick a folder"
```

This script generates a dialog box that allows the user to select a folder. If the user selects a folder, the reference to the folder is placed in the **folder_ref** variable.

Description

You'll use this command when the script requires that the user select a folder. This is the case when you want to process all the files in a folder — for example, a script that looks for new files in a folder and processes them when they arrive — or when you want to move files to a folder.

Value returned

If the user clicks on the button at the bottom of the scrolling list — its name is the name of the current folder — this command returns a reference to the folder, which you can use elsewhere in your script. If the user clicks on the Cancel button, error -128 is posted, and unless you use the **try** statement described in Chapter 12, your script ends. If you get a -108 error, then AppleScript ran out of memory.

Although these commands seem simple, they're sufficient for most of your scripting interface needs. If you need a more complex user interface, you can use HyperCard or FaceSpan, discussed in Chapter 26.

Chapter 10

If: Letting Your Computer Make Decisions so You Can Blame It Later

. . . .

In This Chapter

▶ How to teach your script to make decisions with **if**

▶ All you wanted to know about logical operators like < and **or**

. . . .

*W*hat if you never could make a decision while using your Mac, and as a result, you could never decide which file to use or what an application should do. All in all, your Mac would be pretty useless. The same thing applies to scripts. If your scripts can't make decisions, then they'll be a heck of a lot less useful. Some scripts, such as the one that changes the color depth of your monitor, can get by without you making choices. On the other hand, most scripts, say one that finds all scriptable applications on your disk, need to make decisions. Fortunately, AppleScript includes an easy way to make choices. You saw it before in Chapter 1. It's the ever-famous **if** statement.

The Ever-Famous if Statement

In keeping with AppleScript's near English syntax, the general format of the **if** statement is just

```
if something is true then
    do this stuff
else if something else is true and the first thing wasn't then
    do this other stuff
else if neither of the first two things were true then
    do this final batch of stuff
```

The actual syntax in AppleScript is

```
if some_expression_which_evaluates_to_true_or_false then
   some script lines
else if some_other_expression_which_evaluates_to_true_or_false then
   some other script lines
else
   another set of script lines
end if
```

This looks pretty much like the way you'd say it if you were talking to someone. One of several differences between AppleScript and English is that AppleScript doesn't understand ambiguity. This means that the *some_expression_that_evaluates_to_true_or_false* must be precisely defined — say "if the file is larger than 100K," not something along the lines of "if it's a nice color." Another difference is the need to have that silly **end if** at the end. That's there just to help AppleScript know when the **if** statement ends.

Logical Operators

Before we dive into examples of the **if** control structure, take a look at the operators that are commonly used in the test expression. In general, the operators let you compare two values. Because AppleScript tries to be very much like standard English, or at least American, many comparison operators have multiple versions. For example, to see if two items are equal, you can use **=, equal, is, equals,** and **is equal to**. All of these work just the same. It's an example of — hold your breath, high falootin computerese on the way — *syntactic sugaring.*

syntactic sugaring: Don't worry about your weight . Syntactic sugaring just means that the language has special features that make it easy to write and understand scripts. In AppleScript, the fact that you can use the normal mathematical symbol for equality (=) or the English phrase **is equal to** is an example of syntactic sugaring. If you're a mathematician, you like the =, and if you're human, you probably prefer **is** or **is equal to.**

Most of the logical operators are ones you've run into in high school math, things like > and =, or conversational American, like **greater than** and **less than**.

One other thing to note before plunging into these descriptions is that some of the operators have some representations that don't show up on your keyboard. You can add these operators to your script by using the key combinations shown to the right of the special character. For example, in order to insert the character, you hold down the Option key while pressing down and releasing the = key.

Only the first true condition in an if is executed!

No matter how many different tests there are in an **if** statement, only the script lines associated with the first expression that evaluates to true are processed, even if a later expression is also true. For example:

```
if 3 > 2 then
    set x to 1
else if 2 < 9 then
    set x to 2
```

```
else if 5 < 12 then
    set x to 3
else
    set x to 4
end if
```

When you run this script, the final value of **x** is 1 not 3, even though all three clauses evaluate to true.

---

and

This operator lets you see if two expressions are both true.

```
1 < 2 and 35 > 4
"a" = "A" and 3 > 2.87
```

Both of these examples evaluate to true. The **and** operator works much like English. It has two arguments, one to its left, 1< 2 in the first example, and one to its right, 35 >4 in the first example. The two arguments have to be expressions that evaluate to true or false, which means they generally involve logical operators. If both expressions evaluate to true, then AppleScript replaces the two arguments and the **and** itself with a single value true. Similarly, if either or both of the values are false, then the two arguments and the **and** itself are replaced with false.

You'll find you use the **and** operator when you have multiple conditions that you want to be true at the same time. For example, you may want to pick words in a document that start with a capital letter and are printed in bold.

or

This operator lets you see if one or both of two expressions are true.

```
2 < 3 or 7 < 15        --> true
2 < 1 or 23 > 17.89    --> true
17.9 < 1 or "A" = "b"  --> false
```

Expressions involving the **or** operator evaluate to true if at least one of the two arguments is true. You'll use the **or** operator when you want some items to meet at least one of two possible conditions. For example, you may want to find all customer records in a database where either the customer hasn't made a purchase in the last two years or the customer has purchased less than $100 worth of merchandise in that same period.

=, is, equal, equals, is equal to

You use this to see if two values are equal.

```
7 = 3
"three" = 3
"ABCD" = "abcdef"
```

All of the above expressions evaluate to false, while these next examples

```
3 = 3
"three" = "THREE"
"abcd" = "ABCD"
```

evaluate to true.

For two things to be equal, they have to be the same type of value. Numbers never equal strings, for example. When comparing strings, the case — whether the letters are capitals or not — doesn't make any difference. You can change this behavior by using the **considering** statement discussed in Chapter 21.

≠ (option =), is not, isn't, isn't equal to, is not equal to, doesn't equal, does not equal

This operator lets you see if two values are different.

```
7 ≠ 3
"absce" is not equal to "fgkj"
38 / 2 is not 7
"xyz" ≠ "xyz "
```

All of the above expressions evaluate to true. In every case, the values aren't equal, so this operator, which looks for things that aren't equal, returns true. This operator is just the opposite of the **equal** operator. If **equal** returns true for two values, **isn't equal** returns false, and if **equal** returns false, then **isn't equal** returns true. You may be wondering why the last example isn't true. The reason is that sneaky little space at the end of the string on the right side. Spaces count in comparisons of strings.

When comparing strings spaces, placement before and after the text makes a difference.

>, is greater than, comes after, is not less than or equal to, isn't less than or equal to

This operator lets you determine if one value is greater than another.

```
19 is greater than 7
"def" > "abc"
3.223 comes after 3.222
set x to 32
set y to 97
y is not less than or equal to x
```

All of these examples evaluate to true. When deciding if one string is greater than another, AppleScript uses the standard alphabetical ordering.

Because the various comparison operators, such as **<**, **>**, and **=**, work with strings, you can use them to sort and alphabetize text and to find specific words inside of strings.

Some of the alternative versions of > are more understandable in certain circumstances than others. For example,

```
3.223 comes after 3.222
```

works just as well as

```
3.223 > 3.222
```

It just doesn't seem as easy to understand. Similarly, **is not less than or equal to** and **isn't less than or equal to** tend to be less clear than **is greater than** under most circumstances. But that's my opinion, so feel free to use the version you like best.

<, is less than, comes before, is not greater than or equal to, isn't greater than or equal to

This operator lets you see that one value is less than another.

```
19 < 37
"abcdef" < "bbcdef"
```

These examples evaluate to true. As you've probably guessed, you never need both < and > because, by exchanging the arguments for one of these operators, you can get the same effect as having used the other operator. For example,

```
set x to 37
set y to 93
x < y
```

gives you the same results as

```
set x to 37
set y to 93
y > x
```

≥ (Option-Shift >), >=, is greater than or equal to, is not less than, isn't less than, does not come before, doesn't come before

This operator lets you see if one value is greater than or equal to another.

```
3.12 ≥ 3.1
"abc" is greater than or equal to "abc"
17 is not less than 5
```

All evaluate to true. This operator is very similar to the > operator. The only difference is that if the two values are equal, this operator also returns true.

≤ (Option-,),<=, is less than or equal to, is not greater than, isn't greater than, does not come after, doesn't come after

This operator lets you see if the first value is less than or equal to the second value.

```
3.1415 ≤ 17                      -->true
"a" is less than "b"             -->true
"z" does not come after "a"      -->false
3.1415 ≤ 3.1415                  -->true
```

This operator is similar to the < operator. The only difference is that if the two values are the same, then the comparison returns true.

start[s] with, begin[s] with

This operator lets you check on the value of the beginning of strings and lists.

```
"this is a test" begins with "th"      -->true
{1,2,3} starts with {1,2}              -->true
{1, 2, 3} starts with {1, 2, 3}        -->true
" this is a test" begins with "th"     -->false
```

This operator just compares the two arguments character by character, starting at the first character in the left-hand argument — for strings — or item by item — for lists. If all of the characters or items are equal, then the operator returns true. While this is called **begins with,** the actual comparison is for all of the characters in the right-hand argument, which can be as long as the whole left-hand argument, as shown in the third example. The last example evaluates to false because of the space that starts the left-hand argument. The first comparison is "" on the left to "t" on the right, which is false, so the operator returns false.

ends with

This operator lets you make decisions based on the last part of a string or list.

```
"this is a test" ends with "test"      -->true
{1, 2, 3} ends with {3}                -->true
"this is a test?" ends with "t"        -->false
```

This operator is just like the **begins with** operator, except it looks at the end of the string or list, not the beginning. It checks the last part of a string or list, on the left-hand side of the operator, to see if it's the same as another string or list on the right-hand side of the operator.

contain [s]

This operator lets you see if one item is contained in another.

```
"this is a test" contains "is a"              -->true
{1, "ab", "c", 3} contains "ab"               -->true
{1, 3, 4} contains "1,3"                       -->false
{name:"Melvin", balance:34.56} contains {balance:34.56} -->true
{1, 4, 3, 5, 7} contains {1, 5, 7}             -->false
```

This operator sees if the right-hand argument is contained in the left-hand argument. It works with records, lists, and strings. If the two arguments are of different value types, as in the second example, the operator coerces the values if possible. The best way to think of this is that AppleScript takes the right-hand argument and slides it over the left-hand one until it finds a perfect match, if one exists. As a result, the order of items is important. The last example evaluates to false because even though the left-hand list contains the same items as the right-hand list, they're not contiguous — the 4 and 3 get in the way. The third example is false because the operator coerces "1,3" to {"1,3"}, not {1,3}.

does not contain, doesn't contain

This is just the opposite of the **contains** operator.

```
"this is a test" doesn't contain "is a"           -->false
{1, "ab", "c", 3} doesn't contain "ab"            -->false
{1, 3, 4} doesn't contain "1,3"                    -->true
{name:"Melvin", balance:34.56} doesn't contain {balance:34.56} -->false
{1, 4, 3, 5, 7} doesn't contain {1, 5, 7}          -->true
```

When **contains** returns true, this operator returns false and vice versa. As a result, these next two expressions return identical results.

```
not (some_string contains some_shorter_string)
some_string does not contain some_shorter_string
```

is in, is contained by

This operator is identical to the **contains** operator, except the order of the two arguments is reversed.

```
"This" is in "this is a test"  -->true
{1, 2} is in {4, 3, 1, 2, 7}   -->true
```

This operator is supplied just to make some scripts read more easily. It's functionally identical to the **contains** operator.

is not in, is not contained by, isn't contained by

This operator is identical to the **doesn't contain** operator, except the order of the arguments is reversed.

```
"This" is not in "this is a test"    -->false
{1, 2} is not in {1, 3, 2, 4}        -->true
```

This operator is supplied just to make some scripts easier to read. It's functionally identical to the **doesn't contain** operator.

not

This operator inverts its argument, changing true to false and false to true, much like many politicians.

```
not (true)                       -->false
not (false)                      -->true
not ("this" is in "this is a test")  -->false
```

This operator allows you to invert the logic of any other logical expression. For example, if you build an expression to search for customers who did less than $100 business with your company in the last two years, you can just put a **not** in front of it to search for customers who did more than $100 worth of business.

One last thing that's useful to know about logical operators is that they can be combined. For example, this expression is perfectly reasonable:

```
(x < y and z > 45.3) or (some_string contains "this" or some_string contains "that")
```

This evaluates to true if

- ✔ **some_string** contains either "this" or "that"
- ✔ the value of **x** is less than the value of **y** and the value of **z** is greater than 45.3
- ✔ both of the above conditions are true

You can construct arbitrarily complex logical tests by combining all of the various logical operators. It's a good idea to use a lot of parentheses in order to keep the meaning clear when you read the expression and to ensure that AppleScript doesn't get confused. You may want to rewrite the example above as

```
((x < y) and (z > 45.3)) or ((some_string contains "this") or ¬
        (some_string contains "that"))
```

How Your Script Can Make Up Its Mind

Now that you've seen the syntax for the **if** statement — you may want to jump back a few pages and review it because you've been looking at logical operators for what must seem like hours — and the various logical operators that usually show up in the comparison expressions used in **if** statements, you're probably wondering how you use them in real life. Well, a pretty common use is to deal with the input from the **display dialog** command discussed in Chapter 9. If you've read Chapter 9, you recall that **display dialog** returns a list of values that looks like this:

```
{text returned:"test", button returned:"OK"}
```

You often want to decide what to do based upon which button the user clicked as well as what was typed into the dialog.

Look at an internationalized greeting dialog that takes into account the country of the people using it. The script for a reusable handler — see Chapter 13 — looks like this:

```
on international_hello()
    set user_input to display dialog ¬
        "Please enter your nationality" default answer ¬
        "American" buttons {"Quit", "All Set!"} ¬
        default button "All Set!"
    if button returned of user_input is "All Set!" then
        set nation to text returned of user_input
        if nation is "American" then
            display dialog "Glad to see ya!" buttons {"Same here"} ¬
                default button "Same here"
        else if nation is "English" then
            display dialog "Greetings old chap" buttons {"Well met"} ¬
                default button "Well met"
        else if nation is "French" then
            display dialog "Bonjour Monsieur" buttons {"Bonjour"} ¬
                default button "Bonjour"
        else
            display dialog "Never heard of the place" buttons {"Illiterate peasant"} ¬
                default button "Illiterate peasant"
        end if
    end if
end international_hello
```

TIP

How to type in a script

I've found that I save a great deal of debugging time by typing in the end part of a control statement — such as **end if**, **end repeat**, or **end try** — before I fill in the middle. So if you could watch me type (very boring), you'd see me type in this sequence of lines:

First

```
if x > y then
```

then add the **end if**

```
if x > y then
end if
```

and then

```
if x > y then
    display dialog "x is larger than y"
end if
```

This approach is especially useful when you've got a bunch of nested **ifs** and/or **repeat** statements. By typing the **end if** or **end repeat** first, you make sure that things are properly balanced. Otherwise, you're likely to forget an **end if** after you've typed the 30 script lines that are inside the **if** statement, especially if the **if** is embedded inside another control structure, such as an **if**, **try**, or **repeat**.

Take a minute to read the script and see if you can figure out how it works. If it's not obvious — and don't worry if it isn't — then take a stroll through the following detailed description.

Line 1

```
on international_hello()
```

The first line probably has you a little confused. That's okay, it's covered in Chapter 13. What? You mean you're not reading the book backwards? Oh. Sorry about that.

It turns out that the first and last lines in this script tell AppleScript that this is a function or handler. What that means is that you can *call* this up just as though it were any other AppleScript command, like **display dialog**. This comes in handy when you have big scripts. It also makes it easy to reuse this function in multiple scripts.

call: This is another case of computer nerds hijacking the English language. When you call a function, you're telling AppleScript to invoke it and execute the script lines inside it.

For now, you can just ignore those two lines, though. They don't really affect how the script works. If you want to test the script, you can either remove the first and last lines or add another line

```
international_hello()
```

at the end of your script in order to get it to run properly when you click on the Run button.

This is covered in Chapter 13, but when you click on the Run button, AppleScript executes a function called run. This can be a standard handler which starts with **on** run and ends with **end** run or it can be an implicit **run** handler, which consists of any script lines in a script that aren't in a handler, that is, between an **on** and **end** statement. So, if you just have a function — for example, script lines between **on something** and **end something** — then nothing is executed. However, if you put the name of a function in the script as well

```
on something()
  some script lines
end something
something()
```

the last line calls function **something**, which then executes. So in this sample, the first line to execute is the last one, "something()," which tells AppleScript to execute the function **something**. The function **something** is defined as the script lines called "some script lines" in this example.

Okay, now we can start looking at the part of the script that does something.

Line 2

```
set user_input to display dialog ¬
    "Please enter your nationality" default answer ¬
    "American" buttons {"Quit", "All Set!"} ¬
    default button "All Set!"
```

This just displays a dialog asking the user to enter his nationality. He can then tell the script to continue or to quit by clicking on the Quit or All Set! button.

Line 3

```
if button returned of user_input is "All Set!" then
```

This checks to see that the user didn't decide to quit by making sure he clicked on the "All Set!" button.

Buttons called Cancel automatically stop a script if the user clicks on them. You can use this to make your script a little shorter if you want. The button has to be named Cancel exactly, however; spaces in the name will keep the script from stopping.

Line 4

```
set nation to text returned of user_input
```

This line is just designed to save me typing. If I didn't use this line, I would have had to replace every occurrence of "nation" with "text returned of **user_input**," which would have made the script lines longer and less readable, as well as force me to type more. Using lines like this is entirely up to you.

Line 5

```
if nation is "American" then
```

Egads! An **if** inside an **if**! Talk about an iffy situation. Actually, this sort of thing is so common that there's another term for it. The practice of putting one **if** inside another — or one **repeat** inside another, as shown in Chapter 11 — is called *nesting.* You can actually have many levels of nesting.

So what does this line do? Well, it just checks to see if the value of **nation** is "American." But **nation** isn't American, so how can this ever evaluate to true? The secret is that **is** is an operator just like +. The = is the same as the **is** operator, so that these two lines are the same:

```
nation is  "American"
nation = "American"
```

This means when AppleScript evaluates the expression

```
nation is "American"
```

the first thing it does is replace the variable name **nation** with the value of the variable, which is whatever text the user typed in the dialog. Next AppleScript executes the **is** operator, which compares the value on its right with the value on its left. If the values are the same, then the whole expression evaluates to true. If they differ, then they evaluate to false.

Remember that AppleScript isn't case sensitive, so when you compare two strings, differences in capitalization are irrelevant. You can force AppleScript to consider the case of letters in comparisons by using the **considering** statement discussed in Chapter 21.

If the expression evaluates to true, then the script lines between line 5 and the next **else** or **end if** line, line 7 in this script, are executed. If the expression evaluates to false, then AppleScript hops down to the next **else if** line to see if its expression evaluates to true. If no **else if** line exists, AppleScript hops to the **else** line — only one **else** line can be in an **if** statement — and then processes the lines between the **else** and **end if.** If no more **else if** lines exist and there is no **else** line, then Applescript hops to the **end if** and from there exits the **if** statement and goes on to the rest of the script.

Not everything inside an if gets executed!

Control statements nested inside **ifs** only get executed if they are in the part of the **if** corresponding to the first expression that evaluates to true. For example, the script looks like this:

```
if something then
  if 3 > 2 then
```

```
    script lines (A)
  end if
else if something_else then
    script lines (B)
end if
```

Line 6

```
display dialog "Glad to see ya!" buttons {"Same here"} ¬
    default button "Same here"
```

This line is executed if the user typed in "American" as his nationality. After this line is executed, AppleScript goes directly to line 14.

Line 7

```
else if nation is "English" then
```

If the user didn't enter "American," then this line is evaluated. If the user entered "English," then line 8 is executed. Otherwise, AppleScript skips down to line 9.

Line 8

```
display dialog "Greetings old chap" buttons {"Well met"} ¬
    default button "Well met"
```

I could have used Cheerio, but the cereal company wouldn't pay me an advertising fee. If this line gets executed, then AppleScript jumps down to line 14 because the **if** statement is done, having found a matching condition.

Line 9

```
else if nation is "French" then
```

If the user's entry wasn't "American" or "English," then this line is executed. If the user entered "French," then line 10 is executed. Otherwise, AppleScript hops down to line 11.

Line 10

```
display dialog "Bonjour Monsieur" buttons {"Bonjour"} ¬
    default button "Bonjour"
```

Sadly, this line shows the majority of what I recall from two years of seventh-grade French.

Line 11

```
else
```

This is the catchall case. If none of the previous **else if** lines or the original **if** line expressions evaluated to true, then the script lines between this line and the **end if** are evaluated. This ensures that no matter what is entered, the user gets some sort of reply.

Always use **else**. Even if you're sure that for every possible variable value at least one of the expressions in the **if** and **else if** statements evaluate to true so that you don't need an **else** statement, put one in anyway. Put a **display dialog** command that tells you that an error occurred as the script line to execute. That way, if something funny happens and, contrary to your expectations, none of the expressions do evaluate to true, you'll know about it. Don't feel bad about doing this sort of thing; even the most experienced scripters make mistakes that this little trick catches, especially when user input is involved.

Line 12

```
display dialog "Never heard of the place" buttons {"Illiterate peasant"} ¬
    default button "Illiterate peasant"
```

This line is executed if the user's entry doesn't match any of the test strings. It's the generic reply.

Line 13

```
end if
```

This marks the end of the **if** statement that was making decisions based on the nationality the user entered.

Line 14

```
end if
```

This marks the end of the **if** statement that was making decisions based on which button the user clicked.

Line 15

```
end international_hello
```

This marks the end of the **international_hello** handler.

You'll find that understanding how to use the **if** statement properly is very important. The **if** statement is the only way you can have your scripts make decisions, and just about every script has to make some sort of decisions. It may be deciding which files to use, what the user wants to do, whether a file contains interesting information, or any of a hundred other things, but the capability to automate decisions is one of the key benefits that AppleScript brings to the Macintosh automation arena. If you're not entirely comfortable with how to work with **if**, then I suggest you quickly skim this chapter one more time. You can skip over the logical operators description and then keep reading because many of the example scripts you encounter in this book have **if** statements in them.

The 5th Wave   By Rich Tennant

"I'LL BE WITH YOU AS SOON AS I EXECUTE A FEW MORE COMMANDS."

Chapter 11

Repeat: Going in Circles for Fun and Profit

Computers don't know anything, so why are they so useful? One reason is that they're great for doing repetitive tasks without making mistakes. While you or I may get a tad bored looking at each and every file on all of our hard disks — something like 50,000 in my case — your Mac does it without a qualm and is really fast to boot. Over time, you'll probably find that just about every script you write has some part that you want to execute more than once. It may be looking at every line of text in a file, or every record in a database, or even every file on your hard disk.

The Repeat Statement

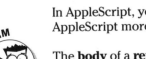

In AppleScript, you use the **repeat** statement to execute some lines of AppleScript more than once.

The **body** of a **repeat** statement is the group of AppleScript lines that lie between the **repeat** and **end repeat** lines.

The syntax for the **repeat** statement version that I tend to use most is

```
repeat with i from n to m [by step_size]
    one or more script lines
end repeat
```

The variable **i** is called the *loop variable*.

loop variable: This is a variable defined in a **repeat** statement whose value changes every time the body of the **repeat** is executed.

Every time the **repeat** statement executes, the value of **i** is increased by the value of *step_value* if the **by** option is used. For example, if *step_value* is less than 0, then the value of **i** is decreased. You see in a bit that you can count backwards (meaning the value of **i** gets smaller with each iteration of the loop in a **repeat** statement) by using the **by** option with a negative value of *step_value*. The default increment, if there is no **by**, is 1. The first value of **i** is **n,** and the last time the loop executes the value of **i** is **m** where the value of **n** and **m** can be any integer, such as -35 or 7 or 1 (but not 3.4 or 8970.5). Also **n** should be less than or equal to **m**. If **n** equals **m**, the **repeat** executes once, and the value of **i** is the value of **n**. If the value of **n** is greater than the value of **m**, the body of the **repeat** statement isn't executed at all.

Here's a simple repeat in detail.

```
set report to ""
repeat with i from 1 to 5
    set report to report & "the value of i is " & i & return
end repeat
return report
```

When you run this script, you see that the value of the variable in the result window is

```
"the value of i is 1
the value of i is 2
the value of i is 3
the value of i is 4
the value of i is 5
"
```

Every time the **repeat** executes the value of the loop, variable **i** is increased by one and the script lines in the body of the **repeat** — just the 1 line in this case — are executed.

The value of **n** has to be less than or equal to the value of **m**, or the **repeat** doesn't execute at all. If you want to have the loop variable change by a value other than 1 every time the **repeat** executes, you can use the following syntax:

```
repeat with i from first_value to max_value by change_amount
    some script lines
end repeat
```

In this case, the first value of **i** is the value of **first_value**. On each successive execution of the body, the value of **i** is decreased by the value of **change_amount**. The script stops when the value of **i** is greater than the value of **m** if **change_amount** is greater than 0, or when **i** is less than **m** if **change_amount** is less than 0. For example, this slight modification to the previous script

```
set report to ""
set change_value to -3
repeat with i from 5 to 1 by change_value
    set report to report & "the value of i is " & i & return
end repeat
return report
```

puts this into the result window:

```
"the value of i is 5
the value of i is 2
"
```

The loop only executes twice because on the third time, the value of the loop variable **i** is 2 – 3, which is –1, which is less than the second limiting value in the **repeat** statement, 1 in this example. If we change the value of **change_value** to 3 from –3 and change the **repeat** statement to

```
repeat with i from 1 to 5 by change_value
```

we get the following result:

```
"the value of i is 1
the value of i is 4
"
```

In this case, the script stops at the second execution because the next value of the loop variable **i** is 4 + 3, which is greater than the upper limit of 5.

The **repeat** statement executes the loop body until the value of the loop variable is outside of the limits specified by the **start_value** and the **max_value** parameters.

Searching for a word that may not be in the text file

You may be wondering how you handle cases where you don't know how many times you want to repeat something. Say you're reading lines from a text file and want to stop if you find the word Aardvark. You don't know in advance where you'll find that word, or even if you'll find it at all, so what do you do? You can try a couple of approaches. The simplest, but least generally useful, is to use an **if** statement in conjunction with the **exit** command as shown in the next example.

In this example, the script is solving a little math problem. The question is, "If I pick a random number between 0 and 1,000, what is the first integer such that the sum of all of the integers up to and including that number is greater than the random number I picked?" For example, if the random number is 4, the answer is 3, because 1 + 2 + 3 is 6, which is greater than 4, while 1 + 2 is 3, which is less than 4. I can't know what the answer is in advance, but a script like this

```
set sum to 0
set limit to random number from 0 to 1000
repeat with j from 1 to 9.0E+6
    set sum to sum + j
    if sum > limit then
        exit repeat
    end if
end repeat
set report to "Limit = " & limit & " sum = " & sum & " integer = " & j
return report
```

returns the answer. The basic idea is to set the upper limit to some huge value and then compute the sum for each loop iteration until you find that the **sum** is greater than the value of **limit**. To do so, you test with the **if** statement. When the value of **sum** is greater than the value of **limit**, then you use the **exit** statement to exit the repeat. When an **exit** statement is executed, AppleScript immediately hops to the first script line after the next **end repeat** statement and continues from there (the line that sets the value of the variable report in this example). If the **exit** statement occurs inside a **repeat** inside a **repeat** (nested **repeats**), then only the innermost **repeat** containing the **exit** statement is exited.

You can do this in more elegant ways, however, by using two other versions of the **repeat** statement. The first one is the **repeat until** version, which has this syntax:

```
repeat until some_expression_that_evaluates_to_true_or_false
  some script lines
end repeat
```

As you probably guessed, this **repeat** loop executes so long as the value of *some_expression_that_evaluates_to_true_or_false* is false. So we can write our little math script as

```
set sum to 0
set limit to random number from 0 to 1000
set j to 0
repeat until sum > limit
    set j to j + 1
    set sum to sum + j
end repeat
set report to "Limit = " & limit & " sum = " & sum & " integer = " & j
return report
```

The loop keeps repeating until the value of **sum** is larger than the value of **limit.** When **sum** becomes larger than **limit,** the expression in the *loop* evaluates to true and the loop stops.

loop: While this is a scenic part of the Chicago downtown scene, in computing lingo, a script that is repeatedly doing something is said to be looping. One of the most dreaded computer errors is the infinite loop where the script is set to loop forever with no exit. That can happen if you set the upper limit to some huge value and then either leave out the **exit** statement or arrange things so that the exit is never called.

The **repeat while** syntax is essentially the inverse of the **repeat until** in that it repeats so long as the expression is true and stops when the expression is false. The syntax is

```
repeat while some_expression_that_evaluates_to_true_or_false
    some script lines
end repeat
```

We can rewrite the little math script using the **repeat while** as

```
set sum to 0
set limit to random number from 0 to 1000
set j to 0
repeat while limit ≥ sum
```

```
    set j to j + 1
    set sum to sum + j
end repeat
set report to "Limit = " & limit & " sum = " & sum & " integer = " & j
return report
```

The only real change is that we had to change the test expression by reversing the two arguments and changing the > operator to the ≥ (option) operator. The operator has to be changed because in the case where the value of **limit** is the same as the value of **sum,** we need to iterate one more time in order to find the integer such that **sum** is greater than the **limit**. For example, if the value of **limit** is 3, then when **j** is 2, the **sum** is 3, 1 + 2. However, we want the value of **j** such that **sum** is greater than **limit** so we want the script to return the value 3, because 1 + 2 + 3 = 6 is the first sum that is greater than **limit**, not 2. If we used the > operator, the test expression evaluates to false if **limit** and **sum** are both 3, which results in the script returning 2 as the answer.

If you're running a script from inside the Script Editor and it's stuck in an infinite loop or is doing something else that's undesirable, you can stop the script by clicking on the stop button or holding down the Command key and pressing the period key.

Once again, make sure to note that you cannot do anything with the **repeat until** or **repeat while** that you can't do with the basic **repeat** statement. The advantage of **repeat until** and **repeat while** is that they make your script simpler to read.

Working with lists and records

Another version of the **repeat** statement is designed to make it easy to work with lists and records. It's the **repeat with** statement whose syntax is

```
repeat with some_item in some_list_or_record
    some script lines
end repeat
```

In this version of the **repeat** statement, the loop variable, *some_item*, is set to the values in the input list or record, *some_list_or_record*, one at a time, starting at the left and going to the right. This example

```
set some_list to {1, "z", 3.24, "this is a test", 19}
set report to ""
```

```
set i to 0
repeat with an_item in some_list
   set i to i + 1
   set report to report & "item " & i & " of the list is " & an_item & return
end repeat
return report
```

sets the variable **report** to

```
"item 1 of the list is 1
item 2 of the list is z
item 3 of the list is 3.24
item 4 of the list is this is a test
item 5 of the list is 19
"
```

You can do the same thing with the basic **repeat** format by getting the length of the list — remember that **length** is one of the properties of the list value class — and using it as the upper limit on the **repeat,** as in this example:

```
set some_list to {1, "z", 3.24, "this is a test", 19}
set report to ""
set num_items to length of some_list
repeat with i from 1 to num_items
   set an_item to item i of some_list
   set report to report & "item " & i & " of the list is " & an_item & return
end repeat
return report
```

This example generates the same value for the report variable as the previous example using **repeat with**. I find **repeat with** to be a great deal simpler to use, though, and given that you often have to work with lists in AppleScript, you'll find it worth your time to make a little mental note about **repeat with**.

Finding files containing keywords

Here's a real world case where **repeat with** is nice. Suppose you want to find all of the files in a folder whose names contain a certain keyword (perhaps those files are associated with a particular contract). You can do that with this little script:

```
set folder_path to (path to startup disk)
set file_list to list folder folder_path
set found_files to {}
set search_term to "system"
repeat with a_file in file_list
   if a_file contains search_term then
       copy (a_file as string) to the end of found_files
   end if
end repeat
return found_files
```

The **list folder** command lists all of the files and folders in the specified folder, which is the top level of the start-up disk in this case. The value of **a_file** is set to each of the items in the list returned by the **list folder** command. If the item, which is the name of the file, contains the string we're searching for, we add the name of the file as a string (to make the resulting list easier to read) to the end of the **found_files** list. Instead of using **copy,** you can write

```
set found_files to found_files & a_file
```

I use **copy** because it's more efficient, but the difference is probably insignificant unless you're working with really big lists. You can use **repeat with** with records as well. When working with records, the **repeat** converts them to lists by removing the property names.

Using repeat times

Another version of **repeat** — don't panic, this is the next to last one — is **repeat times** whose syntax is

```
repeat some_integer times
    some script lines
end repeat
```

where the value of *some_integer* specifies how many times the loop repeats. No loop variable exists, although you can define one by doing something like

```
set i to 0
repeat some_integer times
    set i to i + 1
end repeat
```

Clearly you can duplicate this version's functionality with the standard **repeat** statement by picking the right values for the starting and ending parameters.

Using repeat forever

One last version of repeat is **repeat forever**. Its syntax is

```
repeat
    some script lines
end repeat
```

It repeats forever — or until someone unplugs your computer — unless you put an **exit** statement somewhere inside the loop body. I never use this version. You can get the same effect by setting the upper limit of the standard **repeat** statement to some huge number, so don't worry if you don't have this tattooed on the back of your hand.

Before we exit the exciting world of repeats, I need to mention a few minor things. First, you can't permanently change the value of a loop variable inside a loop. For example, in this script

```
set report to ""
repeat with i from 1 to 10
    set report to report & i & return
    set i to i + 5
end repeat
return report
```

the final value of **report** is

```
"1
2
3
4
5
6
7
8
9
10
"
```

which shows that at the start of each loop the loop variable is set to the next value irrespective of what happened in the repeat body. You can change the value temporarily, as you can see in this example:

```
set report to ""
repeat with i from 1 to 10
```

```
        set report to report & i & return
        set i to i + 5
        if i > 10 then
            exit repeat
        end if
    end repeat
    return report
```

which sets the value of **report** to

```
"1
2
3
4
5
6
"
```

In this case, the value of **i** is changed inside the loop body and a subsequent line checks the new value of **i**, finds that it's greater than 10, and then exits the **repeat**. In general, you should avoid this sort of thing because it'll make your scripts harder to understand.

The other thing to remember about loop variables is that they exist outside of the **repeat** as well. That means that in this script

```
set i to 100
set sum to 0
repeat with i from 1 to 2
    set sum to sum + i
end repeat
return i
```

the final value of **i** is 2, not 100.

Chapter 12

Try: Dealing with Problems without Crashing

*W*hile we all like to think that our scripts are bulletproof and will never generate an error message, even when we write a perfect script, forces beyond our control can cause errors that halt the script and display a cryptic error to the user. A classic example are the various **choose** commands — application, file, and folder. If the user clicks on the Cancel button, an error is generated and the script stops. That's all well and good if that's the behavior we want, but often it isn't. Other common sources of errors are problems that occur when working with applications. But whatever the cause, we'd like to be able to gracefully recover from an error and have the script continue in an intelligent fashion at least some of the time.

bulletproofing: This doesn't have anything to do with getting ready to go into the city. In the scripting world, bulletproofing refers to writing your scripts so that if a problem occurs, the user either does not know that anything happened (because your script deals with the error and continues doing what the user wants) or sees a polite message explaining that the script can't do its job because a problem occurred. If you don't write your scripts in this manner, all the user sees is an often cryptic error message, which doesn't help him or understand what he or she has to do to fix the problem.

Using the Try Statement — the Simple Way

The **try** statement gives us the capability to recover from errors. In its basic form, the **try** statement is not very complex, but when all of its variations are taken into account, the **try** statement is very powerful. In English, **try** works like this:

```
try to execute some script lines
if an error occurs while trying to execute those lines do these other script lines
```

The actual syntax is

```
try
    one or more script lines
on error
    [error_message_variable]
    [number error_number_variable]
    [from object_that_caused_the_error]
    [partial result error_result_list_variable]
    [to expected_type_variable]
    some script lines that execute when an error occurs
end [ error | try ]
```

Sure looks messy, doesn't it? But the good news is that the most common way you use **try** is

```
try
    some script lines
on error
    some script lines to execute if an error occurs
end try
```

I've never had to use the more complex syntax, although it can be useful. I cover some of the options for the technically inclined in a bit, but first I go over the basics that are generally useful.

First, look at a typical example. You'll find that your scripts often need to open a file in order to read it. This is most common when you're using an application but also happens if you use the **open for access** command in AppleScript, discussed in Chapter 14. But if you try to open a file that is already open, say for editing in a word processor, an error occurs. If you don't use the **try** statement, your script just dies with the error message shown in Figure 12-1.

Figure 12-1:
An
AppleScript
error
message
when a file
is already
open for
writing.

While this message does tell the user a problem exists, it doesn't give any options to correct it. Here's an example of one way that the **try** command can deal with this:

```
set file_name to "system:ddta.storage"
set success to false
repeat until success
    try
        set file_ref to open for access file file_name with write permission
        set success to true
    on error
        set temp to display dialog "The file " & file_name & ¬
            " is already open for writing" & return & ¬
--the next line is slid a bit to the right to fit in the book margins
            "Should I close it and then open it for this script?" buttons {"Close and
                Open", "Just Quit"} ¬
            default button "Just Quit"
        if button returned of temp is "Close and Open" then
            close access file file_name
        else
            return
        end if
    end try
end repeat
write "tests tests tests" to file_ref
close access file_ref
```

This example uses the **try** command to see if a problem exists opening the file. If so, the **try** command assumes the problem is that the file was already open.

You can use the **try** command's advanced features to find out what type of error occurred and how to deal with it. However, you'll often find that assuming that a certain type of error has occurred works almost all the time and doesn't require you to use the more advanced syntax. While that's cheating, it's better to have a script that deals politely with most problems than a script that doesn't deal politely with anything.

The **try** command then asks users if they want to close the file and then open it so that it can be written to. If the users say they want to close and open the file, the script does so. Otherwise it quits. Following is a line by line analysis of this sample script.

Line 1

```
set file_name to "system:ddta.storage"
```

This line just sets up the name of the file we're using. In a real script, the file name can be a user choice or it can be defined in another part of the script.

Line 2

```
set success to false
```

The **success** variable is used as a flag to signal the **repeat** when it should stop looping. When it's false, the script hasn't successfully opened the file for writing. When the value of **success** is true, then the script has managed, by hook or crook, to open the file for writing.

Line 3

```
repeat until success
```

This is a **repeat** statement that keeps looping until the value of the variable called **success** is true. In this script, that only occurs when the file has been successfully opened for writing.

Line 4

```
try
```

This marks the start of the **try** statement. If an error occurs in any line between this line and the **on error** statement in line 7, then the script lines between the **on error** statement and the **end try** statement, in line 14, are executed. Remember that **try** only detects errors that can stop your script. It won't detect mistakes you make. For example, if you decide to add two numbers instead of subtracting them, **try** doesn't catch the problem.

Line 5

```
set file_ref to open for access file file_name with write permission
```

This uses the **open for access** command to open a file so that the script can write data into the file. This command is discussed in Chapter 14. The command returns an integer that is used in subsequent commands, see lines 16 and 17, to identify the file being used.

Line 6

```
set success to true
```

If no error occurred when the script tried to open the file, then this line is executed, setting the value of **success** to true. This causes the **repeat** statement, started in line 3, to stop looping.

Line 7

```
on error
```

This marks the beginning of the script lines that execute if an error occurs in lines 5 or 6.

Line 8

```
set temp to display dialog "The file " & file_name & ¬
    " is already open for writing" & return &
    "Should I close it and then open it for this script?" buttons {"Close and
        Open", "Just Quit"} ¬
    default button "Just Quit"
```

This rather long display dialog line puts up the dialog box shown in Figure 12-2 to ask the user what he or she wants to do.

Figure 12-2:
Asking the
user what
to do.

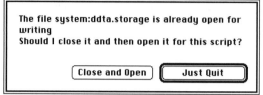

> The file system:ddta.storage is already open for writing
> Should I close it and then open it for this script?
>
> [Close and Open]   [[**Just Quit**]]

Line 9

```
if button returned of temp is "Close and Open" then
```

Remember that **display dialog** returns a record that contains several items or properties. The property whose name is **button returned** contains the name of the button the user clicked. If the user hits the Return key, then the name of the default button (the one with the dark black border) is returned. This **if** statement checks to see which button the user clicked. If it was Close and Open, then line 10 is executed. If not, then line 12 is run.

Line 10

```
close access file file_name
```

If the user wants the file closed, then this line closes the file. The script then continues the **repeat** loop, because the value of the variable called **success** is still false, and opens the file on the next loop.

Line 11

```
else
```

This just separates the script lines that run in the two cases.

Line 12

```
return
```

This just terminates the script if the user selected the Just Quit button.

Line 13

```
    end if
```

This marks the end of the **if** statement.

Line 14

```
    end try
```

This marks the end of the **try** statement.

Line 15

```
end repeat
```

This is the end of the **repeat** statement.

Line 16

```
write "tests tests tests" to file_ref
```

When the value of the variable **success** becomes true, the **repeat** loop ends and the script executes this line next. The only way the script gets to this point is if the file was opened successfully. This line just writes a string to the file the script opened.

Line 17

```
close access file_ref
```

In order to avoid future problems, this line closes the file. If you skip this line, the next time some script tries to open the file — unless the Mac's been rebooted in the interim — a problem occurs.

Now you know pretty much everything you need to know in order to use the **try** statement to bulletproof your scripts. Feel free to go on to the next chapter. If, however, you find a need to have more control over what happens when an error occurs — more than one possible error can occur and you want to respond differently depending upon what the error is, for example — then you should read this next section. Be warned that it's not really all that complicated.

Advanced Try Options

The full syntax of the **try** command is back on the second page of this chapter.

Parameters

error_message_variable: This contains the error message AppleScript generates for the particular problem that has occurred.

error_number_variable: This contains a unique integer identifier for the error.

object_that_caused_the_error: This contains a reference to the object that caused the error. Be warned that the object that causes the error may not always be the source of the error. In any case, this reference gives you a good place to start looking for the source of the problem.

error_result_list_variable: This contains a list that has the results that were returned before the problem occurred. It's useful if the application supports a command such as "get records 1 through 10" and the error occurred with record 8. In that case, this variable contains records 1 through 7.

expected_type_variable: This contains the class that AppleScript was trying to coerce the value of. It's useful if the error is due to AppleScript being unable to correctly coerce a value.

Example

```
set some_string to "this is a test"
try
    repeat with i from 1 to 245.34
       set z to word i of some_string
    end repeat
on error error_message number error_number ¬
    from problem_object to target_class partial result initial_results
    set result to {error_message, error_number, ¬
       problem_object, target_class, initial_results}
    return result
end try
```

In this case, the problem is that the **repeat** command can't use real values, such as 245.34, as input parameters. The value of **result** when this script is run is

```
{"Can't make 245.34 into a integer.", -1700, 245.34, integer, {}}
```

You can use these values to give the user a better idea of what's going on or to decide how the script should procede. The advanced version of **try** isn't all that horrible. But remember, for 99 percent of what you do, the basic **try** syntax is just fine.

Chapter 13

Handlers: Organizing Your Script

*W*hile the script examples you've seen so far are fairly short and simple, real scripts can get fairly large — hundreds of lines long in fact. Most of your scripts will be short, but if you have to write a large script, you'll find that it's nice to be able to break it up into byte-sized — sorry about that pun — pieces. In AppleScript, several different kinds of "mini-scripts," called *handlers,* break a script into manageable pieces.

Getting a Handle on Messages

Handlers get their name because they "handle" messages. But what the heck does e-mail have to do with this, you ask? The answer is nothing. But internally, AppleScript sends lots of messages. When you click on the Run button, AppleScript actually sends a run message to the script. When you drag a bunch of files onto a script icon, an open message is sent to the script. If nothing much is going on, then AppleScript sends idle messages to your active scripts.

Calling a handler with variables

Your script looks for a handler to deal with a received message. The full syntax for a handler is fairly complex — for AppleScript, that is — and I go over it in a bit. However, I first look at the simple version you use 90 percent of the time:

```
on handler_name(input1, input2)
end handler_name
```

arguments, parameters: Both of these terms are used to refer to the inputs of a handler.

The inputs of a handler, of which there can be any number, are pieces of information that are passed to the handler in the message that launches the handler. Before this gets too confusing, look at this simple example:

```
on add(a_number, another_number)
    set sum to a_number + another_number
    return sum
end add
set x to 3
set y to -6
set z to add(x, y)
```

When you run this script, the first line executed is the line that sets the value of the variable **x** to 3. Why is this? The answer is that when you click on the run button, a run message is sent to your script. If you have an **on run. . . end run** handler, then that handler is executed. If you don't, then AppleScript assumes that everything in your script that isn't between an **on** and an **end** statement is really part of an implicit **run** handler. So in this case, AppleScript ignores the stuff between the **on add** and **end add** and starts executing the first line that isn't inside a handler.

An *implicit run handler* is just all of the script lines in a script that aren't in some other handler. Everything that's outside of an **on...end** structure is part of the implicit **run** handler. If a script does not have an **on run...end run** handler, then the script lines in the implicit **run** handler are executed.

The question now is what happens when we reach the line that sets the value of the variable **z**? Well, AppleScript sends a message to your script. The message is add (x,y) — this is referred to as "calling" the **on add. . .end add** handler. AppleScript then sees that you've got an **on add. . .end add** handler in your script, so it runs that handler putting the value of **x** into the first input value of the handler — **a_number** in this case — and the value of **y** into the second input value — **another_number**. The script lines between the **on add** and **end add** lines are then executed using those values of the **a_number** and **another_number** variables.

call: This doesn't mean you're enriching AT&T. It's one way of referring to what happens when AppleScript comes across a script line that invokes the execution of a handler. In this line,

```
set z to add(x,y)
```

a worldly-wise scripter says that the **add** handler was being called.

Calling a handler with values

You can call a handler with values as well as variables, as in

```
set z to add(2,3)
```

In addition, as you've probably already noticed, if you call a handler, you don't have to use the same variable names in the call, which occurs in the line

```
set z to add(x,y)
```

as in the handler definition, the **on add** line.

The **return** statement tells AppleScript that it should replace the add (x,y) in the

```
set z to add(x,y)
```

line with the value of the variable **sum** computed inside the **add** handler. If you don't put in a **return** statement, then the last value computed in the handler is automatically returned. This means that if I write the **add** handler as

```
on add(a_number, another_number)
    set sum to a_number + another_number
end add
```

it works just fine, because the last thing computed in the handler is the value of the variable **sum,** which is automatically returned. Once a **return** statement is encountered, no further script lines in a handler are executed. The **return** statement is a definite exit from the handler.

When you use the **on add** (input1, input2) syntax — that's called using positional parameters — the order of the inputs is critical. While it doesn't matter for the **add** handler, take a look at this **divide** handler:

```
on divide(numerator, denominator)
    set ratio to numerator / denominator
    return ratio
end divide
```

If you call **divide** using the following two script lines, you find that

```
set r1 to divide(8.0, 2.0)
set r2 to divide(2.0, 8.0)
```

r1 is equal to 4 while **r2** is equal to .25.

If your handler doesn't have any inputs, you still need to put an empty set of parentheses after its name when you declare it and when you call it, as in this example:

```
on make_sound()
    beep
end make_sound
sound()
```

subroutine: This isn't what they do on nuclear submarines. It's another name for a handler. Subroutine is the name used in more old-fashioned languages. In AppleScript, a subroutine is a user-defined handler.

So now you know all you need to know about handlers. Well, at least 80 to 90 percent of what you need to know. The only other key thing to understand is variable scope.

Understanding a variable scope

When you define a variable inside a handler, it's only usable in the handler because its scope is restricted to the handler. For example, in this script sample

```
on test1(a, b)
    set x to a + b
    return x
end test1
on test2(c, d)
    set x to c - d
    return x
end test2
set x to 5
set z to test1(3, 4)
set y to test2(3, 1)
return x
```

the value returned is 5. Even though **x** is used inside the handler's **test1** and **test2**, as well as at the top level of the script in the implicit run handler, AppleScript views all three occurrences as different variables. That's because all variables defined inside a handler are local variables, only understood inside that handler.

variable scope or scope: This isn't a telescope designed for observing variable stars. The scope of a variable is the part of the script where its name is recognized by AppleScript.

local variables: These are variables that are only understood inside the handler where they're used. If you want to be sure that a variable is local to a handler, use the **local** statement:

```
local variable_name
```

If you do this, even if there's a global variable of the same name, the variable will be treated as a local one and not have the global value.

In fact, inside the **test1** handler, **x** isn't defined at all until the first line is executed. If I try to add **a** and **b** to **x**, I get the error message shown in Figure 13-1.

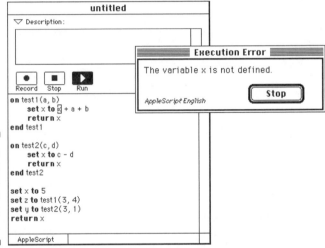

Figure 13-1:
You need to define local variables before you use them.

Because the **x** variable outside of the handlers is only understood by AppleScript in those script lines that are outside of any handler, the **x** used inside the handlers is a completely different variable. One way to look at this is to think about phone numbers. Phone numbers are pointers to phones. You dial the number and you get access to the person at that number, unless they're gone or already on the line. With a variable, you use its name to get the value that's stored in the variable.

You have a phone number, unless you're really antisocial or live somewhere in Outer Mongolia. I've got a phone number. They may be the same. Well, not exactly, because the area code is different. Even though my phone number is 555-8976 and your phone number is 555-8976, your friends don't call me by accident and Arnie's Used Nuclear Weapons salespeople don't call you. Think of each handler as having its own area code. All of the lines that aren't in a handler, such as the ones in an implicit **run** handler discussed in the preceding example, have their own special area code as well. So even though variable names are the same, they represent different phones . . . er, storage locations, if they're used inside different handlers.

Passing data between handlers

But how do you pass data between handlers then? Well, you can do it in two ways. You've already seen how to use the **return** statement. If you want to return more than one value, you can use the following approach:

```
on some_function(x, y)
    set sum to x + y
    set dif to x - y
    set ratio to x / y
    set temp to {sum, dif, ratio}
end some_function
set values to some_function(12, 13)
set difference to item 2 of values
set total to item 1 of values
set divide_result to item 3 of values
```

All you have to do is put the different results into a list and then return the list.

This script doesn't have a return statement, because AppleScript will automatically return the last value set in a script, the variable values in this case, if there is no return statement. If you'd rather type a bit more to make the workings of the script clearer, just add this line:

```
return temp
```

after the "**set** temp **to** {sum, dif, ratio} line.

Another way to share data is by using *global variables*.

global variables: This doesn't have anything to do with the international currency markets. A global variable is a variable that is recognized everywhere in a script.

You declare a variable to be global with this syntax:

```
global variable_name1, variable_name2
```

You can declare any number of variables global by using a single global line. Take a look at this script:

```
global g_monster
on change()
    set new_monster to the first word of g_monster & " Monkey"
end change
set g_monster to "King Kong"
change()
```

What is the result returned by the **change** handler? If you guessed King Monkey, you're right.

In general, if you've got a large script, you should use some naming standard that makes it easy to see which variables are global. You can start or end the name with a g or g_, for example. This'll help avoid problems.

Since global variables are so easy to declare, why wouldn't you use them for everything? Well, in the first years of programming, intrepid pioneer programmers working on their Conestoga 100 computers did use global variables a great deal. When they weren't out hunting buffalo, those same pioneers discovered that global variables are a major source of bugs in software. Take a look at this example:

```
global sum
on total(j, k, m)
    set sum to j + k + m
end total
set sum to 3
total(2, 3, 5)
return sum
```

I declared a variable to be global and then accidentally used its name in a handler. When this script runs, the final value of **sum** is 2 + 3 + 5 = 10, not 3. This is what's known as a *side effect* of the handler. In general, such side effects tend to lead to problems in your script. Because of these problems, you should avoid global variables unless they're absolutely necessary.

side effect: When a handler makes a change to something other than the value it returns, changing a global variable for example, it's called a side effect. Other side effects could be changing some system parameter such as the sound volume or the color depth of a monitor.

Chapter 14

Properties: Storing Data for Awhile

. . . .

In This Chapter

▶ Storing data in a script by using properties

▶ Storing data in a text file

▶ Using all of the AppleScript commands that let you work with files

. . . .

*Y*ou may have been wondering how you can keep track of information from one execution of a script to the next. For example, if you write a script that watches for changes in the items that are in a folder, how can you arrange for the script to remember what it last saw in the folder when it starts up each day? Or if you're writing a script to do periodic back-ups of key files, how do you keep track of when you last backed up? The answer to both of these questions involves properties.

Defining Properties

You've come across the properties that objects, such as strings — see Chapter 4 — can have, so it shouldn't shock you to find out that your scripts can have properties too. A property is like a global variable except that it retains its value between executions of the script. When you run this script

```
property current_value : 0
set current_value to current_value + 1
display dialog "the value is now " & current_value
```

you see that the value of the property **current_value** increases by one each time you run the script. It starts out at one and then keeps getting bigger.

The basic syntax for defining a property is

```
property property_name: initial_property_value
prop property_name : initial_property_value
```

Both ways are equivalent, so you can use the one that is most appealing. The *initial_property_value* can be any legal value, and the **property_name** follows the same rules as used for naming variables.

The one drawback to properties is that whenever you compile a script and use the Check Syntax button, the values of all properties are reset to the initial value specified in the line that defines the property. If that's a problem, then you need to look to other solutions.

Using Read and Write

Another approach to persistently storing data in a script is to use the **read** and **write** commands that come with AppleScript. These commands can be complex and dangerous in that misusing them can lead to a loss of data. However, it's pretty easy to use the **read** and **write** commands to store data without having to find out about the more arcane aspects of their syntax.

I want to make something very clear from a visual perspective. The material in this section can cause you to lose data and destroy or corrupt files that have nothing to do with AppleScript. This occurrence is unlikely if you follow the guidelines I give you, but it can happen if you make an itsy bitsy mistake. So be careful and make sure you back up your critical files often.

Still not scared off, eh? Well, I knew you were made of stern stuff because you've read this far. So on to the fun.

The general mission of the **read** and **write** commands is to give you the capability to read and write data to standard Mac files. With these commands, you can open and edit a Pixel Paint Pro drawing. Of course, it takes you a few years to get the script working properly and the script only runs at a tiny fraction of the speed of Pixel Point Pro, but you can do it. On the other hand, using these commands to write a set of values to a file and then reading those values back the next time you run the script is pretty simple. Before I look at the commands in detail, look at this simple little script, which reads and writes from a file.

```
property storage_file_name : "data storage"
set file_path to ((path to startup disk) as string) & storage_file_name
set file_ref to open for access file file_path
set eof_position to get eof file_ref
if eof_position > 0 then
    set message to read file_ref before return
else
    set message to "No messages entered yet"
end if
```

```
close access file_ref
set user_input to display dialog "Please enter a message" default answer message
if button returned of user_input is "Ok" then
    set message to text returned of user_input
    set file_ref to open for access file file_path with write permission
    write message & return to file_ref
    close access file_ref
end if
```

Pretty trivial, isn't it? Well, if not it will be after you read through this line by line description.

Line 1

```
property storage_file_name : "data storage"
```

This line just defines the name the script uses for the file it's going to write to and read from. I also can use

```
set storage_file_name to "data storage"
```

because the script never changes the name and hence doesn't really need to use a property as opposed to just hardwiring the script. I've found, however, that it aids in script readability if constant information, such as this file name, is at the top of the script in a property. In a real script, I include a comment line to describe the role of the property **storage_file_name** as follows:

```
--storage_file_name is the name of the file where the script stores
--messages
```

Line 2

```
set file_path to ((path to startup disk) as string) & storage_file_name
```

This line just defines a full path for the file. In this case, I've decided to put the file at the top level on my startup disk. You can change this script to hardwire the entire path by saying something like

```
set file_path to "My Disk:My folder:data storage"
```

The script's approach doesn't require you to change the script if you move it to someone else's computer though, because every Mac has a startup disk — well, at least every Mac that's working.

Line 3

```
set file_ref to open for access file file_path
```

This is the first line where we use a read/write related command. **Open for access** opens a file to read or write from. If the specified file path doesn't exist, **open for access** creates a new SimpleText file. This line tells AppleScript to get ready to read from a the file whose path is contained in the variable **file_path**. You need to put **file** in front of **file_path** because **file_path** is a string and the **open for access** command wants a reference to a file.

The **open for access** command returns an integer that uniquely identifies the file so that you can have multiple files open at the same time in a script. That integer is used by all subsequent commands to define the file they're referring to, which is why the integer is saved in the variable **file_ref**, short for file_reference.

Line 4

```
set eof_position to get eof file_ref
```

This line finds out how big the file is. The **get eof** command returns the *EOF*.

EOF (End of File): This isn't the date that you throw the file in the trash. EOF marks the end of a file. In AppleScript, it's the number of bytes in the file for the file. In this context, the number of bytes in the file is the same as the number of characters — counting spaces, tabs, and returns as one character each — in the file if you're using English or any other language that has one-byte characters.

If the EOF is bigger than zero, then something's been written to the file and you need to read back what was there. If the EOF is zero, then the file hasn't been written to so you have nothing to read.

Line 5

```
if eof_position > 0 then
```

If the EOF is larger than 0, then the file has been written to so you should read it.

Line 6

```
set message to read file_ref before return
```

Set the value of the variable called **message** to everything in the file before the first carriage return by using the **read** command. The **before** parameter tells the **read** command to read everything from where it starts — the first character in the file unless you specify otherwise — until it finds a return. The next **read** or **write** starts where this command stopped.

Line 7

```
else
```

This marks the end of the script lines that are executed if the EOF is greater than 0 and the beginning of the script lines that are executed if the EOF is 0.

Line 8

```
set message to "No messages entered yet"
```

This sets the value of the variable **message** to a warning string. This value is used until the user enters some text.

Line 9

```
end if
```

This line marks the end of the **if** statement, which tests the value of the EOF.

Line 10

```
close access file_ref
```

This line closes the file so that other applications (or this script, the next time it runs) don't get an error saying that the file is already open if they try to access the file.

Line 11

```
set user_input to display dialog "Please enter a message" default answer message
```

This displays a dialog, which gives the user the ability to enter a new message. The default message displayed is the one read from the file and stored in the variable called **message**.

Line 12

```
if button returned of user_input is "Ok" then
```

This checks which button the user clicked. If the button was Ok, then the user wants the new message to be used — unless he or she hit the wrong button by mistake.

Line 13

```
set message to text returned of user_input
```

This sets the variable **message's** value to the value of the property called "text returned" of the record returned by the **display dialog** command in line 11.

Line 14

```
set file_ref to open for access file file_path with write permission
```

This line opens the file for reading. The **with write permission** tells AppleScript to give the script authority to write changes to the file. When one application opens a file with write permission, no other application or script can open the file. That's necessary to ensure that two different scripts are prevented from changing a file at the same time, which can lead to confusion. As before, the value returned by the **open for access** command provides a way for other **read/write** commands to specify which file they operate on.

Because the file was just opened, the file mark position is at the very beginning of the file. That means any reads or writes start at the very beginning of the file. If we leave the file open after the initial read, then the file mark is right after the first return in the file. You then have to move the *file mark* — using the option in the **write** command — so that the new message is placed at the beginning of the file.

file mark: This isn't a file that is likely to lose at poker. Rather, it's the place in a file where a **read** command starts reading, unless you specify differently with an optional parameter, and the place where data written by a **write** command is written. The file mark is moved whenever you read from or write to a file. You can also move the file mark by using options in the **read** and **write** commands. All in all, a file mark in a file is a lot like the insertion point in a word processing document.

Line 15

```
write message & return to file_ref
```

This line uses the **write** command to write the value of the variable **message** and a carriage return to the file that was just opened. This action partially or completely overwrites what is currently in the file. When you first open a file, the file mark (the place that new information is written to the file) is at the very beginning of the file so that new information overwrites what, if anything, is in the file. For example, if the file contains "This is a test" and you wrote "Oh no!" the file's contents are "Oh no!s a test" — without the quotes. In this script, we end each **write** with a carriage return, so the file looks like

```
Oh no!
s a test
```

The new message overwrites part but not all of the previous message because the new message is shorter than the previous one. If the new message is longer, then it overwrites the entire old message.

You can move the file mark and write the information at different places in a file so that you can put a new piece of text after the existing pieces of text. (I discuss the full syntax of the **write** command later in this chapter.) However, for this script, we're only storing one message, so overwriting is fine.

Writing numbers or other values

If you want to write numbers or other values, the easiest way is to coerce them to a string when you write them and then coerce them back when you read them back. For example, if **number_of_dogs** is an integer, you can write it to a file with

```
write (number_of_dogs as string) & return¬
    to file_ref
```

and then, assuming you've got the file mark positioned properly, read it back with

```
set number_of_dogs to (read file_ref¬
    before return) as integer
```

Line 16

```
close access file_ref
```

This line closes the file, identified by the value of the **file_ref** variable, so that other scripts or applications can access it.

Line 17

```
end if
```

This just marks the end of the script lines that are executed when the user clicks on the OK button in the dialog asking for a message. If this script gets an error, say you don't have room on the disk to write the data to the file, you might leave the file open. To close an open file just use

```
close access file some_file_path
```

It's simple to extend this script to multiple pieces of data. For example, these two handlers write some data to a file and read it back.

```
on write_to_file of version_number from prefs_file given user_name:u_string,¬
        account_balance:cash
    set file_ref to open for access file prefs_file with write permission
    write (version_number as string) & return to file_ref
    write u_string & return to file_ref
    write (cash as string) & return to file_ref
    close access file_ref
end write_to_file
on read_from_file from prefs_file
    set file_ref to open for access file prefs_file
    set the_version to read file_ref before return
    set the_version to the_version as integer
    set user_name to read file_ref before return
    set cash_balance to read file_ref before return
    set cash_balance to cash_balance as real
    close access file_ref
    return {version:the_version, user:user_name, balance:cash_balance}
end read_from_file
write_to_file of 2 from "system:prefs" given user_name:"Fred",¬
        account_balance:345.56
set user_info to read_from_file from "system:prefs"
```

These two handlers show you how to save multiple items to a file and how to save and retrieve numbers as well as strings. The **write_to_file** handler takes the data passed to it through its input parameters and writes them to a file. The **read_from_file** handler returns a record — just like **display dialog** does — of the data read from the file. If these handlers are not completely obvious, feel free to skim through the more detailed description that follows.

Line 1

```
on write_to_file of version_number from prefs_file given user_name:u_string,¬
        account_balance:cash
```

This defines several different types of input parameters. The direct, unlabeled, input is assigned to the local variable **version_number**, while the only subroutine parameter labeled input, which uses the label **from**, is assigned to the local variable **prefs_file**. The two user labeled parameters are **user_name** and **account_balance**. Line 18 shows an example of how to call this handler.

Line 2

```
set file_ref to open for access file prefs_file with write permission
```

This line opens the file with write permission. An integer that identifies the file is stored in the local variable **file_ref**.

In a real script, it's a good idea to wrap a **try** statement around this line in case the file is already open.

Line 3

```
write (version_number as string) & return to file_ref
```

This line writes the version number, as a string, terminated with a carriage return to the file. Because the file was just opened, the **write** starts at the very beginning of the file.

Line 4

```
write u_string & return to file_ref
```

This writes the value of the **u_string** variable and a return to the file. The first character of **u_string** is written immediately after the return written in line 3 because the file mark is placed immediately after the last character written by a **write** command.

Line 5

```
write (cash as string) & return to file_ref
```

This writes the value of the **cash** variable as a string and a return right after the entry from line 4.

Line 6

```
close access file_ref
```

This closes the file so that other scripts or applications can access it.

Line 7

```
end write_to_file
```

This marks the end of the **write_to_file** handler.

Line 8

```
on read_from_file from prefs_file
```

This marks the start of the **read_from_file** handler. It has one labeled input parameter, which contains the path to the file to be read.

Line 9

```
set file_ref to open for access file prefs_file
```

This opens the file for reading.

Line 10

```
set the_version to read file_ref before return
```

This reads in the value of the first entry in the file. The value of **the_version** is a string.

Line 11

```
set the_version to the_version as integer
```

This line coerces the value of **the_version** to an integer. If you want decimal version numbers, such as 3.01, then you should coerce the value to a real.

Line 12

```
set user_name to read file_ref before return
```

This line reads in the second value placed in the file. Because the second value is supposed to be a string, we don't have to coerce it.

Line 13

```
set cash_balance to read file_ref before return
```

This line reads in the third entry from the file.

Line 14

```
set cash_balance to cash_balance as real
```

This line coerces the string to a real number with a decimal point.

Line 15

```
close access file_ref
```

This closes the file.

Line 16

```
return {version:the_version, user:user_name, balance:cash_balance}
```

This line shows you how to return multiple values in a record. This can be extended to any number of values. You can also use a list and just omit the property labels. Doing so makes the part of the script where the various values are accessed harder to understand because instead of clear property names, you just have items 1, 2, and 3.

Line 17

```
end read_from_file
```

This marks the end of the **read_from_file** handler.

Line 18

```
write_to_file of 2 from "system:prefs" given user_name:"Fred",¬
        account_balance:345.56
```

This line shows you how you can call the **write_to_file** handler. While the parameters can be in any order, the direct parameter, which has a value of 2 in this example, must come directly after the handler name. However, you must make sure all of the parameters are present. Omitting any of them results in an error, and your script crashes.

Line 19

```
set user_info to read_from_file from "system:prefs"
```

This is an example of how to read back the values from the file.

You don't have to read and write a file inside the same script. Different scripts can write and read the same files. For example, a script in your Startup Items folder can write the amount of free disk space at the start of the day to the same file that a script in your shutdown items folder writes the amount of free disk space at the end of the day. You can then keep track of how much more disk space you use each day.

As you can see, writing multiple items to a file is not that complex. You can vary the details in this example without changing the basic structure. For example, I separate entries with carriage returns, but you can use tabs. Just replace **return** wherever it occurs with **tab**. No other changes are required. Similarly, if you want to write more items, just add more **write** and **read** statements. AppleScript takes care of the file size — assuming you don't run out of space on your hard disk.

The Read and Write Commands

You've seen that it's not that hard to write data to a file for subsequent retrieval. If that's all you ever want to do, you don't have to read the rest of this chapter. However, you can do some fairly sophisticated file manipulation with AppleScript's **read/write** commands. While much of this information is for the technically inclined, even average non-nerds will find some things of interest in the detailed syntax of the various commands I'm about to describe. I suggest that if you're not a real computer fanatic, you just skim the definitions and then plan to read them in more detail if you run into a problem that requires more complex read and/or write capabilities.

Don't be intimidated by the extensive list of options for some of these commands, such as **read.** In most cases, the options are fairly simple after you look them over for a bit, and you'll probably never use those options that aren't so simple anyway. One thing to remember is that if a parameter is in bytes, you should supply an integer because AppleScript doesn't understand fractional bytes; humans do — that's when you start to bite into an apple and find a worm.

When working with the contents of a file, it's important to understand the concept of the file mark we discussed in the previous line by line. The file mark is the equivalent of the insertion point in a word processing document. The file mark moves whenever you read from or write to a file. Unless you specify otherwise, **read** and **write** commands start at the current location of the file mark.

The various **read** and **write** commands follow. You don't need to memorize them; just get a general idea of how they work. Unless you want to do something ambitious, the sample script I discussed earlier in this chapter for writing strings to a file and then reading them back is all you'll ever need.

Get EOF

This gets the location of the end of a file.

Syntax

```
get eof some_file_reference
```

Parameters

some_file_reference: This is a reference to a file, such as

```
file "some disk:some folder:some file"
alias "some disk:some folder:some other folder: some file"
```

or a file reference number returned by the **open for access** command.

Example

```
set end_of_file to get eof file "Kate:penguin"
set file_reference to open for access alias "Kate:penguin"
set end_of _file to get eof file_reference
```

Description

This command returns an integer, which tells you the location of the current EOF (end of file). **Get EOF** is useful when you want to add data to a file. You can tell the **write** command where in a file you want to write data. If you tell the **write** command to write after the EOF, then you can append data to the end of the file without overwriting any of the data currently in the file. Following is an example:

```
set file_ref to open for access file "system:test" with write permission
set eof_value to get eof file_ref
write "add on test " & return to file_ref starting at (eof_value + 1)
close access file_ref
```

The first time you run this script, if the file doesn't exist, it is created and its contents are

```
add on test
```

The next time you run the script, the file's contents are

```
add on test
add on test
```

The third time, the contents are

```
add on test
add on test
add on test
```

Are you bored yet? I am, and I'm sure you've got the idea by now. Without the

```
& return
```

after the string I was putting into the file, the "add on test" is all squished together on the same line.

Value returned

This command returns an integer the size of the file in bytes, which happens to be the length in characters if you're using a European language because the Mac only uses one byte to store each letter in a European alphabet. If you're working in a language with lots of characters — say Kanji — then the Mac takes more than one byte to represent each character.

New File

This lets the user define a new file using a standard Mac dialog.

Syntax

```
new file [with prompt some_string] [default name some_other_string]
```

Parameters

some_string: This is some short string, up to 255 characters, which tells the user why he's creating a new file — something like, "Name for a new message file:"

some_other_string: This is the default name for the new file. The user can accept this name, edit it, or type in a completely new name.

Example

```
set ref_to_new_file to new file with prompt "Name for the new file" default name¬
        "Message Central"
```

Description

The example generates the dialog box shown in Figure 14-1.

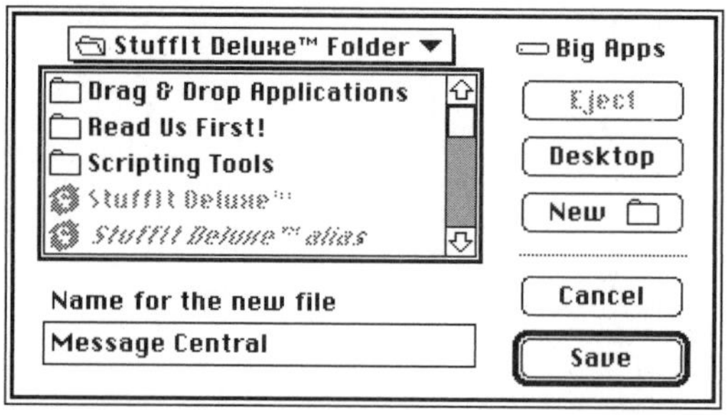

Figure 14-1:
The dialog
box for
letting the
user define
a new file.

```
┌─────────────────────────────────────────────┐
│ 🗁 StuffIt Deluxe™ Folder ▼     ▭ Big Apps   │
│ 🗀 Drag & Drop Applications  ⇧               │
│ 🗀 Read Us First!              │   [ Eject ]  │
│ 🗀 Scripting Tools             │              │
│ 🗘 StuffIt Deluxe ™            │  [ Desktop ] │
│ 🗘 StuffIt Deluxe ™ alias  ⇩   │              │
│                               │  [ New  🗀 ]  │
│ Name for the new file                        │
│ ┌─────────────────────────┐    [ Cancel ]    │
│ │ Message Central         │                  │
│ └─────────────────────────┘    [  Save  ]    │
└─────────────────────────────────────────────┘
```

It's very important to realize that this command does not create a new file. All it does is create a reference to a file of the form

```
file "some disk:some folder:some other folder:some file"
```

which you can then use in a call to **open for access** to actually create the file.

If the user clicks on the Cancel button, an error -128 is generated and the script quits. If you want the script to continue, you need to put the call to **new file** inside a **try** statement — see Chapter 12.

Value returned

This command returns a reference to a file of the form

```
file "disk:folder:folder2:some file"
```

Read

This command reads information from a file.

Syntax

```
read some_file_reference [from starting_location]
[for number of bytes to read | to last byte to read | until some delimiter | ¬
        before some_delimiter]
[as some_class_name [ using delimiter[s] delimiter_list]]
```

Parameters

some_file_reference: This is a standard file reference of the form

```
file "disk:folder:another folder:file"
alias "some disk: some folder: some file"
```

You can also use the value returned by a call to the **open for access** command.

starting_location: This is the first byte, or character if you're using a European language, that's to be read in. Negative values are counted from the back of the file, so a value of -10 means that the read starts at the tenth byte from the end of the file.

number_of_bytes_to_read: This is how many bytes, or characters if you're not using a language which has multi-byte characters, of information are to be read in from the file.

last_byte_to_read: This is the last byte to read. All data between the value of **starting_location** — if specified, otherwise it's the last place something was read from — and the last byte is read.

some_delimiter: This is a character that is used to mark the end of the data to read. Although **tab** or **return** are most common, it can be any character you want, such as *a*. All data is read from the starting point to the first occurrence of the character specified as the delimiter character.

some_class_name: This is the name of a data value class, such as list or record. You use this option to read in data types other than strings. The allowable values are as follows:

> list
>
> record
>
> integer
>
> text
>
> real
>
> short
>
> boolean
>
> data

This requires the data to be in the correct format.

Example

```
set info to read file_ref from 10 for 20
set into to read file_ref as {text} using delimiters {tab,return}
```

Description

This command lets you read information from files. You've seen how to read from a file you've written, but you can also read from files written by other applications. There seems to be a problem with the reading as some class option. You can read as **text**, but there seems to be a problem with reading entries as other classes when the file was written by AppleScript. You can still coerce values to a string before you write them to a file and then coerce them back when you read them as shown above if you want to store values other than strings in files.

Value returned

Generally a string but it can be other values if the **as** parameter is used.

Set EOF

This defines the endpoint of the file.

Syntax

```
set eof some_file_reference  to some_integer
```

Parameters

some_file_reference: This is a reference to a file.

some_integer: This is the new length of the file.

Example

```
set eof file "system:test file" to 100
```

Description

The eof is the number of the last byte in the file so it's the number of bytes long the file is. If you make the file shorter with this command, the information in the file after the new eof is lost. If you're making the file longer, the data in the new part of the file is meaningless.

Value returned

None.

Write

This command lets you write information to a file.

Syntax

```
write info_to_write to a_file_reference [ for number_of_bytes] ¬
        [ starting at byte_number]
```

Parameters

info_to_write: The data you want to write to the file.

a_file_reference: This can be a standard file reference or an integer returned by the **open for access** command.

number_of_bytes: The number of bytes of data you wish to write to the file.

byte_number: The location in the file you want to start writing at.

Example

```
write "this is a test" to file "system:write test" for 4 starting at 3
```

Description

This command lets you write data to a file. The **starting** parameter lets you determine where in the file the write will occur (it resets the file mark to that location), and the **for** parameter lets you specify how many bytes of data you want to write. Remember that if you're using English, each character is 1 byte long.

Value returned

None.

Open for Access

This lets you get a file ready for reading or writing.

Syntax

```
open for access a_file_reference [write permission a_boolean]
```

Parameters

a_file_reference: This is a file reference of the form file "disk:file" or alias "disk:file."

a_boolean: If true then subsequent commands can write data to the file.

Example

```
open for access file "system:a test file"
```

Description

This command gets a file ready for reading and writing. If you want to be able to write to a file, you have to set the **write permission** parameter to true. If the file doesn't exist, it'll be created.

Value returned

An integer that can be used to reference the file in subsequent commands.

Close Access

This command closes files so they can be opened by other applications.

Syntax

```
close access a_file_reference
```

Parameters

a_file_reference: This is a standard file reference or an integer returned by the **open for acccess** command.

Example

```
close access file "system:file"
```

Description

This command closes a file so that other applications or scripts can use it. You should always close all files a script opens. If you open a file using **open for access** and don't close it with the **close access** command, other scripts or applications will get an error if they try to open it.

Value returned

None.

Chapter 15

Droplets: Making Drag and Drop Applications

* *

In This Chapter

▶ Creating a drag and drop script

▶ Testing a drag and drop script

* *

*O*ne of the nice new features of System 7 is the capability to process a bunch of files by dragging them onto an application's icon. This drag and drop support is much nicer than selecting all the files via a standard file dialog inside an application. Drag and drop applications can do lots of things, including changing the file type of a bunch of files. You can set text files to be opened by the word processor of your choice, not just SimpleText or the word processor that created the document. You can also find out how much free space is available in all of the disks dragged onto the application.

Creating a Drag and Drop Script Application

It's really easy to make a drag and drop script application. All you have to do is include an **open** handler, such as the one shown in this script sample, to your script and then save the script as an application.

```
on open the_items
end open
```

The variable **the_items** is a list (even if only one item is dropped on the application) filled with the paths to each of the items — files, folders, and/or disks — that were dropped on the application. In general, an **open** handler consists of a **repeat** that processes each of the items dropped on the script.

The following example changes the file creator of all of the files dropped on it to "ttxt." As a result, when you click on these ttxt files, SimpleText is launched. This comes in handy if you get text files from other people, via eWorld or the Internet for example, which have been created by various word processing applications but saved as text.

```
on open the_files
    repeat with a_file in the_files
        set item_info to info for a_file
        --Make sure the item isn't a folder
        if not folder of item_info then
            tell application "Finder"
                set the creator type of a_file to "ttxt"
            end tell
        end if
    end repeat
end open
```

The script just takes the items dropped on it, checks to make sure they're not folders, and then uses the scriptable Finder — Finder version 7.5 or later — to change the file creator so that the Mac thinks that the files were made by SimpleText.

Line 1

```
on open the_files
```

This defines the handler that responds to the **open** message that the scripting application receives when the user drops one or more files or folders on the application's icon. The variable **the_files** is filled with a list containing references to each of the items dropped on the application.

Line 2

```
repeat with a_file in the_files
```

This line starts a **repeat** loop, which executes once for each of the items dropped on the application icon. On each iteration of the loop, the loop variable **a_file** is set to one of the file references in **the_files**.

Line 3

```
set item_info to info for a_file
```

This line gets a bunch of information about the current loop item. The **info for** command — see Chapter 8 — returns a record with lots of interesting stuff, but all we're interested in is whether or not this item is a folder. If it's a folder, we don't want to try to change its creator type because folders don't have a creator type.

The creator type tells the Finder which application created a file. The Finder uses this information to decide which application to launch when you double-click a file. Because all folders are made and managed by the Finder, no creator type information is required.

Line 4

```
if not (folder of item_info ) then
```

This line checks the folder property of the record contained in the variable **item_info** to see if the item is a folder. If the item isn't a folder, the script lines inside the **if** statement (lines 5 to 7) are executed and the file's creator type is changed. Remember that when you put a **not** in front of something, a true changes to a false and a false changes to a true. In addition, the statements after an **if** statement execute if the expression in the **if** statement is true. In this case, if the folder property is true (the item is a folder), the **not** changes true to false so the statements after the **if** do not execute. On the other hand, if the folder property is false (the item isn't a folder), then the **not** changes false to true and the script lines inside the **if** execute.

Line 5

```
tell application "Finder"
```

This tells AppleScript that the lines from here to the next **end tell** statement — just line 6 in this script — are to be directed to the Finder. The **tell** statement is described in detail in Chapter 17.

Line 6

```
set the creator type of a_file to "ttxt"
```

This line tells the Finder to change the creator type of the current file to "ttxt." The Finder will now treat the file as though it had been created by SimpleText.

Line 7

```
    end tell
```

This marks the end of the lines that are being directed to the Finder.

Line 8

```
    end if
```

This marks the end of the **if** statement.

Line 9

```
    end repeat
```

This marks the end of the **repeat** statement.

Line 10

```
end open
```

This marks the end of the **open** handler.

Testing Your Drag and Drop Script

Making a drag and drop script just consists of writing a regular script with an **open** handler. The one slightly hard thing about drag and drop scripts is testing them. When you click on the run button in the Script Editor window, the **open** handler doesn't get executed. So how do you test your script? One way is to write it, save it as an application, and then drop some files on it and see if it works. Another way is to buy one of the other script editors, such as Script Debugger, to test **open** handlers. The third way is to build a test script that looks something like this:

```
on open file_list
    repeat with an_item in file_list
        --the script lines that you write to deal with each item
    end repeat
end open
set n_test_files to 1
set n_test_folders to 1
set item_list to {}
repeat with i from 1 to n_test_files
    set temp to choose file with prompt "Select test file " & i
    set item_list to item_list & temp
end repeat
repeat with i from 1 to n_test_folders
    set temp to choose folder with prompt "Select test folder " & i
    set item_list to item_list & temp
end repeat
open item_list
```

You develop your script using this little framework, and then when it's working you copy the **open** handler to a new script or delete the test scaffolding script lines if you're really confident. If you've written any handlers that are called from the **open** handler, make sure you either copy them to the new script or avoid deleting them when you delete the test script lines.

The test part of the script works by asking you to pick a set of files and folders in the two **repeat** loops. As each file or folder is picked, it's added to a list of items that looks just like the list that AppleScript will produce when you drop files and folders on a drag and drop script. The last line of the script just calls your open handler with that list as an input parameter.

Now you know all you need to know to make drag and drop scripts. All that's left is for you to figure out useful applications. One common use is to move files. You can make a script that moves all the files dropped on it to a special file for archiving, for example. The possibilities are endless, so take a break from reading and go write a script!

Chapter 16
Agents: Watching, Not Spying

. . . .

In This Chapter

▶ Making scripts that stay open and watch for changes

▶ Executing scripts at fixed intervals

▶ Watching for new files in a folder

. . . .

*O*ne of the hot new buzzwords in software is *agents*. An agent is a piece of software that goes off and does something that you want done without your supervision. People talk about intelligent agents swooping through cyberspace, finding information that interests you, and bringing it back to your screen.

Writing Agents That Do What They're Told

AppleScript provides a slightly more mundane type of agent. In AppleScript, you can write scripts that wake up periodically to perform tasks. For example, suppose you often receive image files from various sources. You can write a script that wakes up every five minutes to check if any new files have appeared in any of several folders. If new files have appeared, that same script can process those files using Canvas or Apple's Photoflash. You can also write a script that wakes up periodically and looks for new text files that contain certain keywords. The possibilities, while not endless, are certainly interesting.

To give you a concrete example of how agents work, look at how I develop a simple but useful script for the following scenario. But first, a little background. Since the advent of the desktop computer, the number of cases of repetitive stress injuries (RSI) seem to be on the rise. While not all doctors agree, the general feeling in the community is that taking a break from typing and mouse clicking once in a while is a good thing. Commercial products advise frequent breaks and also include suggestions for exercises and other activities that may reduce your vulnerability to RSI. Well, AppleScript can't tell you about the exercises, at least not in a short script, but you can write a script that wakes up every 15 minutes and reminds you to take a short break. Not only can the script save you from lifelong crippling injury — not that I know anything about medicine nor should you consider my comments anything more than the mindless ramblings of a totally unprofessional layperson — but more important, it can save you the $40 one of those commercial products costs. Just to make sure the lawyers understand, neither I nor IDG warrant the following script to be able to protect anyone from anything. It's merely here as an example. If your wrist, or anything else for that matter, starts hurting, see a doctor — don't just shorten the reminder interval!

All right, now that you realize that this script is just for fun and not a real medical-type thing, take a look at it.

```
property minutes_between_warnings : 15
on idle
    activate
    set msg to "It's been " & minutes_between_warnings ¬
        & " minutes since you took a break." & ¬
        return & ¬
        "Why don't you stretch and stop using the computer for a bit?"
    display dialog msg ¬
        buttons {"Sounds Good", "Nah I'm indestructible"} ¬
        default button "Sounds Good"
    return (minutes_between_warnings * 60)
end idle
```

In order for this script to work as an agent, you have to save it as an application and select the Stay open option. (See Figure 3-10 in Chapter 3). The Stay open option tells AppleScript to leave the script up and running until you use the Quit item in the script applications menu to stop it.

The script takes advantage of AppleScript sending **idle** messages to active scripts when nothing is going on. If the script has an **idle** handler, then that handler is executed whenever the script receives an **idle** message. AppleScript uses the value returned by the **idle** handler to decide when to next wake up the script. If the **idle** handler returns 60, then the script receives another **idle** message in 60 seconds. If it's 3600, then the script executes its **idle** handler in an hour.

AppleScript is not a real-time operating system. It tries to send **idle** messages at the intervals specified by the values returned by the **idle** handler, but other activity on your Mac can interfere. Treat the wake-up interval as an approximation, not a guaranteed fact.

This script displays a dialog every time the **idle** handler is called and then returns a value, which is the number of seconds to the next wake-up. The user has to click one of the buttons before he or she can do anything else with the computer. Hopefully the user takes a short break and stretches. But that's entirely up to the user. My attempts to send high voltage shocks through the keyboard, while successful on Windows machines — another of those unpublished Microsoft hooks — just don't work on the Mac. So now that you've got a top-level view of what the script does, you may want to walk through the following line-by-line description.

Line 1

```
property minutes_between_warnings : 15
```

This just defines the number of minutes between activations. You can make this fancier by having the script read this value from a file (see Chapter 14) so that the user can change the time without editing the script.

Line 2

```
on idle
```

This is the beginning of the **idle** handler that is run when the script receives an **idle** message.

Line 3

```
    activate
```

This command brings the script to the front so the user can't ignore it.

Line 4

```
    set msg to "It's been " & minutes_between_warnings ¬
        & " minutes since you took a break." & ¬
        return & ¬
        "Why don't you stretch and stop using the computer for a bit?"
```

This line just builds up a long string to go into the dialog that's displayed in line 5. I can put all of this into line 5, but this is just a bit easier for me to read.

Line 5

```
display dialog msg ¬
    buttons {"Sounds Good", "Nah I'm indestructible"} ¬
    default button "Sounds Good"
```

The dialog box the user sees is shown in Figure 16-1.

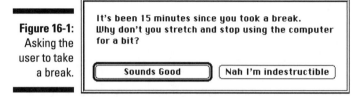

Figure 16-1:
Asking the
user to take
a break.

> It's been 15 minutes since you took a break.
> Why don't you stretch and stop using the computer for a bit?
>
> [**Sounds Good**]   [Nah I'm indestructible]

Notice that the script doesn't do anything with the value returned by the dialog. That's because the script does the same thing no matter what button the user presses. If you want to enforce a break, you can check for the button clicked. If it was the Nah I'm indestructible button, you can shorten the interval between awakenings by temporarily reducing the value of the **minutes_between_warnings** variable. For example, if the baseline interval is 15 minutes and the user decides to not take a break, you can set the next dialog box appearance for five minutes. If the user waves that one off as well, you can wake up the script in one minute. Eventually the user is unable to get anything done unless he or she clicks the Sounds Good button. The user can still keep working, but odds are he or she takes a break. Of course, software that does that sort of thing is the primary cause of gunshot wounds to monitors, so I only recommend doing something like that for people who really want it.

Line 6

```
    return (minutes_between_warnings * 60)
```

This line returns the number of seconds the script wants to wait before it's run again.

Line 7

```
end idle
```

This line marks the end of the **idle** handler.

You can use this type of script in a number of ways. The only similarity is this basic structure:

```
on idle
  return time_in_seconds_till_next_wakeup
end idle
```

In order for an agent to work, it has to be saved as an application. In fact, one of the main problems with developing agents is that you can't test the **idle** handler from inside Script Editor — although Script Debugger does give you a way to do this.

You can do anything you want inside the **idle** handler. You can control applications, including the Finder, and you can read and write files. You're limited only by your imagination. Typical tasks that can be automated include scheduling activities or watching for changes in a folder that can be on a server and then doing something with the new files.

 The timer in a script is reset when the script is restarted. So if you shut down your Mac, the delay starts from scratch when the agent is started again. This means that unless you leave your Mac on all the time, a delay of 24 hours (60*3600*24 seconds) doesn't cause the agent to do something once a day.

Displaying the Startup Screen

One last design issue has to do with whether or not you want to display the startup screen when the agent is started. That screen consists of the text in the description area of the script window and two buttons, Run and Quit, as shown in Figure 16-2. If you expect the user to manually launch the script, this is a nice feature. On the other hand, a typical way to use agents is to place them in the Startup Item's folder inside your System folder so that the agent is automatically launched when your Mac starts up. If the script is being launched automatically, you don't want the Mac to sit around waiting for someone to click on the Run button. So if your agent is launched manually, you should probably retain the startup screen display. If the script is launched automatically, then you should inhibit the display of the startup screen.

Figure 16-2:
A typical
startup
screen.

Here's another example of an agent, and one that you can launch from your Startup Item's folder. This one watches a folder you specify and notifies you when something in the folder changes.

```
property folder_to_watch : ""
property file_list : {}
on run
    if folder_to_watch is "" then
        set folder_to_watch to ¬
            choose folder with prompt "Please select the folder to watch"
        set file_list to list folder folder_to_watch
    else
        set new_file_list to list folder folder_to_watch
        check_files(new_file_list)
    end if
end run
on idle
    set new_file_list to list folder folder_to_watch
    check_files(new_file_list)
    return 1800 --check once every half hour
end idle
on check_files(new_file_list)
    set added_files to {}
    set missing_files to {}
    set missing_flag to false
    set added_flag to false
    repeat with an_item in file_list
        if not (an_item is in new_file_list) then
            copy an_item to the end of missing_files
            set missing_flag to true
        end if
    end repeat
    repeat with an_item in new_file_list
        if not (an_item is in file_list) then
            copy an_item to the end of added_files
            set added_flag to true
        end if
    end repeat
    set error_message to ""
    if missing_flag then
        set error_message to (folder_to_watch as string) & return & "Missing files:"
        repeat with an_item in missing_files
            set error_message to error_message & an_item
        end repeat
```

```
      end if
   if added_flag then
      if error_message is "" then
         set error_message to (folder_to_watch as string) & return & "Added files:"
      else
         set error_message to error_message & return & "Added files:"
      end if
      repeat with an_item in added_files
         set error_message to error_message & an_item
      end repeat
   end if
   if error_message is not "" then
      display dialog error_message
      copy new_file_list to file_list
   end if
end check_files
```

Pretty long script, isn't it? To keep it in perspective, a C program often has
thousands of lines. But as you peruse the detailed line by line, you'll see that
the script isn't all that complex.

Line 1

```
property folder_to_watch : ""
```

This line uses the persistent storage capability of script properties to keep
track of the path to the folder that the user wants the script to watch between
script executions. The value is initialized to the empty string, "", so that the
script can tell when it has to ask the user which folder to watch. After all, you
don't want to ask the user every time the script runs — unless you're giving it
to someone you don't like and you want to annoy them.

Line 2

```
property file_list : {}
```

This line stores the list of files that are in the folder. The script works by
detecting changes in this list. As a result, the script needs to store this list
between script executions, which is why the script uses a property. An empty
list is used so that the files found in the folder can just be appended to the
initial value of the list.

Line 3

```
on run
```

Remember how script lines that aren't in a handler are considered to be part of an implicit **run** handler? Well, I generally use that implicit **run** handler, but just to show you another way to do things, I've used a real **run** handler. The **run** handler is executed whenever the script gets a **run** message. Because a script is launched whenever a **run** message is received, the **run** handler is used for initializing the script. Most of the actual work is done by the **idle** handler.

Line 4

```
if folder_to_watch is "" then
```

When the script is launched, this line checks to see if the user has already picked a folder to watch. If he or she hasn't, then the script lines inside this **if** statement are executed. This approach doesn't give the user any way to change the selected folder, so you can think about how you want to do that without bothering the user too much. I use the empty string as the initial value, but you can use any value that can't be confused with a file path.

Line 5

```
set folder_to_watch to ¬
    choose folder with prompt "Please select the folder to watch"
```

This line uses the **choose folder** command to let the user select the folder he or she wants to watch.

Line 6

```
set file_list to list folder folder_to_watch
```

This line uses the **list folder** command to get all of the files and folders contained in the folder the user wants to monitor. If you have the scriptable Finder, you can use

```
set file_list to every item of folder_to_watch
```

Line 7

```
else
```

This just separates what the script does when a folder hasn't been selected from what it does when a folder has been selected. Lines 8 and 9 are executed if the script starts up and the user has already selected a folder to watch.

Line 8

```
set new_file_list to list folder folder_to_watch
```

This line gets the current list of files and folders in the folder that's being watched.

Line 9

```
check_files(new_file_list)
```

This calls a handler that compares the current list of files and folders with the reference list. If there are any differences, the user is notified.

Line 10

```
end if
```

This just marks the end of the **if** statement that checks to see if the user has selected a folder to watch.

Line 11

```
end run
```

This marks the end of the **run** handler.

Line 12

```
on idle
```

This is the beginning of the **idle** handler, which AppleScript runs at user-defined intervals.

Line 13

```
set new_file_list to list folder folder_to_watch
```

This gets a list of the current contents of the folder being watched.

Line 14

```
check_files(new_file_list)
```

This calls the **check_files** handler, which looks for changes and notifies the user of any.

Line 15

```
return 1800 --check once every half hour
```

This tells AppleScript to send another idle message to this script in 1800 seconds, which happens to be half an hour. If you want to make this script more flexible, you can ask the user what the monitoring interval should be when he or she picks the folder to monitor. You also need to add a new property so the interval is remembered between script executions. Finally, you need to add another **display dialog box** command to ask the user to enter the value of the wake-up interval.

Line 16

```
end idle
```

This ends the **idle** handler. It's so short because most of the script lines have been moved to the **check_files** handler. I moved them because the script needs to check the file lists in two places, the **run** and **idle** handlers. I can just repeat the script lines at those two places, but that means that I have to make changes in two places — one in **run** and one in **idle** — if I want to change one of the lines that compare the new and old file lists.

Line 17

```
on check_files(new_file_list)
```

This starts the handler that actually compares the new list of files and folders to the reference list.

Line 18

```
set added_files to {}
```

This initializes a list that stores the names of files and folders added to the watched folder since the last time it was checked.

Line 19

```
set missing_files to {}
```

This initializes a list that stores the names of files or folders that were in the watched folder the last time it was checked but aren't there now.

Line 20

```
set missing_flag to false
```

This is a *flag* that the script uses to see if any files or folders have disappeared since the last time the folder was checked.

flag: This isn't what you find on a flagpole. In scripting lingo, a flag is a variable that indicates a certain condition. If the value of the variable is true, the script does one thing. If it's false, the script does something else.

Line 21

```
set added_flag to false
```

This is the flag used to indicate if files and/or folders have been added to the watched folder since the last time the folder was checked.

Line 22

```
repeat with an_item in file_list
```

This sets the value of **an_item** to each of the items that was in the folder the last time it was checked. This **repeat** loop checks for items that are in **file_list** but that aren't in **new_file_list**. Those are the items that have been removed from the watched folder since the last time it was checked.

Line 23

```
if not (an_item is in new_file_list) then
```

If an item that was in the folder before, so that it is in **file_list**, isn't in the folder now, you need to add it to the list of missing items, called **missing_files**, and set the missing item flag.

Line 24

```
copy an_item to the end of missing_files
```

This line makes a copy of the contents of **an_item**, which is just the name of a file or folder, and places it at the end of the **missing_files** list.

Line 25

```
set missing_flag to true
```

This line sets the value of the **missing_flag** variable to true so that the script knows when it's generating the user report that some files or folders are missing. It can figure that out by checking to see if **missing_files** is empty, but the script is then a little bit harder to understand.

Line 26

```
end if
```

This marks the end of the **if** statement that deals with items missing from the folder.

Line 27

```
end repeat
```

This marks the end of the **repeat** over the items that had been in the folder.

Line 28

```
repeat with an_item in new_file_list
```

This **repeat** loops over the items currently in the folder. This loop is used to check for files that are in **new_file_list** but not in **file_list**. Those items have been added to the watched folder since it was last checked.

Line 29

```
if not (an_item is in file_list) then
```

If an item is in **new_file_list** but not in **file_list,** the script needs to add it to the list of added files.

Line 30

```
copy an_item to the end of added_files
```

This copies the name of the added item to the end of the **added_files** list.

Line 31

```
set added_flag to true
```

This sets the flag that indicates that at least one item has been added to the watched folder since the last time it was checked.

Line 32

```
end if
```

This marks the end of the **if** that handles looking for newly added files.

Line 33

```
end repeat
```

This marks the end of the **repeat** that looks for newly added files.

Line 34

```
set error_message to ""
```

This initializes the string that displays to the user if anything has been changed.

Line 35

```
if missing_flag then
```

If some files or folders have disappeared, perhaps to go hide with Elvis, the script sets the value of **error_message** to notify the user.

Line 36

```
set error_message to (folder_to_watch as string) & return & "Missing files:"
```

The first step is to tell the user which folder is being watched and that that folder is missing some files. This is important because you can have multiple copies of this script watching multiple folders at the same time. Even if only one folder is being watched, unless files are changing fairly frequently, the user tends to forget the folder path over time.

Line 37

```
repeat with an_item in missing_files
```

This **repeat** loops over the items that are missing so that the script can give the user a detailed report of what's gone.

Line 38

```
set error_message to error_message & an_item
```

This adds the name of the missing item to the error message.

Line 39

```
end repeat
```

This marks the end of the **repeat** that builds up the individual item entries in **error_message.**

Line 40

```
end if
```

This marks the end of the script region that deals with missing files.

Line 41

```
if added_flag then
```

This **if** checks to see if any files or folders were added. If so, then the error message must be properly configured.

Line 42

```
if error_message is "" then
```

If **error_message** is the empty string, then the folder name has to be added. On the other hand, if the script has already put in the folder name because some files or folders were missing, the watched folder name is not shown twice.

Line 43

```
set error_message to (folder_to_watch as string) & return & "Added files:"
```

This puts the watched folder name and the header indicating that at least one item has been added to the watched folder.

Line 44

```
else
```

This divides the script lines that are processed if the folder name hasn't been written to **error_message** from those that are executed if the folder name has been added.

Line 45

```
set error_message to error_message & return & "Added files:"
```

This line just puts in a label indicating that the names that follow it are for files or folders that have been added since the last time the folder was checked.

Line 46

```
end if
```

This marks the end of the script lines that deal with putting an initial label into the error message for the entries associated with added items.

Line 47

```
repeat with an_item in added_files
```

This loops over all of the added items so that their names can be added to the error message.

Line 48

```
set error_message to error_message & an_item
```

This adds the name of an added item to the error message the user sees.

Line 49

```
    end repeat
```

This is the end of the **repeat** that adds the names of files or folders that have appeared in the watched folder to the message the user sees.

Line 50

```
   end if
```

This marks the end of the script lines that deal with preparing a user message.

Line 51

```
    if error_message is not "" then
```

If **error_message** is still the empty string, then no changes were discovered and the script doesn't need to display a message to the user. You can also use

```
if missing_flag or added_flag then
```

Line 52

```
     display dialog error_message
```

This line actually displays the error message. Although the **display dialog** command only displays 255 characters in the message, this script doesn't check message length. Think about how you can deal with a situation where a bunch of items is changed.

 This is also the place where you can customize the script's behavior. For example, instead of notifying the user, you can send the lists of added and/or missing files to some handler that automatically processes them, such as a script that enters the data from the files into Excel.

Line 53

```
     copy new_file_list to file_list
```

This copies the list of files that is currently in the folder to the reference list. The assumption here is that the user doesn't want to be continually reminded about changes. On the other hand, if this is a security program looking for unauthorized changes, you may want to eliminate this line so that the user is notified until the folder is returned to its original state.

Line 54

```
end if
```

This marks the end of the **if** statement that checks to see if changes need to be dealt with.

Line 55

```
end check_files
```

This is the end of the **check_files** handler.

Now that you understand how this script works, think of any tasks you can automate using this agent as a starting point. You may want to watch a folder on a server so that as soon as a fellow worker puts his or her inputs inside, you know and can incorporate them into your work. Doing so can save time over the traditional approach of manually checking the folder occasionally. Depending upon what information your colleague supplies, you can even write a script that automatically incorporates his or her inputs while you're off at a meeting.

Testing Agents

One last thing to consider is how do you test agents? When you click the Run button in the Script Editor, the **idle** handler isn't invoked. So what do you do? As with drag and drop scripts, you've got three options. You can just write the script, save it as an application, launch it, and see if it works. You can buy one of the commercial script editors, such as Script Debugger, which lets you test **idle** handlers. Or you can build a test script very similar to the one you saw in Chapter 15 for testing drag and drop scripts. Such a sample script looks like

```
property wake_up_interval : 10
on idle
    set next_delay_time to wake_up_interval + 2
    display dialog "It's been " & wake_up_interval & " seconds since I last ¬ showed up"
```

```
    return next_delay_time
end idle
on wait(t_in_seconds)
   set start_time to current date
   set delta_time to 0
   repeat until delta_time > t_in_seconds
      set delta_time to (current date) - start_time
   end repeat
   return delta_time
end wait
repeat with i from 1 to 10
   activate
   set wake_up_interval to idle
   wait(wake_up_interval)
end repeat
```

This script calls the **idle** handler ten times at intervals defined by the value returned by the **idle** handler. You can test any idle handler with this test script to make sure it works. If you ever need to delay a script, you can use the **wait** handler shown here. It just records the clock time when it's called and then keeps checking the difference between when it was called and the current time until the delay specified as an input argument, in seconds, has elapsed. The **wait** handler then returns, and the rest of the script can proceed.

One last thing that's of interest is that you can send messages to agents. If an agent called "melvin" contains a handler called "compound_interest," you can cause that handler to run from another script by using something like this:

```
tell application "melvin"
   compound_interest()
end tell
```

So now you know all of the arcane secrets necessary to develop agents with AppleScript. Think you can develop intelligent agents that wander the Internet looking for information that's of use to you? Sounds a bit far-fetched, doesn't it? But by using the power of scriptable Internet applications such as Netscape, you can actually put together some very interesting scripts that save you a great deal of time surfing the Net looking for items of interest.

The 5th Wave By Rich Tennant

"Now, when someone rings my doorbell, the current goes to a scanner that digitizes the audio impulses and sends the image to the Mac where it's converted to a Pict file. The image is then animated, compressed, and sent via high-speed modem to an automated phone service that sends an e-mail message back to tell me someone was at my door 40 minutes ago."

Chapter 17

Taking Charge of Applications

· ·

In This Chapter

▶ Using the dictionary

▶ Controlling applications via AppleScript

▶ Discovering Apple Events, the Object Model, and the OSA

▶ Recording your actions as a script

· ·

The Basics of Bossing Around Apps

AppleScript's main reason for being is to give you the capability to control applications, including the Finder. You can use AppleScript by itself or as an internal scripting language for HyperCard or FaceSpan (seee Chapter 26) to do some interesting things, but the meat and potatoes of AppleScript is controlling other applications. Controlling other applications was the original motivation for developing AppleScript. While I love my Mac's point-and-click interface, sometimes, like when I'm opening the 57th picture to translate from MacPaint to PICT, I like to automate my applications. The DOS/Windows/UNIX folks have a command line interface that gives them some automation capability for Finder-like activities — copying files and so on — but little or no control over applications. Apple, however, has defined the Open Scripting Architecture (OSA) standard for scripting language. Apple has created Apple Events and Object Model for defining and transferring data between applications, which makes it possible for vendors to write applications that can seamlessly integrate with AppleScript and each other. Apple Events specifies how applications talk to each other, and Object Model specifies how applications describe information so that they can understand what is being said. This is no small feat; no other operating system has a system in place that provides standardized plug-and-play interapplication messaging and automation like you can use today on the Mac.

Great conversation topics for parties

Open Scripting Architecture (OSA): This has nothing to do with constructing buildings out of failed sitcom scripts. This is a standard that Apple has defined for system-level scripting languages. Any language that complies with this definition is able to interoperate with other OSA-compliant languages. For example, if you happen to have QuicKeys or UserLand's Frontier on your Mac, the pop-up menu in the script window's lower left-hand corner in the Script Editor gives you the option of editing scripts written in those programs' native languages. In general, you don't have to worry about OSA, you can just benefit from how easy it is to use.

Apple Events: This standard for messages that can be exchanged between applications defines how to send commands and data between applications. Because Apple Events is a standard, applications from any vendor that support it can exchange messages and information. Vendors can follow this standard and define their own messages.

Object Model: This is another standard that Apple has defined. It specifies how applications should talk about information. It's very similar to standard object-oriented programming concepts. Once again, you don't have to worry about the theoretical details. The bottom line is that most of what you see in AppleScript and in the applications' additions are objects with properties, such as strings or lists, that behave just like those that are part of AppleScript itself. For the technically inclined, the Object Model specifies how to find an object, or its property, based upon the object's location in a hierarchy of containers.

One of the Mac's key advantages is that once you know how to use one application, you know how to use them all — unless they're from Microsoft — because they all have basically the same look. The applications use the same key combinations for common activities, for example. In the world of those other, less-advanced operating systems such as Windows 1895, such commonality is, well, uncommon. As a result, it's harder to catch on to new applications, and the poor folks who are stuck on those platforms have to waste more time figuring out how to make the computer work and less time actually doing something useful.

The OSA and the Object Model allow Mac users — that's us — to go the step beyond standard application interfaces. These standards let you combine and automate application activities so that you not only save the tons of time that Windows users spend learning an application, but also the time you currently spend on repetitive tasks. For example, suppose you want to monitor news stories for information on corn futures. You can manually log on to GEnie and search around for items of interest, but every day that takes 10 to 15 minutes, most of which are wasted looking at business news stories that aren't relevant. With AppleScript, you can use SITcomm — a telecommunications program —

to log on and get all of the news stories, search those stories for relevant keywords, such as corn and futures, with Word or WordPerfect, and stuff the relevant articles into a FileMaker Pro database that you can easily search by date and keyword for items of interest. Such a script is not that hard to write and can save you a great deal of time. Similarly, you can write scripts to automate the separation of the interesting stuff from the tons of information that comes from Internet newsgroups.

Because you're working with Apple, writing scripts that make use of applications is easy, not some arcane rocket science. The way scripting works is that each and every scriptable application has a dictionary, which effectively contains definitions of all of the commands and data value types that the application supports. When you want to use those commands, you use the **tell** statement to let AppleScript know which dictionary to use to figure out the command's meaning. For example, if I want to use the Finder to determine what disks are currently available, I just have to write

```
tell application "Finder"
   set the_disks to disks
end tell
```

The value of **the_disks** on my Mac is

```
{startup disk of application "Finder", disk "Peter the Man" of application
"Finder", disk "Kate" of application "Finder", disk "Ted the man" of application
"Finder", disk "Big Apps" of application "Finder", disk "Big Games" of application
"Finder", disk "MetroWorks" of application "Finder", disk "Book related stuff" of
application "Finder", disk "Ted" of application "Finder", disk "Mary" of applica-
tion "Finder", disk "therese" of application "Finder", disk "Archive" of applica-
tion "Finder", disk "Games" of application "Finder", disk "Programming" of
application "Finder", disk "Source Code" of application "Finder", disk "Applica-
tions" of application "Finder", disk "Text archives" of application "Finder", disk
"Telecom" of application "Finder", disk "Who knows" of application "Finder", disk
"Multimedia" of application "Finder"}
```

which is a list of references to each of my hard disk partitions. With just plain old AppleScript, if I try to do something similar, such as

```
set the_disks to disks
```

I get the error message shown in Figure 17-1 because AppleScript doesn't know what the word *disks* means.

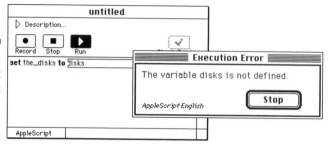

Figure 17-1:
AppleScript
doesn't
know the
word *disks*.

But the Finder does. I bet you're wondering how I figured out that the Finder understands the word *disks*. I guessed. Just kidding. Actually all you have to do is check out the Finder Dictionary by choosing Open Dictionary from the File menu in Script Editor. Figure 17-2 shows the entry for the disk data value type, which shows that you can use the plural of disk when you're working with the Finder. The entry's remaining information is explained in a bit, but for now, just get a feel for how much information you can glean from a dictionary entry.

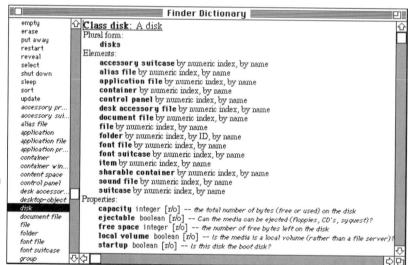

Figure 17-2:
A piece of
the Finder
Dictionary.

Sometimes when you compile a script with **tell** statements, you get a standard file dialog box asking you to locate the application you've directed the **tell** at. AppleScript needs to find the application when it compiles the script. By doing so, AppleScript can read the application's dictionary to understand the commands that occur inside the **tell**. If AppleScript can find the application on its own, then it won't bother you with this dialog box.

To direct script commands to an application, all you have to do is use the **tell** statement.

Yep, it's really that easy to control applications. All you do is read their dictionary, decide what commands you need, write a script that tells the application what you want it to do (using the commands and data structures in the application's dictionary) and then run it. These steps work with any scriptable application, even the newest one released a year after AppleScript hit the streets.

Because it's so easy to work with scriptable applications, you get a strong foundation for automating most of the uninteresting tasks you do on your Mac. That's because most of your time on the Mac is spent working with applications. If you can automate these tasks, you can automate much of what you do.

Clearly you can't automate complex tasks that involve complex decision-making and that use your uniquely human strengths. After all, even the most hardened scripting fanatic — that's me — wouldn't suggest that you write a script that writes letters to your best friend. On the other hand, most of you have regular tasks that are neither mentally challenging or fun. The first step in seeing if you can save time through AA — Application Automation — is to find out if the applications you use are scriptable.

Differentiating Between Good Applications and Pond Scum

Even though Apple introduced the wonders of AppleScript a millennium ago — in software years, which are 39 human seconds long — many applications aren't scriptable. Making an application fully scriptable involves a great deal of effort. Vendors weren't sure how important it was to support scripting because Apple, in its usual low-key way, hadn't really been grabbing people by the throat and shaking them until they admitted that AppleScript is better than sliced bread. You also have the old chicken-and-egg issue. Until someone made scriptable applications, AppleScript didn't have a whole lot of use. But until people started using AppleScript, vendors didn't feel a whole lot of pressure to make applications scriptable.

Fortunately, the fact that the Finder is very scriptable starting with version 7.5 (earlier versions have limited scripting support) means that you can do tons of useful things if all you've got is System 7.5. That fact, combined with the success of scripting in areas such as publishing, has increased the momentum behind scripting. The big software packages are starting to support scripting these days. Word, Excel, WordPerfect, FileMaker Pro, MacWrite Pro, and QuarkXPress, among others, are providing the type of scripting support you need to save time through automation.

So the first step in seeing if an application is good in the context of scripting is to see if it has any scripting support at all. You can do this in several ways. The easiest is to look in Chapter 27. While not all scriptable applications are listed, a reasonable fraction of the most common ones are. If you already have the application, you should check to see if scripting is covered in its documentation. Many scriptable applications come with sample scripts and separate scripting documentation, normally in electronic format on the disk. If you don't find any scripting documentation for your application, you can tell if it's scriptable with AppleScript by checking for a dictionary. To do so, just choose the Open Dictionary command from the File menu in the Script Editor. If the application doesn't show up in the file selection dialog box that the Open Dictionary command puts up, then your application doesn't have a dictionary and isn't scriptable.

Applications can use Apple Events and the Object Model without being scriptable with AppleScript. Unless the application has a special resource, an 'aete,' AppleScript doesn't have any way to determine what message formats the application supports. As a result, AppleScript can't work with applications that lack dictionaries. Well, that's not entirely true. If an application supports the required events — open, run, quit, print — you can send them to it using the **tell** statement, even if the application doesn't have a dictionary. If you know the message formats, you can use UserLand's Frontier — now called Aretha — but that's not a task for a typical scripter.

Don't Trust Aliases

It turns out that aliases, even those of nonscriptable applications, show up in the Open Dictionary dialog box. When you select the alias of a nonscriptable application, you get the error message shown in Figure 17-3.

Figure 17-3:
If you select a nonscriptable item from the Open Dictionary dialog box, you get this error.

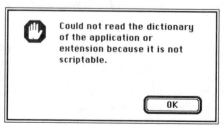

Could not read the dictionary of the application or extension because it is not scriptable.

OK

After you've determined that the application has a dictionary, the next step is to check to see if it's one of the dreaded "not really scriptable" scriptable applications. Those applications have a dictionary with only four commands, as shown in Figure 17-4.

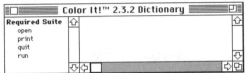

Figure 17-4:
A basically useless dictionary for an otherwise great application.

Unfortunately, you can't do a whole lot with such an application from inside AppleScript — see Chapters 25 and 26 for dealing with nonscriptable applications.

The next step up is an application with just a few — even as few as one — commands. Figure 17-5 shows the dictionary for Adobe PageMaker. It looks pretty pitiful, doesn't it? But because it has the **do script** command, PageMaker's dictionary turns out to be fairly useful.

Figure 17-5:
A limited but usable dictionary.

do script: This command usually lets you invoke by name a script written in an application's internal, non-AppleScript, scripting language. You can use this command to combine the functionality of an application's scripting language with that of AppleScript.

To use the **do script** command effectively, you need to understand the application's internal scripting language as well as AppleScript. As a general principle, applications that let you access most of their functionality without having to use a **do script** command are easier to automate and require less development and testing effort.

If the application has a reasonable number of commands, the next thing to do is to see what the commands let you do. Some applications give you access to all their functionality via AppleScript, and others only provide support for a limited subset. You can't always tell what commands you can use from the number of scripting commands, but a general rule of thumb is the more commands, the better. In the next section, I tell you how to read a dictionary's contents in detail, so just assume for the moment that you know how to do that. In addition to looking at commands, look at the data types — those are the items in the dictionary window that show up in italics, such as *file descriptor* and *window* in Figure 17-6.

Figure 17-6:
Value
classes
defined in an
application
show up in
italics in the
dictionary
window.

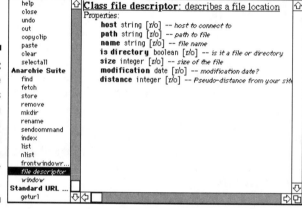

In general, applications without data types are harder to work with than those that have data types designed for the application's functional area. A word processor that has data types for pages, text flow, and so on is easier to work with than one that doesn't.

If the application has a reasonable number of commands and data types, the next thing to determine is the level of scriptability supported. I discuss this stuff in Chapter 2, but here's a quick recap of scriptability levels:

✔ **Scriptable:** The application has more than the four basic script commands.

✔ **Recordable:** You can build scripts by doing actions manually. AppleScript watches what you do and transcribes your actions to a script.

✔ **Attachable:** You can attach new commands, such as menu items, to an application.

✔ **Tinkerable:** You can change the basic functionality of application commands, such as menu items, with scripts.

The bad news is that you can't tell which of these levels an application supports, other than the fact that it's scriptable, by looking at its dictionary. Two sections from now you'll see how to record scripts. A simple way to see if an application is recordable is to try to record a script and see what happens. To find out if an application is Attachable or Tinkerable, you need to check with the vendor or see if the application comes with scripting documentation that tells you how to make use of the application's Attachable or Tinkerable features.

Using a Dictionary without Knowing How the Words Are Spelled

Now that you know how important dictionaries are to scripting applications, you're probably wondering how to decipher the various entries in a dictionary. Well, you've come to the right place.

The first thing to realize is that two different types of dictionary entries exist. One type is just like AppleScript's commands, and the other type — value classes or data types— is just like AppleScript's value types. Commands are basically verbs that the application says it will perform, and value types are the ways that the application groups information.

Look through the Finder Dictionary, part of which is shown in Figure 17-7, to see how to interpret the different entries.

The first thing to note is that the commands and value types are separated into groups — the Standard Suite and the Finder Suite. These partitionings just group commands that are, or should be, standard to all applications and those that are specific to the Finder. The same is true of the value types. You might see the same name in each group — *file* appears in both groups, for example. But the two entries will have different properties. That's because the file value class in the Finder Suite is specific to the Finder application, so it has many Finder-specific properties, while the file value class in the Standard Suite has only properties that are applicable in all applications. There's no way to distinguish the two definitions in a script, and AppleScript will always use the right one, so don't worry about it. You can combine commands from different suites in the same script line, and you can access all of these commands from inside a single **tell** command directed at the application.

Use the **move** command to find out a dictionary command's syntax. You can get the dictionary entry by clicking the command name in the scrolling list on the dictionary window's left-hand side. The entry is highlighted, and the description appears in the right-hand side window, as shown in Figure 17-8.

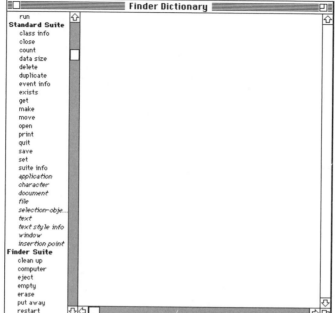

Figure 17-7:
Part of the
Finder
Dictionary.

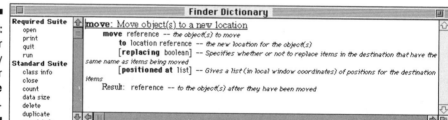

Figure 17-8:
The Finder
Dictionary
entry for
the **move**
command.

The first line of any command's entry contains the command name followed by a short description of what the command does. Next is the command syntax's description, which uses a format very similar to what you've already seen in this book. Stuff enclosed in square brackets, [ ], is optional, and comments (text preceded by the --) that aren't part of the command are shown in italics. The entry concludes with a description of the command's result, the value the command returns.

The simplest usage of the **move** command is

```
tell application "Finder"
    move file "System:test" to folder "System:scripting folder:"
end tell
```

This little script moves a file named test, which resides at the top level of a disk called System, into the scripting folder, which resides on the top level of the disk called System. While it doesn't say so in the dictionary, the folder named scripting folder has to exist before you execute the **move** command or you get an error. Another thing to note is that even if a command returns a value, you don't have to use it. That means I didn't need to write

```
set x to move file "System:test" to folder "System:scripting folder:"
```

The optional parameters can be used either separately or together.

That looks fairly straightforward, doesn't it? Unfortunately, things can get a   bit complex for a number of reasons. The most bothersome is when a vendor changes AppleScript support but doesn't update the dictionary. You should consider this possibility when you use a command as it's stated but get an error message either when you check the script syntax or run the script. Before assuming the vendor has a problem, though, make absolutely sure that you've used the right types of values. For example, if you just use a string, "System:scripting folder:," instead of a reference folder, "System:scripting folder:," the command doesn't work. In that case, it would be your mistake, not the vendor's.

Another type of problem occurs when the vendor doesn't list special cases in the dictionary. For example, I originally intended to use the **make** command as the example for reading the dictionary entries for a command. You use the **make** command fairly often to create new folders and such, but it has a small problem as you'll see in a moment. The dictionary listing is shown in Figure 17-9.

Figure 17-9:
The syntax
of the **make**
command.

```
╔═╦═══════════════════════ Finder Dictionary ═══════════════════════╦═╗
║ Standard Suite  ⇧ │make: Make a new element                       ⇧ ║
║   class info       │     make                                        ║
║   close            │        new type class -- the class of the new element
║   count            │        at location reference -- the location at which to insert the element
║   data size        │        [to reference] -- when creating an alias file, the original item to create an alias to
║   delete           │        [with data anything] -- the initial data for the element
║   duplicate        │        [with properties record] -- the initial values for the properties of the element
║   event info       │     Result: reference -- to the new object(s)
║   exists           │                                              ⇩ ║
║   get              │                                                 ║
║   make           ⇩ │                                                 ║
╚════════════════════════════════════════════════════════════════════╝
```

If you read the entry, it's clear that the format for a command to make a new file at the top level of a disk named System is

```
tell application "Finder"
    make new file at disk "System:"
end tell
```

Unfortunately, when you check the syntax of this script you get the error shown in Figure 17-10.

Figure 17-10:
The wages
of following
the
dictionary.

You get the answer if you read the AppleScript Finder Guide, which comes with the AppleScript CD from Apple. You discover that if the type of item you're creating is a file, you can't use the word **new** even though that word is shown to be a part of the required syntax. So the correct way to do use the **make** command is as follows:

```
tell application "Finder"
    make file at disk "System:"
end tell
```

Unfortunately, you can't figure out the syntax of this special case just by reading the dictionary. However, once you get the hang of debugging scripts, you'll have a set of tools for figuring out how to identify and fix problems like this. I walk you through the process of dealing with this particular problem in Chapter 18.

I know the thought of dictionary errors is bothersome, but to put it into perspective, they're very infrequent. Don't let the possibility of a problem keep you from reaping the benefits of scripting. In any case, I've tried to identify all of the problems of this type that I'm aware of, and vendors presumably fix these sorts of errors as they release new application versions.

Time to move on to the value type entries. Figure 17-11 shows the entry for the **disk** value type.

The definition of the **disk** value type in Figure 17-11 may appear a bit intimidating at first, but don't panic — save that for what happens if the check you used to pay for this book bounces. All items for any value type fall into three categories, not all of which are present for every value type. The first is what, if any, the plural form of the value is. Not all values have plurals. If a value type has a plural, you can use it to access all of the items of a given type, as in this example:

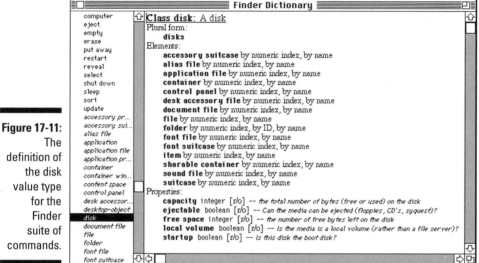

Figure 17-11:
The definition of the disk value type for the Finder suite of commands.

```
tell application "Finder"
    set disk_list to disks
end tell
```

This script sets the value of **disk_list** to a list containing references to all of the disks that are currently available.

The second type of entry is called Elements. Elements are other value types that can be contained in the value type being defined. The list is long for a disk because disks can contain pretty much anything the Finder deals with. Each entry under Elements gives the name of the value class and how it can be accessed. The possible ways to access an element are described in Chapter 7 because they're just the standard reference forms. For example, next to files, it says "by numeric index, by name." That means that you can refer to files on a disk by numeric index, as in these samples:

```
tell application "Finder"
    set z to the first file of disk "System"
    set x to the file 4 of disk "System"
    set y to the files 1 through 3 of disk "System"
end tell
```

Or you can refer to files on a disk by name, as in these examples:

```
tell application "Finder"
    set z to file "activity log" of disk "System"
end tell
```

One particularly useful way to access elements is by using a **whose** clause. For example, this next script returns a list of references to all files on the top level of the disk called "System" that contain the string "test."

```
tell application "Finder"
    set z to every file of disk "System" whose name contains "test"
end tell
```

The bad news is that you can't figure this out from anything in the dictionary. What you expect to see is something like "satisfying a test" next to the element name. The important thing isn't how good the dictionary is, though; it's what you can do with the commands and value types in it. So resign yourself to doing some experimentation. When a script you're writing would benefit from a value class supporting test that doesn't show up in the dictionary, write a simple sample script like the preceding one and see if it works. If so, great. If not, you've only wasted a minute or so. But be of good cheer. As time goes on, application dictionaries will get better.

The third type of information that appears are properties. These are just like the properties of AppleScript's built-in classes, such as strings. You can access properties by using their name, as in

```
tell application "Finder"
    set z to capacity of disk "system"
end tell
```

This sets **z** to the formatted capacity of the disk called "System" in bytes. The [r/o] next to the property name means it's read-only, so you can't change it. While the disk value type doesn't have any editable properties, the **file** value type, shown in Figure 17-12, does.

Notice that the **locked, creator type, file type**, and **stationary** properties don't have [r/o] next to them. That means you can set them as in this next script, which unlocks locked files that are dragged on it — that's why it has the **open** handler, which I discuss in Chapter 15.

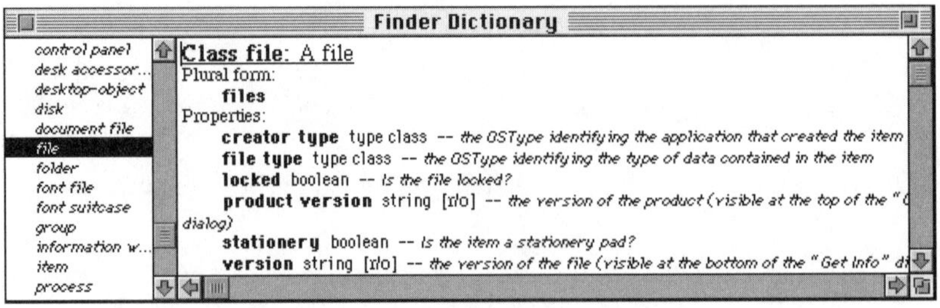

Figure 17-12:
The file data type in the Finder.

```
on open dropped_files
    tell application "Finder"
        repeat with a_file in dropped_files
            if kind of a_file is not folder then
                set locked of a_file to false
            end if
        end repeat
    end tell
end open
```

When you drag a locked file onto the icon for this script after it's been saved as an application, a dialog box appears, as shown in Figure 17-13, to ask you if you really want to open the file. This de-automates this script a bit. Even though the dialog box says you can't change the file, the script above does unlock it.

Figure 17-13: The locked file warning.

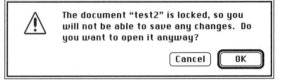

See how easy it is to set a property? Just use the syntax

```
set some_property_name of some_item to some_value
```

Getting the value of a property is just as easy. The script checks to see what the value of the **kind** property of the item is in this line

```
if kind of a_file is not folder then
```

in order to avoid trying to set the **locked** parameter of a folder. Folders don't have the **locked** property, and if you try to set a property that doesn't exist, you get an error.

Now you know how to read the dictionary entries for both commands and data items. In general, the dictionary gives you reasonable insight into automating an application. You've also seen how the dictionary can let you down at times. When that happens, what do you do? Well, you read this book, which has lots of examples in Part III for a wide variety of applications. Another thing you can do is buy one of the commercial script-editing packages. They all improve the dictionary in one way or another. But one of the best things you can do, if the application is recordable, is to make a recording and let the application tell you the proper scripting syntax.

How to Make a Good Recording — Even If You Can't Sing

When AppleScript was under development, the capability to record user actions and turn them into scripts was one of its most ballyhooed features. The lack of recordable applications first dimmed the glow of this feature. While it's fairly easy to add some level of scripting support to an application, making it fully recordable is much more complex and time consuming. The second problem that has put recording on the back burner in terms of cutting-edge technology is that this feature can't capture loops or decisions. Recorded scripts never contain **repeat** or **if** statements, which clearly limits their utility. For example, if you're working with SITcomm, which is recordable, and you log on to CompuServe, look at the first three news items, and then log off, the recorded script looks like this (without the comments that I've included so you can figure out what's going on):

```
tell application "SITcomm™"
    activate
    -- get the connection info for CompuServe
    Load Address "CompuServe"
    --connect to CompuServe
    Connect
    --start capturing the text coming from CompuServe
    -- into a file
    Turn On Capturing
    --wait for a prompt from CompuServe
    Wait For Text " more !"
    --tell CompuServe you want to read the first news item
    -- this line sends the character 1 to compuserve just as though you'd
    -- typed it
    Send Text "1"
    --this time item 1 was more than 1 page long so we have to hit return
    Wait For Text "more !1"
    -- this line is sending a return to Compuserve just as though you'd hit
    -- the return key
    Send Text "
"
    --since the first article has more than 2 pages we've got to
    -- send Compuserve another return
    Wait For Text "nload !"
```

```
    Send Text "
"

    Wait For Text "nload !"
    Send Text "
"

    Wait For Text " more !"
    --here we ask for article 2
    Send Text "2"
    Wait For Text "more !2"
    Send Text "
"

    Wait For Text "nload !"
    Send Text "
"

    Wait For Text "nload !"
    Send Text "
"

    Wait For Text " more !"
    Send Text "3

    Wait For Text "nload !"
    Send Text "
"

    Wait For Text "nload !"
    Send Text "
"

    --we're done so we stop capturing the messages into the file
    Turn Off Capturing
    --these next lines send bye followed by return to Compuserve in
    --order to log off
    Wait For Text " more !"
    Send Text "b"
    Wait For Text "more !b"
    Send Text "y"
    Wait For Text "ore !by"
    Send Text "e"
    Wait For Text "re !bye"
    Send Text "
"

end tell
```

The first thing to notice is that depending upon a news item's length, you may or may not have to send one or more carriage returns to CompuServe in order to get the article's whole text. Unfortunately, if I run this script tomorrow, the number of pages in the first, second, or third news item may be different and the script would break. What I really need is an **if** statement that looks at the prompts — the text that CompuServe sends to SITcomm. If those prompts indicate that another page to view exists, the **if** branches to a script line that sends a return. If another page doesn't exist, the **if** branches to a different script line. That way the script works no matter how long, or short, a news item is.

A similar problem is that this recorded script always reads the first three news items. It is a lot clearer and a lot easier to extend to more news items, if instead of having the individual commands for getting each message, you have a **repeat** loop of the form

```
repeat with i from 1 to the_number_of_news_items_to_read
```

A well-designed version of this script looks like this:

```
set the_number_of_news_items_to_read to 3
repeat with i from 1 to the_number_of_news_items_to_read
    read_message() --this has the script lines necessary to read a single message
end repeat
```

All right, if recording is so useless, why is it there at all? The answer is that you can use recording to find out the syntax of obscure scripting commands and as a quick way to get a script skeleton, which you can then improve by adding **repeats** and **if** statements. For example, the SITcomm dictionary for the Set Tool Config command is shown in Figure 17-14.

Figure 17-14:
The
SITcomm
dictionary.

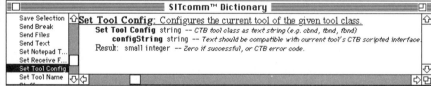

I'd be mighty impressed if you could figure out how to change the number of columns of text from 132 to 80. Fortunately, SITcomm is recordable, so you can have SITcomm show you the right way to do this. The first thing you do is open a new script window in Script Editor. Next you click the Record button in the window between the script and description areas. In order to make it easy for you to know that AppleScript is watching what you do and recording everything inside a scriptable application, a special recording icon, as shown in Figure 17-15, starts alternating with the standard Apple menu Apple icon on the left-hand side of the menu bar. At this point, anything you do inside a recordable application, such as the Finder, starts showing up in the script window. You may have a bit of a lag, so don't bother looking at the window until you've finished what you want to record. When you're done with the actions you want to record, switch back to the Script Editor and click the Stop button. This is the script I get when I switch to SITcomm, choose the Terminal command from the Session menu, and change the number of columns from 132 to 80:

```
tell application "SITcomm™"
    activate
    Set Tool Name "tbnd" toolName "TTY Tool"
    Set Tool Config "tbnd" configString "FontSize 9 Width 80 Cursor Block Online
            True LocalEcho True AutoRepeat True RepeatControls False AutoWrap True
            NewLine False Scroll Jump ShowControls False SwapBackspaceDelete False"
end tell
```

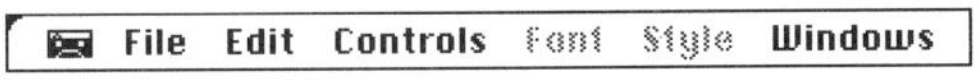

Figure 17-15:
The
recording
icon.

File   Edit   Controls   Font   Style   Windows

Now I don't know about you, but I sure wouldn't have figured out how to change the number of columns from the dictionary. Fortunately, because SITcomm is recordable, I don't have to.

Another example of a good use of recording is in Microsoft Word. While Word has pretty good scripting support, as you see in Chapter 23, many of its features are only accessible via its built-in scripting language, Word Basic. You can access those features by using the **do script** command, but they're only documented electronically. In any case, you don't really want to have to understand Word Basic if you can avoid it. The solution, as you've probably guessed by now, is to use recording to discover what the appropriate **do script** commands are. For example, suppose I want to replace all instances of a certain phrase. No **find** command is in Word's scripting dictionary, so recording seems to be a good answer. Following the same general procedure that I used to record the SITcomm sample, I open a new script, click the Record button, switch to Word, press Command-F (which launches the Find dialog box, as shown in Figure 17-16), enter the string to search for, enter the string to replace things with, and click the Replace All button. I then switch back to Script Editor, click the Stop button, and am rewarded with the next script.

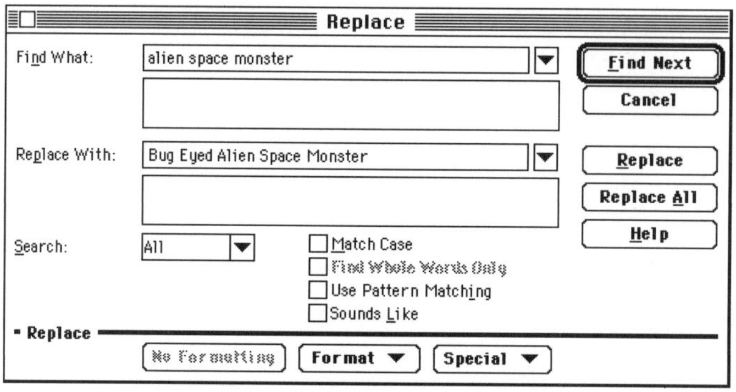

Figure 17-16:
The Find and
Replace
dialog box
in Word.

```
tell application "Microsoft Word"
   activate
   do script "EditReplace .Find = \"alien space monster\", .Replace = \"Bug Eyed
        Alien Space Monster\", .Direction = 0, .MatchCase = 0, .WholeWord = 0,
        .PatternMatch = 0, .SoundsLike = 0, .ReplaceAll, .Format = 0, .Wrap = 1"
end tell
```

All I have to do is copy that last command inside the **tell** and use it in my script.

The bottom line is that recording is a nice tool for building preliminary scripts that you improve by adding **repeats** and **ifs.** Recording is also very useful for figuring out the proper syntax of application commands.

Tell: How to Get Applications to Pay Attention

You've seen how you use the **tell** statement to direct commands to applications. Now it's time to discover the full syntax of this wondrous command. The basic syntax for the compound statement is

```
tell a_reference_to_some_object
  some script lines
end [tell]
```

The parameter *a_reference_to_some_object* can be an application, system object, or a script object — see Chapter 20.

Most of the time that you use the **tell** statement, you use an application as the target object, and the statement looks like this:

```
tell application "Finder"
  some script lines
end tell
```

You can also use the **tell** statement to direct commands to documents as in

```
tell document "stupid scripting book" of application "MacWrite Pro"
```

In order to reference an application, you can put in any string you want. For example, say you want to script DeltaGraph Pro, a graphing program. The application name on my hard disk is DeltaGraph® Pro 3.5. If I write the following script line

```
tell application "DeltaGraph Pro"
```

where I just use DeltaGraph Pro for the application name, everything still works just fine. When I click the Check Syntax button, AppleScript looks for an application called DeltaGraph Pro and doesn't find it. AppleScript then displays the dialog box, shown in Figure 17-17, asking me to use a standard Mac file dialog to locate the application I want to use. I could have even used DGP for the application name and things would have worked out fine. After you tell AppleScript where the application is, AppleScript changes the application's name in the **tell** statement to the application's real name. After being compiled, the **tell** line looks like this:

```
tell application "DeltaGraph® Pro 3.5"
```

You can nest **tell** statements inside of other **tell** statements as in this next example.

Figure 17-17:
AppleScript
asks you
to find
DeltaGraph
Pro.

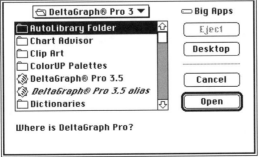

```
tell application "Finder"
   --some script lines (1)
   tell application "MacWrite Pro for Power Mac"
      --some other script lines(2)
   end tell
   --yet another set of script lines(3)
end tell
```

The script lines labeled 1 and 3 are directed to the Finder, while those labeled 2 are directed to MacWrite Pro. You can also use nested **tells** to complete partial references. In this example

```
tell application "Finder"
   tell window 1
      set bounds to {40, 52, 300, 423}
   end tell
end tell
```

the bounds *rectangle* of window 1 of application "Finder" are set. AppleScript looks at the **set** bounds line and determines that it doesn't have a complete reference, so it goes to the first **tell**. Using the information from that **tell**, AppleScript knows it's supposed to set the bounds of window 1, but it still doesn't know which window 1. Because it still doesn't have a complete reference, AppleScript goes to the next **tell** and ends up realizing that it's supposed to set the bounds of window 1 of application Finder.

rectangle: You describe the bounds rectangle — that's the rectangle that defines the outer boundary of an object — of a window or any other object as a four-item list. The first item is the distance in pixels from the left edge of the screen to the left side of the window. The second term is the distance in pixels of the top of the window from the top of the screen. The third item is the distance of the right-hand side of the window from the left-hand edge of the screen. The fourth item is the distance from the top of the screen to the bottom of the window.

Inside a **tell** statement, you can use two special variables. The first is **it,** which is a reference to the object the **tell** is targeting. So this script

```
tell application "Finder"
   set z to frontmost of it
end tell
```

sets the value of **z** to true if the Finder is the frontmost application and false otherwise.

The second value is **me,** or **my,** which refers the script, actually the script object if you want to get technical, that the **tell** is in. For example,

```
property name : "melvin"
tell application "Finder"
    set z to my name
end tell
```

sets **z** to the string "melvin," as does

```
property name : "melvin"
tell application "Finder"
    set z to name of me
end tell
```

The most common use of **my** is to tell AppleScript that some commands inside a **tell** aren't to be interpreted with the application's dictionary. For example, in this script

```
on add(x, y)
    set sum to x + y
    return sum
end add
tell application "Finder"
    --get the number of files on the top level of the first disk
    set n_files to the number of files in item 1 of disks
    --get the number of folders on the top level of the first disk
    set n_folders to the number of folders in item 1 of disks
    set total to add(n_files, n_folders)
end tell
```

I want to use the **add** handler defined in the script inside the **tell** statement. This script compiles with no errors, but when I run it, I get the error shown in Figure 17-18. That's because the Finder doesn't have an **add** command in its dictionary, so when it gets an **add** message, it throws up its hands and says, "I don't have the foggiest idea of what you're talking about." This problem can be fixed by putting **my** in front of add, as in this line

```
set total to my add(n_files, n_folders)
```

The **my** tells AppleScript to direct the following command to the script itself, not to the object of the **tell** statement.

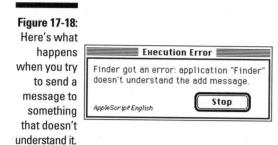

Figure 17-18:
Here's what happens when you try to send a message to something that doesn't understand it.

By now, you should have a good idea of how easy it is to work with applications. True, you've discovered that the dictionary isn't as wonderful as it can be in some cases, but in Part III you get concrete proof that working with dictionaries isn't that hard.

Chapter 18

Debugging: Fixing Problems without DDT

. . . .

In This Chapter
▶ Tracking down and eradicating problems in your scripts
▶ Using the Event Log window to help isolate problems
▶ Scripting defensively so that you're less likely to encounter bugs

. . . .

Scripting is a creative activity, such as writing a paragraph, and the most creative part is figuring out what went wrong. As you develop scripts, you discover that they either won't compile, they crash when they run, or, worst of all, they run but produce the wrong result. These things don't occur because you're some sort of idiot; they happen to all scripters. Writing a script can be a very complex activity, and the Mac has no common sense. If you don't tell the Mac exactly what you want it to do in exactly the way it wants to hear it, you have problems. But don't panic. As you get more scripting experience, you'll be able to avoid problems; but even when you're a scripting guru, long, complex scripts will have their share of teething problems. The secret is to master the art of debugging.

The Art of Debugging

The commercial script editors, described in Chapter 28, have some really nice tools to aid you in debugging scripts — tools that Apple's bare-bones, but free, Script Editor doesn't. That's reason enough to shell out the money for one of those non-Apple tools if you're going to be doing any serious scripting. This chapter only covers techniques that you can use with Script Editor.

Because debugging is an art, you really can't lay out a detailed process guaranteed to squash all bugs under all circumstances. Instead, I show you some proactive and reactive techniques that get you started in the debugging business.

Not using global variables

Global variables can be useful in passing information between handlers, but years of experience have shown that sooner or later you're going to run into a problem when the name of a variable in a handler happens to be the same as that of a global variable — see Chapter 13 for details. Even if this only happens once in a very long while, it can be very painful because it's very hard to track down this sort of error. Instead of using global variables, you should pass data around by using parameters. For example, instead of this

```
global x, y,sum
on add()
    return x + y
end add
on add_up()
    set x to 3
    set sum to add()
end add_up
set y to 4
add_up()
set total to sum
```

you should write something like this

```
on add(x, y)
    return x + y
end add
on add_up(y)
    set x to 3
    set sum to add(x, y)
    return sum
end add_up
set y to 4
set total to add_up(y)
```

Labeling variable names clearly

Your script doesn't break because you use cryptic names for variables. At least not just because you use cryptic variable names. But what happens is that as you write the script, you forget what type of value is in a variable, and you use that value in a place in your script where it doesn't make sense. For example, this script compiles just fine

```
set x to "this is a test"
set y to 3
--20 or 30 script lines
set sum to x + y
```

but when you try to run it, kaboom! Some languages protect you from this error with *strong type checking*. I prefer the flexibility AppleScript brings to the table, but it does mean that you need to be a bit careful with how you use variables. A corollary to this is that if you give variables very specific names, you tend to put only one kind of value into them. For example, a variable called **user_name** probably never contains an integer, while one called **yacht_weight** doesn't tend to harbor a string.

strong type checking: This doesn't mean that you have your variables lift weights. It means that the language requires you to define a variable's value type and then you can never put a different value type into that variable. This is common in "real" programming languages because it helps avoid bugs.

Breaking large scripts into modular handlers

You should try to break large scripts into a bunch of small, modular handlers, which helps to avoid bugs in several ways. First, it makes your script easier to understand because each handler does one little thing and all of the script lines that are needed to do that one little thing are grouped together where you can see them. In addition, you can read the following script easier.

```
tell application "Microsoft Word"
   activate
   open file (find_most_recently_modified_file of me given folder:book_folder)
end tell
```

Because the script lines needed for finding the latest file in a given folder have been moved to their own handler, which isn't shown, the preceding script is easier to read than

```
property book_dir : "Mary:Files:AppleScript for Dummies Book:text:"
tell application "Microsoft Word"
   activate
   set latest_date to date "Saturday, September 1, 1990 00:00:00"
```

(continued)

(continued)

```
    set file_list to list folder book_dir
    set file_to_open to "error"
    repeat with a_file in file_list
        set file_info to info for file (book_dir & a_file)
        if modification date of file_info > latest_date then
            set file_to_open to a_file
            set latest_date to modification date of file_info
        end if
    end repeat
    if file_to_open is not "error" then
        set file_to_open to book_dir & file_to_open
    end if
    open file file_to_open
end tell
```

This difference is important because the easier it is to read a script, the easier it is to spot bugs before they bite and to figure out where they're hiding after they catch you. Another advantage of this approach is that it limits the scope of variables. If you use a common variable name such as **temp** or **sum** and then forget to initialize it before you use it again, you can run into problems. If you break your script into chunks, the value of **sum** in one handler doesn't affect the value of **sum** in another. For example, this next script has problems.

```
set sum to 0
repeat with i from 1 to 10
    set sum to sum + i
end repeat
-- a bunch of unrelated script lines and then another loop where ¬
I want to compute the
-- sum of the integers from 1 to 100 but instead I'll get the sum ¬
of the integers from 1 to
--100 plus the sum of integers from 1 to 10 because the value of the ¬
variable sum didn't
--start out as 0
repeat with j from 1 to 100
    set sum to sum + j
end repeat
```

On the other hand, the following script works just fine.

```
on some_handler()
    set sum to 0
    repeat with i from 1 to 10
        set sum to sum + i
    end repeat
end some_handler
on some_other_handler()
    set sum to 0
    repeat with j from 1 to 100
        set sum to sum + j
    end repeat
end some_other_handler
```

But wait. You say this script initializes **sum** before **sum** is used the second time. The first script still works if you do that. But look closely. When I run the first version, it appears to work just fine. Only the answer isn't right. If I try to run the second version without setting the value of **sum** in the second handler, I get the error shown in Figure 18-1.

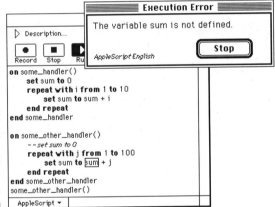

Figure 18-1: Getting caught making a mistake.

Another advantage of breaking your script is that it's easier to incrementally test it.

Incrementally testing your script

Incremental testing may sound fancy, but it just means that you don't write 200 lines of script and then see if it all works. Instead, write pieces of the script and see if they work. For example, say you want to do some processing with all of a folder's files that contain "help" in their name. Instead of writing all of the script lines first, you just write this:

```
set the folder_to_use to choose folder with prompt "Which folder should I process?"
set found_files to {}
tell application "Finder"
repeat with an_item in folder_to_use
    if the name of it contains "help" then
        set found_files to found_files & an_item
    end if
end repeat
end tell
return found_files
```

When you run the script, you can look at the value of **found_files** to make sure that you're getting the files you want. After you're sure it's working, you can throw away the **found_files** variable and start writing the script lines that process the files whose names contain "help," secure in the knowledge that the right files are being selected.

Don't forget that when you use **contains,** the comparison is case sensitive. If the file name is "Help," AppleScript says that it didn't contain "help."

Using rapid prototyping

Rapid prototyping is closely related to incremental testing. The idea is to quickly throw together part of your script that you're not sure how to write so that you can see what you need to do. For example, suppose you want to use the Finder and a **whose** clause to get all of the files whose names contain help instead of a **repeat** statement. What's the proper way to write that? Well, you can put that inside of your big script and run the whole script every time you want to test a potential approach. On the other hand, you can save time and effort by creating a new, temporary script window to try that one script line. For example, the rapid prototype for using the Finder and a **whose** clause can be this script:

```
set the folder_to_use to choose folder with prompt "Which folder should I process?"
tell application "Finder"
    set file_list to every file in folder_to_use whose name contains "Help"
end tell
return file_list
```

You can run this script, verify that the result is what you want, and then put the **set** line back into your main script. The basic idea is to try things that you're not sure will work in a minimal environment to avoid problems due to other parts of your script. By doing so, you make those problems easy to modify and can rapidly retest prototype solutions. You don't have to restrict rapid prototyping to a single line; you can apply it to a whole handler if you want.

Use lots of comments

Most of the scripts in this book lack comments. That's because they're usually short. I've also found that when you're not familiar with scripting, a lot of comment lines tend to obscure the script flow. In addition, detailed, line-by-line descriptions of scripts are associated with most long scripts. When you're writing a script, though, the only documentation you have is what's in the script itself. If you're writing a script in a few minutes and you're never, ever going to change it, you can get by without comments. On the other hand, if the script is a large one that you modify over time, comments can really help you avoid problems. Comments can be used to tell you what type of information a variable should contain. For example, if the script uses a variable called **user_education,** it may not be obvious whether or not this variable should contain a string — high school or college, for example — or a number representing the number of years of education. A simple comment like this

```
--user_education contains the number of years of school, including
--Kindergarten, the user has completed.
```

helps avoid problems when you change the script. Comments are especially useful in handlers that you may want to use in more than one script. If the handler is well commented, it's easy to figure out what the handler does and how to use it in your script. Here's a well-commented version of a handler. See if you can figure out what it does.

```
on find_latest_file given folder:book_dir
    --Inputs:this takes a folder path, as a string, as input in ¬
        the book_dir parameter
    --Outputs:a string containing the path to the file in the folder
    --defined by book_dir which was most recently modified
    --Function: Find the file in a folder which was most recently modified
    --Additions Used: None
    --Applications Used: None
    --set the latest_date variable to a date early enough so that
```

(continued)

(continued)

```
--some file in the folder has been modified more recently than
--that date
set latest_date to date "Saturday, September 1, 1990 00:00:00"
--get the files in the folder
set file_list to list folder book_dir
set file_to_open to "error"
--check files to see which was most recently modified
repeat with a_file in file_list
    set file_info to info for file (book_dir & a_file)
    if modification date of file_info > latest_date then
        --if the file was modified more recently than the previous
        --record for latest_date then set file_to_open to this
        --just discovered file and set the latest_date to the
        --modification date of this file
        set file_to_open to a_file
        set latest_date to modification date of file_info
    end if
end repeat
if file_to_open is not "error" then
    set file_to_open to book_dir & file_to_open
end if
return file_to_open
end find_latest_file
```

In general, it's a good idea to specify a handler's inputs, the value or values the handler returns, what it does, what nonstandard scripting additions it uses, and what applications it calls on. Scripting additions, which I talk about in Chapter 19, are special items that let you extend the syntax of AppleScript. Scripting additions commands are a lot like those in an application's dictionary, but they don't have to be used inside a **tell** statement. Because users may not have all of the third-party freeware, shareware, and commercial scripting additions on their Mac, it's a good idea to keep track of which, if any, nonstandard additions a handler requires.

Savvy Troubleshooting

Now suppose you follow these good scripting practices, but you get a problem when you try to run your script. What do you do? Well, I don't have a surefire 30-day, money-back-guarantee approach to fixing problems, but the following path is useful in a lot of cases:

1. **Understanding what the problem is.**
2. **Figuring out where the problem occurs in the script.**
3. **Pinpointing why the problem occurs.**
4. **Fixing the problem.**
5. **Testing the solution.**

Understanding the problem

The first thing to do is figure out what's wrong. If your script generates an error message, that's one indication that your script is less than perfect. Another way is to run the script and discover that it doesn't do what you want. In general, errors that AppleScript catches are easier to track down than those that you catch because AppleScript helps isolate the error for you. For example, in Figure 18-1, the problem was that the variable **sum** hadn't been initialized, and when AppleScript tried to execute this script line

```
set sum to sum + 1
```

it realized it couldn't because it didn't know what to replace the right-hand instance of **sum** with. Not only did AppleScript highlight the right-hand instance of **sum**, it also told you in the error message that the **sum** hadn't been defined. With an error description like that, you can't go wrong. Unfortunately, you can't always count on AppleScript being this helpful. Figure 18-2 shows a less-helpful error message.

Figure 18-2: Trying to use a reserved word as a variable.

It's far from obvious what the problem is here until you realize that **repeat** is a reserved word and you therefore can't use it as a variable. That's why it sometimes takes a bit to understand what the problem is, even when AppleScript is telling you that it is confused. The situation is worse when you discover that a script isn't producing the expected results. In that case, you don't know where in the script the problem lies. You don't know if it's a scripting problem, if you told AppleScript the wrong thing, or if it's a more fundamental problem with the script's basic concept. An example of telling AppleScript the wrong thing is that you use the variable **x** when you mean to use **y**. An example of a fundamental problem with the script's basic concept is that you intend to select the most recently modified file in a folder, but you mistakenly think that the creation date of a file was updated when it was modified, and so you use that file property to select the file.

Figuring out where the problem occurs in the script

After you know what's wrong, or at least have decided that given the information you have you can't figure out the error, the next step is to try to figure out where the error occurs. When AppleScript tells you about the error, it's usually fairly easy to track down the problem because AppleScript highlights the place the problem occurs. Unfortunately, what is highlighted may not always be the source of the problem. In Figure 18-3, the script compiles just fine. However, when I try to run the script, it dies with an execution error — which is desirable for hard-core criminals but bad news for honest scripters.

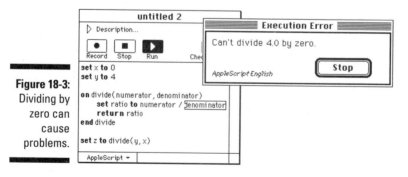

Figure 18-3:
Dividing by zero can cause problems.

The problem is that I'm dividing a number by 0, but no error exists in the **divide** handler — unless you want to count that I don't check to make sure that the denominator isn't zero before dividing and that I don't have a **try** statement to catch a problem like this. The error is in the script's first line, where I set **x** to 0. Alternatively, you can say the error is in the call to **divide,** where I use an inappropriate parameter value. The bottom line is that while the place

AppleScript highlights in your script tells you where AppleScript had a problem, it doesn't tell you the problem's source. Unfortunately, you can't take a magical path to get from where AppleScript detects the problem to the problem's origins. You have to look at your script to figure that out on your own. This is especially true when you, not AppleScript, detect the problem.

Pinpointing why the error occurs

After you've isolated where the problem occurs — including problems where only the script's results are wrong — you have to figure out what's going on. Why does the error occur? Sometimes this is easy to figure out, as in Figure 18-3. Other times, it is very complex. In general, the more complex your script, the more complicated the errors. While I can't give you any easy-to-use yet infallible process for figuring out what's wrong, I can give you some tips.

✔ Figure out what the script line that contains the error is supposed to do.

✔ Find out the values of the variables used in that script line.

In the earlier example, the line with the problem is supposed to divide two numbers. Figure 18-3's error message says the denominator is 0, so it's not rocket science to figure out the problem. Figure 18-4 shows a more complex problem, which occurs when I compile the script.

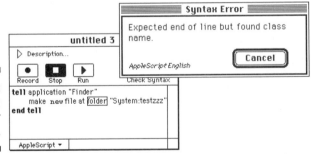

Figure 18-4: A puzzling error message.

At first glance, the error message seems strange. If I end the script line after the **at**, it hardly makes sense. After all, where does the Finder make the new file? In addition, "make new file at" just doesn't sound right, which is a usual indication of some problem because AppleScript tends to be very English-like. So what is the problem? The purpose of the line is to make a new file. No variables are used, so I skip over checking the variable values and go directly to checking the values of the constants used. The first thing I do is check to make sure a disk called "System" exists. It does, so what next? Well, at this point, it's time to go to the application dictionary to look up the **make** command's syntax, shown in Figure 18-5.

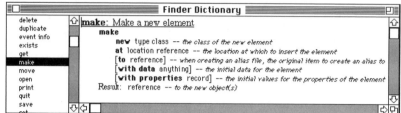

Figure 18-5:
The **make**
command
syntax.

Unfortunately, after reading the **make** command's syntax, it seems fairly clear that the syntax in the example is correct. So what's there to do? Remember that sometimes application dictionaries are wrong, so try to modify the command syntax a bit and see what happens. I know I need to use **make** and I need to specify what it is I want to make, so I've got to keep **file**. Similarly, I've got to tell the Finder where to make the new file, so I need to keep the **at** "System:testzz." The only item that I can possibly get rid of is **new**. New is slightly redundant because **make** seems to imply creating something new, so get rid of it and see what happens. Amazingly enough, that works. It turns out this is a quirk of the Finder's syntax. The approach I followed is obviously not universally applicable, but it should give you an idea of how to attack a script error that pops up during compilation.

If the error occurs when the script is running, you have some additional tools available. This next script tries to get the name of the disk a file is on and the file name by looking at the file's path.

```
property file_path : ""
property file_name : ""
property disk_name : ""
on get_disk_name(file_path)
    set old_delims to AppleScript's text item delimiters
    set AppleScript's text item delimiters to ":"
    set file_name to file_path as string
    set file_name to the first text item of file_path
    set AppleScript's text item delimiters to old_delims
    return file_path
end get_disk_name
on get_file_name(file_path)
    set old_delims to AppleScript's text item delimiters
    set AppleScript's text item delimiters to ":"
    set file_name to file_path as string
    set file_name to the last text item of file_path
    set AppleScript's text item delimiters to old_delims
    return file_name
end get_file_name
```

```
set file_path to "system:system folder:finder"
set file_name to get_file_name(file_path)
set disk_name to get_disk_name(file_path)
return file_name
```

The script sets the property **file_path** to the path to a file. It then uses the two handlers **get_file_name** and **get_disk_name,** discussed in Chapter 20, to set the properties containing the file name and disk name. When the script is run, it should return "finder" because that's the name of the file in the path. Unfortunately, when this script is run, it returns "system." This is clearly a mistake. The silly script has it completely backward. But what to do? AppleScript, that friendly idiot, gleefully and accurately followed my instructions, but somewhere I managed to give the wrong instructions. It turns out problems like this are ideal places to use the ever exciting Event Log.

So I'm going to interrupt our regularly scheduled debugging session to take a gander at the wonders of modern Apple Event monitoring.

A diversion: using the Event Log Window to see what's going on in your script

The first thing to do is to open the Event Log window in Script Debugger by choosing the Open Event Log command from the Controls menu (the shortcut is Command-E). When a script is run in the Script Editor and the Event Log window is open, all of the Apple Events being sent are recorded in this window. The two check boxes at the top of the window let you select what type of information is displayed in the log. The first box, labeled "Show Events," enables the display of the basic messages your script sends. These messages don't include those sent internally in AppleScript, such as **if** or **repeat.** For example, when this script runs, the Event Log looks like Figure 18-6.

```
set disk_name to "system:"
tell application "Finder"
    set temp to disks
    set temp_1 to items in disk disk_name
end tell
```

Figure 18-6:
The Event
Log for a
simple
script.

You should notice a couple of things. First, the script's first line, the one that sets the value of the local variable **disk_name,** doesn't generate any entry in the Event Log. That's because only messages sent out of AppleScript are recorded. The second is that the information in the Event Log window can look a bit different from what you wrote in your script. For example, the first line inside the **tell** statement sets the value of the local variable **temp** to the value of the **disks** property of the Finder. The **set** doesn't show up here anymore than it did in the first line of the script. The "**get every** disk" line is the message that is sent to the Finder by the **disks** property in the script. In order to replace **disks,** the Finder has to be asked to "get every disk." A similar logic leads to the second entry in the Event Log where the Finder has to send every item of the disk "system:" in order to replace "items of disk disk_name" with a value.

You can get more information out of the Event Log by using the Show Event Results option, available only if you select the Show Event Results check box. When both options are on, the results — the data returned to AppleScript by whatever got the message — as well as the messages are shown. When I run the same little script with the second option on, the Event Log looks like Figure 18-7.

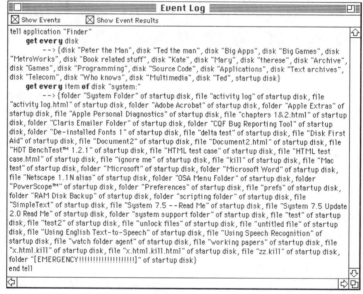

Figure 18-7:
Showing the results of messages as well as the messages themselves.

As you can see, the results of messages can be a great deal larger than the messages themselves. The amount of information that can show up in the Event Log window can be overwhelming — if it is more than 32K of characters, you'll get an error — which is why you have commands for starting and stopping the capture of events to the Event Log. These commands' full syntaxes are given later in this chapter. I've never used those commands, but if you've got a large script and you're only interested in the events that occur in one handler, you can use an approach like this:

```
on some_handler()
    start log
    tell application "Finder"
        set z to disks
    end tell
    stop log
end some_handler
tell application "Finder"
    set z to every item of disk "system:"
end tell
some_handler()
```

When this script is run with neither option checked in the Event Log, you see something like Figure 18-8.

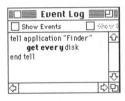

Figure 18-8: Using **start log** and **stop log** to control the contents of the Event Log window.

If you check both boxes and uncheck the Show Events box, which leaves the Show Event Results box checked but dimmed, and then run the script, you get the display shown in Figure 18-9.

Figure 18-9: Getting event results under script control.

```
Event Log
□ Show Events    ☒ Show Event Results
tell application "Finder"
    get every disk
        --> {disk "Peter the Man", disk "Ted the man", disk "Big Apps", disk "Big
Games", disk "MetroWorks", disk "Book related stuff", disk "Kate", disk "Mary", disk
"therese", disk "Archive", disk "Games", disk "Programming", disk "Source Code", disk
"Applications", disk "Text archives", disk "Telecom", disk "Who knows", disk
"Multimedia", disk "Ted", startup disk}
end tell
```

In this case, the results are displayed because the Show Event Results option was on, even though the Show Events option was off. In this mode, only events and their results that are generated in the script after a **start log** command and before a **stop log** command, if any, show up in the Event Log. You can think of the **start log** and **stop log** commands as doing nothing more than toggling the Show Events option. Unlike you, though, they can do it while the script is running, based on what the script is doing.

No matter what you do, if the Event Log window isn't open, then nothing shows up in the Event Log.

Only scripts that execute inside the Script Editor can use the Event Log window. If you've got the Event Log window open and you run a script application, nothing shows up in the log even though your script application may be sending 100,000 messages every second.

Following is the full scoop on the **start log** and **stop log** commands.

Stop Log

This stops the writing of events and event results to the Event Log window.

Syntax

```
stop log
```

Parameters

None.

Example

```
stop log
```

Description

This command stops the logging of events to the Event Log window. It comes in handy under two circumstances. The first is when you only want to look at the events associated with one part of the script, say a specific handler. The second is when you've got **log** commands in your script that are hard to read because so much stuff is being written from the normal show events processing. This command doesn't stop the **log** commands from writing to the Event Log.

Value Returned

None.

Start Log

This command starts the display of events in the Event Log window.

Syntax

```
start log
```

Parameters

None.

Example

```
start log
```

Description

This command starts the writing of events to the Event Log window. You can use it in conjunction with the **stop log** command to only log events associated with specific pieces of your script.

Value Returned

None.

Now that you know about the Event Log window, we can continue. Let's see, where was I? What, you mean you don't remember either? Oh, dear. Fortunately, I can just scroll back up the screen . . . ah, yes.

When you're trying to track down why the script doesn't give the right answer, the Event Log is obviously a good thing to try. Unfortunately, in this case, all of the script lines are internal to AppleScript, so nothing shows up in the Event Log. All is not lost, however. The **log** command allows you to write to the Event Log from anywhere in your script.

Log

This command lets you put comments into the Event Log window.

Syntax

```
log some_string
```

Parameters

some_string: This is any string bounded by quotes, as in "This is a comment."

Example

```
set folder_ref to "Mary:"
set num_items to the number of items in (list folder folder_ref)
log "found " & num_items & " files/folders in " & folder_ref
```

When this script is run, it puts the text after the **log** command into the Event Log window, as shown in Figure 18-10.

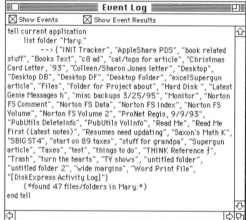

Figure 18-10:
Inserting user-defined information into the Event Log.

Description

This command is very useful when you're looking for the cause of problems in a script — called debugging. By putting in **log** commands, you can find out where the script is running into problems as well as see the values of variables as the script executes. This is the most commonly used Event Log-related command.

Value Returned

None.

So by using the **log** command, you can spy on a script in action. Following is the problem script modified with the addition of some **log** commands that let you see what's going on while the script is running.

```
property file_path : ""
property file_name : ""
property disk_name : ""
on get_disk_name(file_path)
```

```
    set old_delims to AppleScript's text item delimiters
    set AppleScript's text item delimiters to ":"
    set file_name to file_path as string
    set file_name to the first text item of file_path
    set AppleScript's text item delimiters to old_delims
    return file_path
end get_disk_name
on get_file_name(file_path)
    set old_delims to AppleScript's text item delimiters
    set AppleScript's text item delimiters to ":"
    set file_name to file_path as string
    set file_name to the last text item of file_path
    set AppleScript's text item delimiters to old_delims
    return file_name
end get_file_name
set file_path to "system:system folder:finder"
log "value of file_name before calling get_file_name is " & file_name
set file_name to get_file_name(file_path)
log "value of file_name after calling get_file_name is " & file_name
set disk_name to get_disk_name(file_path)
log "value of file_name after calling get_disk_name is " & file_name
return file_name
```

After running this version of the script, notice the three lines with **log** commands in the implicit **run** handler. The Event Log window looks like Figure 18-11.

Figure 18-11:
Using the
log
command to
watch what
happens in a
script.

As we expect, before the **get_file_name** handler is called, the value of **file_name** is "". After **get_file_name** is called, the value of **file_name** is "finder." But for some reason, after the script calls **get_disk_name,** the value of **file_name** has been changed to "system." This is a strong indication that the next place to look is inside the **get_disk_name** handler. The following is the **get_disk_name** handler with some added **log** statements.

```
on get_disk_name(file_path)
    log "value of file_name at first line of get_disk_name " & file_name
    set old_delims to AppleScript's text item delimiters
    set AppleScript's text item delimiters to ":"
    log "value of file_name at middle of get_disk_name " & file_name
    set file_name to file_path as string
    set file_name to the first text item of file_path
    set AppleScript's text item delimiters to old_delims
    log "value of file_name just before return of get_disk_name " & file_name
    return file_path
end get_disk_name
```

When the script is run with these log lines added, the Event Log looks like Figure 18-12.

Figure 18-12:
Isolating the
source of
the problem
using the **log**
command.

As you look at the Event Log, it's clear that the problem occurs somewhere between the middle and end of the **get_disk_name** handler. This narrows the problem down to these lines:

```
log "value of file_name at middle of get_disk_name " & file_name
set file_name to file_path as string
set file_name to the first text item of file_path
set AppleScript's text item delimiters to old_delims
log "value of file_name just before return of get_disk_name " & file_name
```

See anything fishy? Notice how **file_name** is being used as a local variable? Unfortunately, it isn't explicitly declared local by using the **local** statement described in Chapter 13. As a result, when the script is run, AppleScript uses the property called **file_name** — because properties are global in scope — and changes its value rather than make a new local variable. This is the type of problem that can happen with global variables and properties.

Fixing the Problem

You can avoid this problem in several ways, including

- ✔ Giving properties distinctive names such as **p_file_name**
- ✔ Always declaring local variables inside handlers as local

While this might seem to be a pretty stupid mistake, it's from a real script I was writing. The reason the problem occurred was that I copied most of the script lines inside the **get_disk_name** handler from another script, which didn't have the **file_name** property. Because the script lines worked where they came from, I didn't check them too carefully when I put them in this script. But my poor judgment at least did some good by giving you an example of how to use the Event Log window and the **log** command to track down problems.

Testing the solution

The last step is to rerun the script with whatever corrective actions you feel are necesssary in place. If it works, then you can march on. If not, just repeat the process until you fix the problem.

As you script, you'll find that it becomes easier to track down problems. You'll have a better intuition, even if you're an intuition-challenged person, where problems might lie. You'll find that you can figure out where to put **log** statements in order to try to isolate problems. But debugging will never become trivial. Even though AppleScript has been written to minimize the chances of really obtuse errors, you'll find times that you spend a long time, more than 15 minutes, tracking down some obscure problem. Fortunately, these situations don't happen often, so don't worry about them. But if you do run into a tough one, remember the techniques I've shown you here for tracking problems down and eradicating them like the worthless pond scum they are.

Chapter 19

Scripting Additions: Taking AppleScript to New Heights

. . . .

In This Chapter

▶ Making AppleScript more powerful by adding new commands

▶ Finding useful scripting addition collections

. . . .

*Y*ou've seen how powerful AppleScript is and how applications can extend the list of usable commands, so it shouldn't surprise you that Apple provides a mechanism for extending the language's basic capabilities. When you install AppleScript, a new folder called Scripting Additions is added to the Extensions folder inside your System folder. That new folder contains a bunch of files with dictionaries that extend the AppleScript syntax in a manner very similar to scriptable applications. The primary difference is that you don't have to use a **tell** statement to inform AppleScript of where to look for the definition of the commands contained in these scripting additions files.

scripting additions: This isn't a more complex way to do math with scripting, but it is the name used for files that contain commands that extend the basic AppleScript syntax. Many commands that come with AppleScript, such as the **read** and **write** commands, are implemented in scripting additions files. In addition, third parties can write scripting additions that can be added to AppleScript just by dropping them in the Scripting Additions folder.

Figure 19-1 shows you the read/write scripting addition, which looks just like an application dictionary. The only difference is that scripting addition commands are directly available in AppleScript and you don't need to use a **tell** statement to access them.

Because scripting additions are so seamlessly integrated into AppleScript, you normally don't have to worry if commands are built in or come from scripting additions unless you're trying to find the command syntax online. You can find out about the syntax of scripting addition commands by reading the scripting

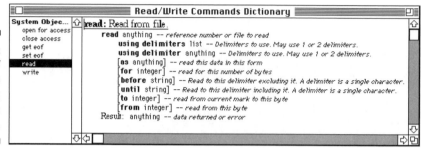

Figure 19-1:
The read/
write
scripting
addition
dictionary.

additions dictionary just as you would read the dictionary of any scriptable application (see Chapter 17). The reason I've got this chapter is that tons of third-party freeware and shareware scripting additions can help make AppleScript even more powerful.

In general, the scripting additions that are available are freeware — you can use them without paying anything — or shareware — you're honor bound to send the author the requested shareware fee if you like the additions and end up using them. I recommend paying the shareware for two reasons. First, if you don't, you're stealing. Second, if you pay, the chances are the author will keep the additions up-to-date as new system software comes out and he or she will probably come up with some new additions as well. A couple of scripting additions collections are on everyone's list of nice things to have. I can't cover them all, but here's a list of the more interesting collections:

✔ **Acme Script Widgets:** Tons of useful scripting additions.

✔ **Donald's Commands:** Several useful additions including ones that get the state of the mouse button.

✔ **GTQ Scripting Library:** Large library of additions including some to make and use a database.

✔ **Jon's Commands:** Most useful if you don't have the scriptable Finder.

You can get scripting additions from a variety of sources. If you've got a modem and access to the Internet or one of the major online services, such as eWorld or America Online, you can get hundreds of scripting additions with little or no trouble. Because many of these scripting additions are produced by hobbyists who have neither the time nor resources to perform extensive testing — after all, they usually distribute these scripting additions for free — you need to be aware that you may encounter problems, such as crashing your Mac. Therefore, you may need to reboot when you use third-party scripting additions. Don't let this scare you off. Such crashes are unlikely, but when you're developing a script that uses non-Apple scripting additions, you should save your script and any other open application files fairly often, just in case something does go wrong.

Chapter 20

Script Objects: Recycling Scripts for a Healthy Environment

● ●

In This Chapter

▶ Making script objects that let you recycle your scripts

▶ Making libraries of useful functions

▶ Using the **continue** statement

▶ Using **Store Script**, **Load Script**, and **Run Script**

● ●

*S*cript objects are just scripts that you can stuff into a variable. Through the magic of AppleScript, you can take all the stuff in a script and squish it into a little variable. What good is that? Well, you get a couple of benefits. First, you can put these script objects into a file that you load into your script where you can use the handlers in the script object without cluttering your script window with all the script object's script lines. Second, you can create new value classes inside a script. Thirdly, since a script object can be stuffed into a variable, you can send it to other scripts where they can use it.

Creating a Script Object

Creating a script object is very easy. The syntax is

```
script [variable_name]
    --anything you'd find in a normal script
end [script]
```

If you supply the variable name parameter, AppleScript stuffs the script into that variable. You may be wondering how you can put a script inside a variable. I'd like to tell you, but then, because this is a major Apple secret, I'd have to kill you. Actually, you can think of a script object as being much like a mini-application. When a script object is put into a variable, AppleScript is just giving this mini-application a name that can be used to access the script object's properties and handlers — which brings us to what can go into a script object. Anything that you put into a script, such as properties, handlers, and **tells** directed to applications, can be inside a script object. Following is a very simple example:

```
script name_caller
    property insult_to_use : "Aardvark"
    on insult(victims_name)
        display dialog victims_name & " is an " & insult_to_use
    end insult
    on change_insult(new_insult)
        set insult_to_use to new_insult
    end change_insult
end script
tell name_caller
    insult("Fred")
    change_insult("atrocious cad and buffoon")
    insult("Melvin")
end tell
```

This script displays two dialog boxes, shown in Figure 20-1 and Figure 20-2. While this sample uses a handler to change the value of the **insult_to_use** property of the script object, you can also use this approach:

```
set insult_to_use of name_caller to "whatever"
```

Figure 20-1:
Insulting
aardvarks
everywhere.

Fred is an Aardvark

Cancel   OK

Figure 20-2:
A
compliment
for Melvin
when the
truth is
considered.

Melvin is an atrocious cad and buffoon

Cancel   OK

Interestingly enough, the scope of a script object's property is restricted to the script object, so in this next case, the value returned is 2, not 4.

```
property test_value : 2
script some_test
    property test_value : 4
end script
return test_value
```

For some strange reason, however, global variables defined outside of a script object are usable inside a script object, so this script

```
global x
set x to 5
script test_script
    on add(y)
        return x + y
    end add
end script
tell test_script
    set sum to add(3)
end tell
return sum
```

runs and returns a result of 8, even though **x** isn't defined anywhere in the script object.

All right, now that you've seen the basics, you're probably wondering how script objects are useful in real life. I'm going to define a script object that parses file paths to get the various components, such as the disk and file name, which are often of interest. Following is a script that defines such an object and a handler to make copies, called *instances,* of the script object.

instance: When you make a copy of a script object, or any other object for that matter, it's called an instance of that class. You can think of a class as a form, such as a driver's license application. While you have only one original form, thousands or millions of copies of that form with different values in the various slots, such as name and age, can be made. AppleScript has the same capability, but it copies objects, not paper.

```
on make_file_path(path_to_file)
    script file_path
        property file_name : ""
        property folders : ""
        property disk : ""
        property full_path : ""
```

(continued)

(continued)

```
property in_folder : ""
on init(path_to_file)
  set file_name to get_file_name(path_to_file)
  set folders to get_folders_only_path_string(path_to_file)
  set in_folder to get_in_folder(folders)
  set disk to get_disk_name(path_to_file)
end init
on get_disk_name(file_path)
  set old_delims to AppleScript's text item delimiters
  set AppleScript's text item delimiters to ":"
  set file_path to file_path as string
  set temp to the first text item of file_path
  set AppleScript's text item delimiters to old_delims
  return temp --> was using file_name instead of temp
end get_disk_name
on get_file_name(file_path)
  --log "in get_file_name input is " & file_path
  set old_delims to AppleScript's text item delimiters
  set AppleScript's text item delimiters to ":"
  set file_path to file_path as string
  set temp to the last text item of file_path
  set AppleScript's text item delimiters to old_delims
  --log "in get_file_name output is " & temp
  return temp
end get_file_name
on get_folders_only_path_string(file_path)
  set old_delimiters to AppleScript's text item delimiters
  set AppleScript's text item delimiters to ":"
  set folders_only to ""
  set n_text_items to the number of text items in file_path
  repeat with i from 1 to n_text_items
    if i < n_text_items then
      set folders_only to folders_only & text item i of file_path & ":"
    else
      if the last character of file_path is ":" then
      set folders_only to folders_only & text item i of file_path & ":"
      end if
    end if
```

```
        end repeat
        set AppleScript's text item delimiters to old_delimiters
        return folders_only
    end get_folders_only_path_string
    on get_in_folder(folders_to_use)
        set old_delims to AppleScript's text item delimiters
        set AppleScript's text item delimiters to ":"
        set n to the number of text items in folders_to_use
        set temp to text item (n - 1) of folders_to_use
        set AppleScript's text item delimiters to old_delims
        return temp
    end get_in_folder
  end script
  tell file_path
     init(path_to_file)
  end tell
  return file_path
end make_file_path
set z to make_file_path("system:system folder:finder")
set y to file_name of z
set y1 to folders of z
set y2 to disk of z
set y3 to in_folder of z
return {y, y1, y2, y3}
```

Don't be intimidated by the length of this script. Look at each handler to see if you can figure out what it does. The overall flow is that when the **make_file_path** handler is called, AppleScript makes a new copy — or instance, if you want to get technical — of the script object defined inside the **make_file_path** handler. That instance is initialized by the **init** handler, defined inside the script object, which sets the values of the various properties of the script object. The instance is copied into the local variable **z**. The rest of the script just gets the values of the various properties inside the script object.

Using Inheritance

Another interesting and useful feature of script objects is *inheritance*.

inheritance: This isn't what you hope to get from your eccentric but rich Uncle Sydney, who thinks that his house is infested with space aliens of the bug-eyed variety. Script objects contain handlers and properties. With inheritance, one script (the child) can get copies of the properties and handlers of another script (the parent). The child script object acts as though the parent's handlers and properties are part of the child script object.

Using inheritance can save you from writing lots of script lines by letting you reuse script lines you've already written. This next script shows the previous script rewritten to take advantage of inheritance.

```
script path_parsing_handlers
  property file_name : ""
  on get_disk_name(file_path)
    set old_delims to AppleScript's text item delimiters
    set AppleScript's text item delimiters to ":"
    set file_path to file_path as string
    set temp to the first text item of file_path
    set AppleScript's text item delimiters to old_delims
    return temp
  end get_disk_name
  on get_file_name(file_path)
    --log "in get_file_name input is " & file_path
    set old_delims to AppleScript's text item delimiters
    set AppleScript's text item delimiters to ":"
    set file_path to file_path as string
    set temp to the last text item of file_path
    set AppleScript's text item delimiters to old_delims
    --log "in get_file_name output is " & temp
    return temp
  end get_file_name
  on get_folders_only_path_string(file_path)
    set old_delimiters to AppleScript's text item delimiters
    set AppleScript's text item delimiters to ":"
    set folders_only to ""
    set n_text_items to the number of text items in file_path
    repeat with i from 1 to n_text_items
      if i < n_text_items then
        set folders_only to folders_only & text item i of file_path & ":"
      else
        if the last character of file_path is ":" then
          set folders_only to folders_only & text item i of file_path & ":"
        end if
      end if
    end repeat
    set AppleScript's text item delimiters to old_delimiters
    return folders_only
  end get_folders_only_path_string
  on get_in_folder(folders_to_use)
    set old_delims to AppleScript's text item delimiters
    set AppleScript's text item delimiters to ":"
```

```
            set n to the number of text items in folders_to_use
            set temp to text item (n - 1) of folders_to_use
            set AppleScript's text item delimiters to old_delims
            return temp
        end get_in_folder
end script
on make_file_path(path_to_file)
    script file_path
        property parent : path_parsing_handlers
        property folders : ""
        property disk : ""
        property full_path : ""
        property in_folder : ""
        on init(path_to_file)
            set my file_name to get_file_name(path_to_file)
            set folders to get_folders_only_path_string(path_to_file)
            set in_folder to get_in_folder(folders)
            set disk to get_disk_name(path_to_file)
        end init
    end script
    tell file_path
        init(path_to_file)
    end tell
    return file_path
end make_file_path
set z to make_file_path("system:system folder:finder")
set y to file_name of z
set y1 to folders of z
set y2 to disk of z
set y3 to in_folder of z
return {y, y1, y2, y3}
```

The script has been reorganized. Most of the handlers from inside the script object defined in the **make_file_path** handler have been moved to a new script object that's defined at the beginning of the script. The other changes are the addition of the **parent** property to the script object defined inside of **make_file_path** and the addition of the **my** in front of file_name in the **init** handler. The parent parameter tells AppleScript that the **file_path** script object should inherit all of the handlers and properties of the **path_parsing_handlers** script object. That means that the **file_path** script object behaves as though it has all of the handlers and properties of **path_parsing_handlers**. You can see this by noting that the **init** method in the **file_path** script object looks pretty much the same as before (ignore the **my** for a second). No **tell** statements are around the handlers, such as **get_file_name**, that are no longer in the **file_path** script object. But the script still works because the **get_file_name** handler is inherited from the parent script object, **path_parsing_handlers**. This is really handy if you've got multiple script objects that all share some handlers. You can move the handlers that appear in all of the script objects into a new script object and have it be the parent of the existing script objects. That way, the handlers only appear once in your script rather than once in each of the existing script objects. Inherited properties work pretty much the same way, except you have to put a **my** in front of them so that AppleScript knows you're referring to the inherited property and not some local variable of the same name. Don't worry if inheritance isn't intuitively obvious. Lots of heavy duty full-time programmers have had trouble understanding how to harness inheritance (other than Uncle Sydney's kind). You may find it useful to come back and glance over this section again after a few days. I find that things like this are easier to recall if I read about them once, go away for a while, and come back and read about them again.

Using the continue statement

There's one last thing you should know about inheritance. Suppose you want to use some, but not all, of the handlers from a script object. Do you have to make a new script object with only the handlers you want to reuse? No, not at all. You can always *override* any handler that is inherited. In fact, you can do one better than that. If you want to use the inherited method but modify it slightly, you can use the **continue** statement. The **continue** statement lets you call a parent handler from inside the child handler that overrides it. In the following script, the **test_case** handler in the child script, **test_child**, processes the incoming string.

```
script test_parent
    on test_case(sentence)
        return the first word of sentence
    end test_case
end script
script test_child
    property parent : test_parent
    on test_case(sentence)
        if the first character of sentence is "t" then
            set n to the number of characters in sentence
            set temp to "T" & characters 2 through n of sentence
            continue test_case(temp)
        else
            continue test_case(sentence)
```

```
        end if
    end test_case
end script
tell test_child
    set z to test_case("this is a test")
end tell
```

The **continue** statement makes sure that the letter that starts the sentence is capitalized and then invokes the parent handler by using the **continue** statement. The script returns "This" and not "this" when it runs. The full syntax of **continue** is

```
continue handler_name input_parameters
```

What this basically means is that you put a call to the handler, with all of the required arguments in either positional or labeled mode depending on how the handlers are defined in the parent script object, after the **continue**. So for positional parameters, it may look like

```
continue some_handler(parameter1, parameter2, parameter3,)
```

while a handler that uses labels may look like this:

```
continue some_handler with x given some_label:14
```

TERM

override: That's what a ham of a horse does in a Western. Actually, when a child script object has a handler that's the same name as a handler in the parent script object, AppleScript uses the handler in the child script object. The handler in the child script object is said to override the handler in the parent script object. For example, the final result of this next script is 4, not 9.

```
script test_parent
    on test_case()
        return 9
    end test_case
end script
```

```
script test_child
property parent:test_parent
    on test_case()
        return 4
    end test_case
end script
tell test_child
    return test_case()
end tell
```

The **test_case** handler in the **test_child** script object overrides the **test_case** handler in the **test_parent** script object.

Before we leave the unobjectionable world of script objects, you can use one other nifty feature to recycle scripts. It turns out you can save a script object to a file and then load it into a script where it can be used. The first step in this process is to use the **store script** command to store a script object to a file. Following is the general syntax of **store script.**

Store Script

This lets you store a script object in a file.

Syntax

```
store script some_variable_containing_a _script_object ¬
        [in some_file_reference] ¬
        [ replacing option]
```

Parameters

some_variable_containing_a_script_object: This is a variable that contains the script object you want to save to a file.

some_file_reference: This is a reference to a file, such as file "disk:folder:file."

option: The three allowable options are ask (if the file already exists, the user is asked via a dialog box if he or she wants to replace the current file contents with this script object, rename the file, or cancel the save); yes (if the file already exists, the script automatically replaces its current contents with this script object); and no (no matter what, don't replace the current file contents, if any, with this script object).

Example

```
store script path_parsing_handlers ¬
   in file ¬
   ("Mary:Files:AppleScript for Dummies Book:scripts under construction:" & ¬
      "path_parsing_handlers") replacing yes
```

Description

This command lets you store a script object in a file. This function is useful because you can then read the script object into a script, using the **load script** command, and make use of the script objects handlers and properties.

Value Returned

None.

This next script shows how you can save the **path_parsing_handlers** script object to a file.

```
script path_parsing_handlers
  on get_disk_name(file_path)
    set old_delims to AppleScript's text item delimiters
    set AppleScript's text item delimiters to ":"
    set file_path to file_path as string
    set temp to the first text item of file_path
    set AppleScript's text item delimiters to old_delims
    return temp --> was using file_name instead of temp
  end get_disk_name
  on get_file_name(file_path)
    log "in get_file_name input is " & file_path
    set old_delims to AppleScript's text item delimiters
    set AppleScript's text item delimiters to ":"
    set file_path to file_path as string
    set temp to the last text item of file_path
    set AppleScript's text item delimiters to old_delims
    log "in get_file_name output is " & temp
    return temp
  end get_file_name
  on get_folders_only_path_string(file_path)
    set old_delimiters to AppleScript's text item delimiters
    set AppleScript's text item delimiters to ":"
    set folders_only to ""
    set n_text_items to the number of text items in file_path
    repeat with i from 1 to n_text_items
      if i < n_text_items then
        set folders_only to folders_only & text item i of file_path & ":"
      else
        if the last character of file_path is ":" then
          set folders_only to folders_only & text item i of file_path & ":"
        end if
      end if
    end repeat
    set AppleScript's text item delimiters to old_delimiters
    return folders_only
  end get_folders_only_path_string
  on get_in_folder(folders_to_use)
    set old_delims to AppleScript's text item delimiters
    set AppleScript's text item delimiters to ":"
    set n to the number of text items in folders_to_use
    set temp to text item (n - 1) of folders_to_use
    set AppleScript's text item delimiters to old_delims
    return temp
  end get_in_folder
```

(continued)

```
(continued)
end script
store script path_parsing_handlers ¬
    in file ¬
    ("Mary:Files:AppleScript for Dummies Book:scripts under construction:" & ¬
       "path_parsing_handlers") replacing yes
```

Notice that I only have to add the **store script** command. No changes to the script object are required. By the way, you can have multiple **store script** commands storing different script objects to different files, or even to the same file if you want to waste computer time, in a single script.

Using a stored script object is just as easy as storing it. You just use the **load script** command.

Load Script

This loads a script object from a file into a script.

Syntax

```
load script a_file_reference
```

Parameters

a_file_reference: A reference to a compiled script or a file containing a script object.

Example

```
set a_script_object to load script file "system:some useful handlers"
```

Description

This command allows you to load a script object saved with the **store script** command into a script. You can also load any compiled script into a script. For example, if I save the script

```
on test()
    return "AppleScript is fun!"
end test
```

as a compiled file, not as a script object, I can use the **test** handler in a script such as this:

```
set a_script_object to load script file "system:a"
tell a_script_object
    set x to test()
end tell
return x
```

I still have to use a **tell** statement, but even though the **load script** handler
returns a script object, the file that it reads in doesn't have to be created with
the **store script** command. You can't use a text file, however.

Value Returned

A script object.

After you load a script object, you can use it the same way you used it in the
script. Following is our fun-filled **file_path** object definition when the
path_parsing_handlers script object is loaded in from a file:

```
global path_parsing_handlers
on make_file_path(path_to_file)
    script file_path
        property parent : path_parsing_handlers
        property file_name : ""
        property folders : ""
        property disk : ""
        property full_path : ""
        property in_folder : ""
        on init(path_to_file)
            set file_name to get_file_name(path_to_file)
            set folders to get_folders_only_path_string(path_to_file)
            set in_folder to get_in_folder(folders)
            set disk to get_disk_name(path_to_file)
        end init
    end script
    tell file_path
        init(path_to_file)
    end tell
    return file_path
end make_file_path
set path_parsing_handlers to ¬
    load script file ("Mary:Files:AppleScript for Dummies Book:" & ¬
        "scripts under construction:path_parsing_handlers")
set z to make_file_path("system:system folder:finder")
```

(continued)

```
(continued)
set y to file_name of z
set y1 to folders of z
set y2 to disk of z
set y3 to in_folder of z
return {y, y1, y2, y3}
```

Looks a lot simpler this way, doesn't it? Not only that, but you can recycle the **path_parsing_handlers** script object in any number of scripts. In general, it's a good idea to build up libraries of useful handlers in script objects, or just in compiled files, that you can load into your other scripts. Doing so saves you significant amounts of development time in the long run. One thing to note: While the definition of the **file_path** object occurs before the script loads in the **path_parsing_handlers** script object, AppleScript doesn't execute the **file_path** script object definition lines until the **make_file_path** handler is called. Fortunately, the **path_parsing_handlers** script object is loaded in prior to **make_file_path** being called. If that wasn't the case, an error occurs because **path_parsing_handlers** isn't defined when needed in the **parent** property statement inside the definition of the **file_path** script object.

Now you've seen how to modularize your scripts and reuse handlers by using script objects and inheritance as well as by loading libraries of handlers into your scripts with the **load script** command. While these are very powerful tools that make professional script development easier, you don't have to use them. Don't let this object-oriented stuff faze you. Pick and choose which of these recycling tools fit your scripting style best, and use them when you think they'll save you work. Certain Apple employees probably wish that they could cause meteorites to fall on my house because I say that I don't use these tools, but it's the truth. That's because I mostly script for fun or for my own needs. As a result, I can get by without using these tools. But any major scripting project takes less effort in the long run if you develop a library of handlers that do common tasks — such as getting the file name from a file path — that you can develop and test once and use often.

One last topic I want to cover, which isn't really related to script objects but is related to recycling scripts, is the use of the **run script** command. This command lets you execute the **run** handler of a script. The full syntax follows.

Run Script

This lets you run a script.

Syntax

```
run script a_reference_or_a_string [ with parameters some_list ]¬
[ in script_language]
```

Parameters

a_reference_or_a_string: This is either a reference to a script file, such as file "system:a script," or a string that is a valid script, such as "beep 2." If you provide just a file name instead of a full path, AppleScript tries to find a file in the current directory.

some_list: This is a list of the parameters passed to the **run** handler of the specified script.

script_language: This specifies which scripting language — actually which OSA-compliant scripting component — is used to translate the string into something your Mac can understand.

Example

```
run script "beep 2"
set z to run script "set z to \"this is a test\"" in AppleScript
set z to run script file "system:a script"
```

Description

This command lets you run a script file. When this command is encountered, AppleScript sends a **run** message to the script. The value returned by the **run** handler of the script is the value this command returns. You can use this command to make use of scripts that aren't part of your current script. You can also use it to execute short scripts that you can fit in a string. This command is probably most useful when you need to integrate some non-AppleScript capabilities, such as a QuicKeys macro, into a script. If you want to get really, really fancy, you can use this command to build a script on the fly, in a string, as part of your script's execution and then execute that custom-built script by using this command. That's not something that most normal human beings do, however.

Value Returned

Whatever value is returned by the **run** handler of the script that is run.

I never use this command, but it comes in handy under certain circumstances. If you never use it, though, you shouldn't feel that you're not doing your share to use AppleScript to its maximum potential.

Chapter 21
Miscellaneous Advanced Stuff

• •

In This Chapter
▶ Handling application commands that take a long time to execute
▶ Customizing the way AppleScript compares things

• •

AppleScript has a number of features that aren't of interest to most scripters or that are a bit complex. I've grouped them all together in this chapter. If you want, you can skip over this chapter until you see a script that uses one of these features. If you're lucky, you'll never need any of them.

Timeout: Dealing with Slowpoke Applications

I bet you didn't know that AppleScript times every command. Well, it does. If a command takes more than 60 seconds — that's one earth minute — to complete, then AppleScript returns an error. That's fine if you're waiting for a response from an application running on a Mac that's just been crushed by King Kong, but it's a real shame if it just happens to take the Finder 60.01 seconds to copy that 44MB file to another disk. Fortunately, the **with timeout** statement lets you control how long AppleScript should wait for a command to complete before declaring a problem. The general syntax is

```
with timeout [ of ] some_integer seconds[s]
    some script lines
end [timeout]
```

Any commands that are directed at objects in some application, such as a paragraph in Word, and that are between the **with timeout** and **end timeout** statements, get up to the value of *some_integer*, in seconds, to respond before AppleScript issues an error. The new waiting period doesn't apply to

AppleScript commands or commands directed at objects that aren't in some application. The basic idea is that many of the tasks you ask an application to do take more than 60 seconds, while the stuff you do inside AppleScript doesn't take anywhere near that long for any single command. Here's an example of the **with timeout** statement being used to ensure that Word has time to replace all of the instances of a common word in a large document.

```
tell application "Microsoft Word"
    activate
    with timeout of 500 seconds
    do script "EditReplace .Find = \"them\", .Replace = \"they\", .Direction = 0," & ¬
    " .MatchCase = 0, .WholeWord = 0, .PatternMatch = 0, .SoundsLike = 0, "& ¬
    " .ReplaceAll, .Format = 0, .Wrap = 1"
    end timeout
end tell
```

Remember that the new time applies to each command so that if you have a **repeat** statement, as in the following example, each command inside the **repeat** statement gets the full 500 seconds to complete.

```
tell application "Microsoft Word"
    activate
    set i to 0
    with timeout of 500 seconds
        repeat with current_word in words_to_replace
            set i to i + 1
            set new_word to item i of words_to_use
            do script "EditReplace .Find = \"" & current_word & "\"," & ¬
                " .Replace = \"" & new_word & "\", .Direction = 0, .MatchCase = 0," & ¬
                " .WholeWord = 0, .PatternMatch = 0, .SoundsLike = 0, .ReplaceAll," & ¬
                " .Format = 0, .Wrap = 1"
        end repeat
    end timeout
end tell
```

Every command directed to Word inside the **with timeout . . . end timeout** gets 500 seconds to complete. The script continues on to the next command as soon as the previous one finishes. Because the script doesn't wait for 500 seconds for each command, setting a large value for the timeout doesn't slow your script down. However, setting a large value for the timeout does increase the time from when a problem occurs to when you get notified. For example, if the longest search and replace you ever have takes ten seconds and you set the timeout value to 500 seconds and a problem occurs seven seconds into the search, you aren't notified that something has gone awry until 500 seconds after the **do script** command starts. On the other hand, if you set the timeout period to 20 seconds, you're notified within 20 seconds of the start of the **do script** command.

You'll find that you use the **with timeout** command mainly when working with applications that take a long time to execute a single command. For example, sorting a large FileMaker Pro database can take longer than 60 seconds, as can recalculating a set of very large, linked Excel spreadsheets.

Considering and Ignoring: Changing the Rules

Some ad campaigns tell you there are no rules. Well, tell that to the guys in Sing-Sing. In AppleScript, as in life, you've got to follow certain rules. Some of these rules can be changed, though, by using the **considering** and **ignoring** statements. For example, one AppleScript rule is that it's case insensitive — it thinks *A* and *a* are the same. That means that

```
"Test" = "tEst"
```

evaluates to true. But suppose you want to make case-sensitive comparisons? Suppose you want to use a different rule? Well, you can just write this:

```
considering case
    if "Test" = "tEst" then
        set z to "it's true"
    else
        set z to "it's false"
    end if
end considering
```

When this script is run, the final value of **z** is "it's false." That's because inside the **considering** statement, AppleScript considers the case, upper or lower, of letters when making a comparison, because you specified case as something to be considered. You'll see in just a bit that a number of different attributes, such as case, can be considered or ignored, but first look at the general syntax for considering, which is

```
considering an_attribute [, another_attribute....]
    [but ignoring some_attribute [,some_other_attribute....]]
    some script lines
end considering
```

Essentially, you can have a list of attributes that should be considered followed by an optional list of attributes that should be ignored. The attributes are

- ✔ **case:** This causes string comparisons or tests, such as = and contains, to take into account the case of letters, so that *A* is not considered the same as *a*.

- ✔ **white space:** Normally the strings "tank truck" and "tanktruck" wouldn't be the same because of the space. If you ignore this attribute, then tabs, spaces, and returns aren't taken into account when comparing strings.

- ✔ **diacriticals:** These are the weird marks that appear on top of characters in foreign languages, such as ^ or ¨. These are normally considered when comparing strings so that *e* and *é* are considered different. If you ignore diacriticals, then *e* and *é* are considered the same.

- ✔ **hyphens:** Normally hyphens are considered when comparing strings so that "non-combustible" and "noncombustible" are considered different. If you ignore hyphens, then those two words are considered the same.

- ✔ **expansion:** This is important if you use œ, æ, Œ, and Æ a lot. Normally when comparing strings, AppleScript treats *œ* as the same as *ae,* but if you ignore this attribute, then *oe* and *œ* are considered different.

- ✔ **punctuation:** Normally, when AppleScript compares strings, it takes into account punctuation (, ! . : ; ? \ ' " `). If you ignore this attribute, then the string "Hello?" is the same as the string "Hello."

- ✔ **application responses:** When a command in a script is directed at an application, AppleScript normally sits around twiddling its virtual thumbs waiting for a reply. In fact, as you noticed in the previous section on the **with timeout** statement, if AppleScript doesn't get a response within some fixed time, it generates an error message. If you ignore this attribute, however, AppleScript sends off the command and then immediately proceeds to the next command. Any results or error messages that may come back as a result of the command are pitched into the electronic void never to be seen again. This attribute does not affect AppleScript commands, only those found in application dictionaries.

The syntax is basically very English-like. If I want to consider case but ignore punctuation — something I've worked hard to do since high school English — I just write

```
considering case but ignoring punctuation
    --some script lines
end considering
```

The ignore statement is essentially the opposite of the considering statement. Its syntax is

```
ignoring an_attribute [, another_attribute....]
    [but considering some_attribute [,some_other_attribute....]]
    some script lines
end ignoring
```

If I want to consider case but ignore punctuation again, I can write

```
considering case but ignoring punctuation
    --some script lines
end considering
```

You can nest **considering** and **ignoring** cases just as you nest **if** or **repeat** statements. When inner and outer **considering** or **ignoring** statements have the same attributes, then the innermost statement has precedence. In this case

```
ignoring case
    considering case
        --some script lines (1)
    end considering
end ignoring
```

the script lines labeled 1 take the case of letters into consideration. If the statements have different attributes, then they all apply. In this case

```
ignoring punctuation
    considering case
        --some script lines (1)
    end considering
end ignoring
```

the script lines marked 1 are evaluated considering case and ignoring punctuation.

The first six attributes — case, white space, diacriticals, hyphens, expansion, and punctuation — only apply to AppleScript comparisons. AppleScript performs all comparisons where the first element is a value in a script. If the first item is a reference to an application or a system object, then the comparison is done by the application or the Finder. So if the name of the startup disk is "System-," then the following script

```
tell application "Finder"
    considering case
        if the name of the startup disk contains "Y" then
            display dialog "Eureka!"
        end if
    end considering
end tell
```

displays the dialog box, even though no capital Y is in the disk name. That's because "name of the startup disk" is not a script value; it's a Finder value. On the other hand, this script

```
tell application "Finder"
    set x to the name of the startup disk
end tell
considering case
    if x contains "Y" then
        display dialog "eureka"
    end if
end considering
```

doesn't display the dialog box because **x** is a script value. That means the case attribute applies to the comparison because AppleScript is performing the comparison, whereas in the previous case, the Finder performs the comparison.

Part III
How to Control the World — or at Least Some Common Programs

In this part . . .

This part of the book shows you how to apply the things you've discovered in Parts I and II to writing scripts that automate real applications. While you can just read the chapters that cover applications you're interested in, I recommend that you try to at least skim all of these chapters. There are two reasons behind this advice: The first is that you'll see what sort of scripting capabilities the other applications have, which might give you some ideas for new scripts. The second reason is that every chapter has sample scripts that demonstrate how to use AppleScript to do things. Even if you don't use the specific application, you'll learn more about designing real scripts.

Chapter 22

Finder Tricks without Touching the Mouse

- -

In This Chapter

▶ Understanding the value classes and commands the Finder defines

▶ Controlling the Finder in order to automate a wide variety of tasks

- -

*T*he scriptable Finder is a wonderful thing. It's very scriptable and record-able, so you can automate just about anything that involves files, folders, and applications, as well as other fun tasks, such as changing the monitor's setting from black and white to millions of colors. I talk about the Finder in more detail than the other applications because lots of your scripts involve the Finder, often in conjunction with other applications.

Before diving into sample scripts, it's a good idea to understand the tons of commands and data types in the Finder dictionary. Take a moment to use the Script Editor to peruse the Finder dictionary. Don't be overwhelmed by the number of items, though. They all correspond to the Finder objects you work with every day, such as files, windows, applications, and folders. Skim the dictionary pausing just long enough to get an idea of the function of each value class, such as window, and command, such as count. Figures 22-1 through 22-4 will help you understand how.

Figure 22-1 shows part of the class hierarchy of the Finder.

REMEMBER

Just what is the Finder?

Yes, Virginia, the Finder is an application. Just as Photoshop works with pictures, Excel works with spreadsheets, and MacWrite Pro with text, the Finder works with files and folders. Some people tend to forget that Finder is an application be-cause it seems to always be present. But Finder can be replaced. If you're old enough, you'll re-member the mini-Finder, or if you're a mere tod-dler, you're probably familiar with Edmark's KidDesk or Apple's At Ease products, which are both Finder replacements.

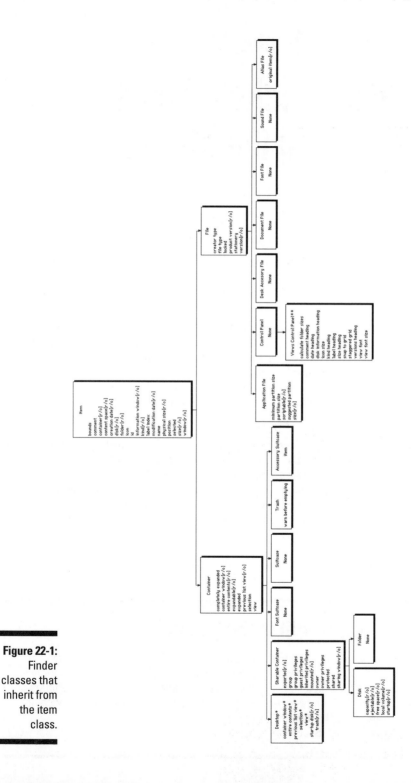

Figure 22-1:
Finder
classes that
inherit from
the item
class.

If Figure 22-1 looks very complex, don't panic. If you're not familiar with inheritance, you may want to flip back to Chapter 20. What you're seeing is an inheritance chart. Each different class — type of information — is shown along with its properties. When a class shows *None* for its properties, it just means that the class has no unique properties of its own — they're all inherited from parent classes. A class that's below another class is a child class. For example, the **item** class is the parent to two children classes, **file** and **container**. A child class inherits the properties of its parent. So the **file** class has the properties that show up in its box, such as **file type**, as well as the properties in the **item** class's box, such as **size**. The [r/o] means the property is read only, just as it does in an application's dictionary. A * next to a class name or property means that for some reason, the class doesn't inherit all of its parent's properties, only those that are shown. One last thing: Don't confuse an inheritance chart with a containment chart. A **folder** object can contain **files,** but **files** don't inherit properties from **folders**. You can find out more about what other classes a class can contain later in this chapter where each class is discussed.

Figure 22-2 shows the inheritance hierarchy for classes that are children, or grandchildren, of the **window** class.

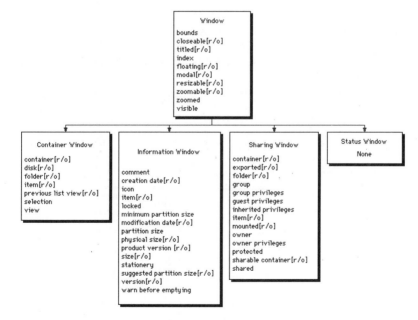

Figure 22-2:
Finder classes that inherit from the Window class.

Figure 22-3 shows the classes that inherit from the **process** class.

process: A process is some piece of computer code that's running on your Mac. When you launch an application by double-clicking it or one of its files, the Mac creates a process. Anytime your Mac does anything, it launches a process. Just think of a process as a running desk accessory or application.

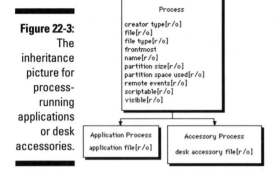

Figure 22-3:
The inheritance picture for process-running applications or desk accessories.

Figure 22-4 shows a grab bag of classes that don't inherit from anything, not even rich old Uncle Melvin. Don't cry for them, though, because they have interesting properties — albeit not beachfront ones — of their own.

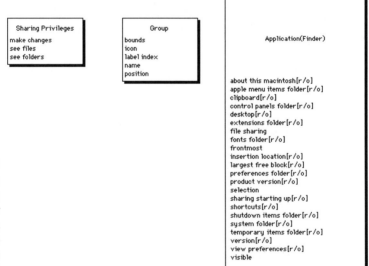

Figure 22-4:
Miscellaneous Finder classes, including the application itself.

Some Quick Finder Tricks

Here are some simple examples of things you can do with the scriptable Finder. The next script shows you how to use the copy command to copy files from one location to another.

```
tell application "Finder"
   copy file "system:test" to folder "system:apple extras:"
--this copies all files on the top level of the startup disk whose name includes
--the string "html"
--to a folder called WWW on a disk called system.
   copy (files whose name contains "html") of startup disk to folder
         "system:WWW:"
end tell
```

This following script shows you how to see if something exists and how to make something new, such as a file or folder.

```
--if the folder "system:test folder:" doesn't exist make a new folder with that name
tell application "Finder"
   if not (folder "system:test folder:" exists) then
      set temp to (make folder at disk "system")
      set the name of temp to "test folder"
   end if
end tell
```

For some strange reason, you can't use **new** when making a new file or folder, so this next script doesn't even compile.

```
tell application "Finder"
   make new file at disk "system"
end tell
```

Instead, you need to ditch the **new**, as follows, when you're making a new file or folder.

```
tell application "Finder"
   make file at disk "system"
end tell
```

Here are some more examples of how to make new files and aliases.

```
tell application "Finder"
    set new_file to (make file at (disk "system"))
    --make a new file called "system:untitled file"
    set the name of new_file to "test 1"
    --changes the name of the new file to "test 1"
    --make a new file with the name already set to "test 2"
    set newer_file to make file at disk "system" with properties {name:"test 2"}
    make alias file to file "system:test 1"
    --make an alias of the file in the same directory
end tell
```

The following is a simple script for a drag and drop script application that will reveal the original files that aliases are associated with.

```
--Put this in a drag and drop application.
--It'll reveal the originals of alias dropped on it by
--opening a window for the folder that contains the original.
--It will only work with aliases
on open file_list
    repeat with a_file in file_list
        tell application "Finder"
            reveal a_file
        end tell
    end repeat
end open
```

This last example shows you how to set multiple properties in a single line by using a list.

```
tell application "Finder"
    set name of selection to "this is a test"
    --this sets both the name and position of the selections icon in one step
    set {name of selection, position of selection} to {"another test", {100, 100}}
end tell
```

Playing Hide and Seek with Finder

You can hide Finder manually by using the Hide Finder command in the Application menu on the far right-hand side of the menu bar. Just make sure Finder is the frontmost application. However, you sometimes will want to hide the Finder automatically. This script does the job:

```
tell application "Finder"
    set visible to false
end tell
```

Run this script and all of your Finder windows disappear. How did I know how to write this script, though? Well, someone posted a question asking about it. I then looked through the property list for the application class in the Finder dictionary until I found one whose name looked relevant, **visible** in this case. I then read the description of the property and noticed that it could be changed by a script (no [r/o] next to the property indicated this). After a quick experimental script, the one you see here, I can send a message telling the solution to the person who asked.

Cleaning Up the Desktop by Tiling Windows

I don't know about you, but when I work on the Mac, the number of Finder windows that are open tends to grow over time. After a bit, my desktop is a total mess with windows all over the place. It's hard to find anything, and I have to waste time finding the window I want. Well, this little script cleans up all of the Finder windows and tiles them neatly on the side of the screen, as shown in Figure 22-5.

Figure 22-5:
A neatly
tiled
desktop.

Here's the script that accomplishes this organizational miracle:

```
tell application "Finder"
    set window_list to windows
    set base_bounds to {10, 40, 180, 150}
    set v_increment to 20
    set h_increment to 0
    set window_list to reverse of window_list
    repeat with a_window in window_list
        set bounds of a_window to base_bounds
        set item 1 of base_bounds to (item 1 of base_bounds) + h_increment
        set item 3 of base_bounds to (item 3 of base_bounds) + h_increment
        set item 2 of base_bounds to (item 2 of base_bounds) + v_increment
        set item 4 of base_bounds to (item 4 of base_bounds) + v_increment
    end repeat
end tell
```

Not too complex, is it? But because you've just started at this, I give you a walk through of how the script works in detail.

Line 1

```
tell application "Finder"
```

This just tells AppleScript to look in the Finder dictionary for the meaning of items, in the script lines that lie between the **tell** and the **end tell,** that it doesn't understand.

Line 2

```
set window_list to windows
```

This gets a list of references to all of the open Finder windows.

Line 3

```
set base_bounds to {10, 40, 180, 150}
```

In the Finder, rectangles that define the bounds of windows are lists of the form {left edge, top, right edge, bottom}. This line just sets up the bounds of the first window that's tiled. You can set this to anything you want. For example, by increasing the value of the third entry, you make the window wider, so you can read longer folder names. Similarly, making item 4 larger makes the window taller.

The coordinate system starts at the upper left-hand corner of the screen. The values of the horizontal coordinate increase as you go to the right, while the value of the vertical coordinate increases as you go down the screen. The menu bar takes up the first 40 or so pixels, so if you set the top edge of a window to less than 40, part of the window may hide under the menu bar. If you put the entire top of the window under the menu bar, you aren't able to use the mouse to drag the window around.

Line 4

```
set v_increment to 20
```

This defines the value that the script uses to vertically offset a window from the previously tiled window. In this example, where the windows are right on top of each other, I use 20 because that's the height of the window title bar. With this vertical offset, the names of the windows are easily visible. You can change this to any value you want.

Line 5

```
set h_increment to 0
```

This defines the horizontal offset each window has with respect to the previous window. You can set this to whatever you want.

Line 6

```
set window_list to reverse of window_list
```

I talk about the **reverse** property of lists in Chapter 4. The **reverse** property of a list returns a copy of the list in reverse order, with the first item in the original list as the last item in the new list, and so on. You're now probably wondering why I did this. I certainly didn't think of it when I first wrote the script. When I ran the script, though, I discovered a slight problem. Instead of things looking like Figure 22-5, they looked like Figure 22-6.

Figure 22-6:
Backwards
tiling makes
it hard to
see window
titles.

This occurs because the list Finder returns has the windows ordered by the distance from being frontmost. The first entry is the frontmost window and the last entry is the window furthest in the back. If the script tiles them in that order, doing the frontmost window first, the front window covers up the back windows. By reversing the order of the list, the script tiles from the backmost window to the front, ensuring that no title bars are obscured.

Line 7

```
repeat with a_window in window_list
```

This **repeat** loops over all of the windows. One way to customize this script is to put an **if** after this line, which selects the windows to tile. For example, you may want to leave the window that contains the files you work with most untitled. You can do this by using an **if** statement to test the name of the window.

Line 8

```
set bounds of a_window to base_bounds
```

This sets the bounds property of the window to the current value of the variable.

bounds: This is the rectangle that forms the outer limit, the boundary, of a window.

The first window uses the value of **base_bounds,** defined in line 3. Subsequent windows use new values of **base_bounds,** set by script lines 9 to 12.

Line 9

```
set item 1 of base_bounds to (item 1 of base_bounds) + h_increment
```

This increments the left-hand edge of **base_bounds** by the horizontal increment. Because **h_increment** is 0, this line can be left out of the script. This way, however, you can try different tiling schemes just by changing the values of **h_increment** and **v_increment**. This new value is used on the next window to be tiled.

Line 10

```
set item 3 of base_bounds to (item 3 of base_bounds) + h_increment
```

This increments the right-hand side of the boundary. This ensures that the windows' widths stay constant.

Line 11

```
set item 2 of base_bounds to (item 2 of base_bounds) + v_increment
```

This increments the top position in **base_bounds.**

Line 12

```
set item 4 of base_bounds to (item 4 of base_bounds) + v_increment
```

This increments the position of the entry in **base_bounds** that determines the bottom of the next window to be tiled.

Line 13

```
end repeat
```

This ends the loop over the windows.

Line 14

```
end tell
```

This marks the end of the lines that are directed at Finder.

Now that you see how the script works, you can customize it, by changing the horizontal and vertical increments, to tile windows the way you want them tiled.

Showing Free Disk Space

The way the Mac works, the bigger your hard disk is, the larger the smallest file. This happens because the Mac can only divide your hard disk up into a finite number of pieces, 64K to be exact, and two files can't share the same piece of the disk. As a result, a file with one letter in it has to take at least one 64,000th of your hard disk. So a 64MB partition on your hard disk has a piece size, called an *allocation block size,* of 1KB, which means that a file with one letter in it takes up the same amount of space as a file with 999 letters in it. On a 640MB disk, the minimum value, unless you partition it, is 10KB. If you've got a lot of small files, you can waste a lot of disk space this way. As a result, many people have several hard disks or hard disk partitions on their desktop. The problem is that it's hard to find out how much free space you have on all the drives. Oh, sure, you can open up the top level window for each drive and manually add up the numbers, but that's something only a Windows 1895 fan likes to do.

Fortunately, AppleScript and the Scriptable Finder make finding out how much free disk space you have easy when you use the following script.

```
tell application "Finder"
    set free_space to 0
    repeat with t_disk in disks
        if local volume of t_disk then
            set free_space to free_space + ¬
                (round ((free space of t_disk) / 1000000))
        end if
    end repeat
    display dialog ¬
        "Total space free on all disks is: " & free_space & ¬
        " Megabytes" buttons {"Ok"} default button "Ok"
end tell
```

The only really new thing in this script is the use of the **free space** and **local volume** properties of disk objects. The former property is the free space, in bytes, available on that hard disk. That's the number you see in the upper right-hand corner of the disk's top level window. The **local volume** property is true if the disk is directly attached to your Mac and false if it's connected via a network. Figure 22-7 shows the dialog box that this script generates on my system. Of course, that was before I had to install Microsoft Word and Excel.

Figure 22-7:
The free space dialog box, right after I got my new 2.2GB drive.

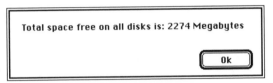

Total space free on all disks is: 2274 Megabytes

Ok

Moving Files through Cosmic Wormholes

I don't know about you, but in order to keep my hard disks organized, I've got about a jillion folders. Well, maybe half a jillion. As a result, it can take a great deal of clicking to get to the deeply nested folder that I want to store some file in. It seems to be one of Murphy's laws that the folder you want to store something in is always the mostly deeply buried one. Fortunately, AppleScript can help you here. In science fiction and theoretical physics, which are often hard to tell apart, the concept of a wormhole in space time, which lets the hero skip from one place to another in an instant, exists. I've developed a wormhole script for your Mac. Drop a file on it and poof, in a flash, the file is transported to its destination buried in the depths of your file system.

The way the script works, you can make multiple copies of it and have each one directing the files dropped on it to a different destination. To make life easier the first time the script is used, it renames itself to let you know where the files dropped on it go. For example, if files dropped on a copy of the script are moved to a folder called "hard disk:storage:," the script is renamed to "Port to storage." Because we can leverage the power of the scriptable Finder, this script isn't all that complex, as you can see.

```
property destination : ""
on open file_list
    if destination is "" then
        set destination to choose folder with prompt "select destination"
        set old_delimiters to AppleScript's text item delimiters
```
(continued)

(continued)

```
set AppleScript's text item delimiters to ":"
    set n_items to the number of text items in (destination as string)
    set new_name to text item (n_items - 1) in (destination as string)
    set AppleScript's text item delimiters to old_delimiters
    rename_me(new_name)
  end if
  tell application "Finder"
    repeat with a_file in file_list
      try
        set new_file to move a_file to destination with replacing
        if a_file exists then
          if new_file exists then
                delete a_file
          else
                display dialog "Problem: File " & a_file & "¬
                wasn't moved!"
          end if
        end if
      on error
        display dialog "Couldn't copy " & (name of a_file)
      end try
    end repeat
  end tell
end open
on rename_me(new_script_name)
  tell application "Finder"
    set n_procs to the number of processes
    repeat with i from 1 to n_procs
      if the name of process i is "wormhole" then
        set app_file to file of process i
        set new_name to "Port to " & new_script_name
        if length of new_name > 32 then
          set new_name to characters 1¬
          through 32 of new_name
        end if
        set the name of app_file to new_name
        exit repeat
      end if
    end repeat
  end tell
end rename_me
```

The script has two handlers. The **open** handler is the standard form for a drag and drop script. It does the work of moving files to the desired directory. It also makes sure the user has said where he wants the files to move to. The **rename_me** handler is the one that changes the name of the script application to reflect the destination of the files. This script has to be saved as an application, using the pop-up menu at the bottom of ScriptEditor's save dialog box, called "wormhole." To see why it needs to be called that, take a glance through these detailed descriptions.

Line 1

```
property destination : ""
```

This defines a place to store, between script executions, the path to the folder that the files are moved to. Remember that when you recompile a script, the values of all properties are reset. If you decide to enhance this script, you have to retell it which folder to move the files to. You may wonder why I didn't set the value of this to some path, such as folder "hard disk:some folder:." That works, but then whenever I want to make a new wormhole I have to edit the script, change the value of the path, and save it to a new name. That's the problem with hard wiring the destination into the script. A better approach is to have the script see if it's been given a destination and then ask the user to specify one if one doesn't exist. You can make new wormholes to new destinations by just copying the original, uninitialized script application and then dropping a file or folder on it. No editing required. Just make sure you've got one uninitialized copy (it'll be called wormhole) lying around. If you accidentally initialize all of your copies, you can get a new uninitialized copy by editing an initialized one and saving it as a script application called "wormhole."

Line 2

```
on open file_list
```

This is the start of the open handler. It's invoked whenever files or folders are dropped on the script application. The variable called **file_list** contains a list of references to the files and folders that were dropped on the script application.

Line 3

```
if destination is "" then
```

This line tests to see if a destination has been specified. If the variable called **destination** hasn't been initialized (it's still ""), then the script asks the user to choose a destination folder.

Line 4

```
set destination to choose folder with prompt "select destination"
```

This uses the **choose folder** command to have the user select a folder to move the files/folders to.

Line 5

```
set old_delimiters to AppleScript's text item delimiters
```

This line stores the current value of the text item delimiters into **old_delimiters,** so the script can restore them after it's through.

Line 6

```
set AppleScript's text item delimiters to ":"
```

By setting the text item delimiters to a colon, I can easily parse the path of the destination folder. Remember that elements in a file or folder path are separated by colons, "hard disk:folder:another folder:file." If the text item delimiters is a colon, each folder, disk, and file in a path name is a text item.

Line 7

```
set n_items to the number of text items in (destination as string)
```

Here the script gets the number of text items in the destination folder's path.

Line 8

```
set new_name to text item (n_items - 1) in (destination as string)
```

This line gets the name of the folder. Because a folder path always ends with a colon, the last text item in a folder path is always "", which is the stuff after that last colon. To get the name of the folder, the script needs the second to last text item. By subtracting one from the number of text items, the script can get the folder name.

Line 9

```
set AppleScript's text item delimiters to old_delimiters
```

This line restores the value of the text item delimiters.

Line 10

```
rename_me(new_name)
```

This calls the second handler, which, hopefully but not surprisingly, renames the script application. When it's done, the script application's name is changed.

Line 11

```
end if
```

Line 12

```
tell application "Finder"
```

Line 13

```
repeat with a_file in file_list
```

This **repeat** just loops over the files/folders that have been dropped on the application. If a folder is dropped on the script, only one reference, the one to the folder, is provided.

Line 14

```
try
```

This **try** handles any errors that occur when the script tries to copy the files or folders. The **replacing** option eliminates one potential error, but others exist, such as the destination disk not having enough free space. The **try** ensures that the user doesn't get an ugly error dialog box and that the script gracefully tells the user that a problem has occured.

Line 15

```
set new_file to move a_file to destination with replacing
```

This uses Finder's **move** command to move a file or a folder to the user-selected destination. Because the **replacing** option is used, if a file or folder with the same name already exists in the destination, it's replaced. A reference to the newly created file in the destination folder is placed into the **new_file** variable.

Line 16

```
if a_file exists then
```

If the destination refers to a folder on a different hard disk (or hard disk partition) than the location of the file or folder dropped on the script application, then AppleScript copies the file to that new location and leaves the original file in place instead of moving it. If that's the case, then after the **move** command is finished, the file that was "moved" is still in its original location. This command tests for that by using Finder's **exists** command. If the original file still exists, the script deletes it.

Line 17

```
if new_file exists then
```

Because deleting a file can have serious consequences — Can you spell total disaster? — this line checks to be sure the file exists at its new destination. If it doesn't, the user is warned that a problem has occurred. If the file does exist at its new destination, then the original is deleted. This still may not be safe enough if you are replacing a file that already exists. In that case, you may want to check that the file exists and that its modification date is the same as the file that you tried to move. These script lines show how you can test the file's modification dates:

```
set mod_date to the modification date of a_file
set existing_mod_date to the modification date of new_file
if mod_date is existing_mod_date then
```

Line 18

```
delete a_file
```

This line uses Finder's **delete** command to delete the original file. If it's very important that the file be deleted, you may want to put a **try** statement around this line to catch cases where the file can't be deleted.

Line 19

```
else
```

Now that you're becoming a scripting guru, I'm going to save space by not talking too much about script lines that just contain **else**, **end if**, **end repeat**, and so on.

Line 20

```
display dialog "Problem: File " & a_file & "¬
wasn't moved!"
```

This halts the script's execution until the user clicks one of the dialog box buttons. If you want the script to run when no one's around — say you want to move very large files over the network and you plan to get a soda while the copy is going on — you may want to use the **write** command to write the error message to a file and then notify the user when the script is done that he or she should read the error file.

Lines 21 and 22

```
end if
end if
```

Just ending some ifs.

Line 23

```
on error
```

This marks the beginning of the script lines that are executed if an error occurs in lines 15 through 23.

Line 24

```
display dialog "Couldn't copy " & (name of a_file)
```

This tells the user that something has gone wrong. The most likely problem is that the file can't be copied. I can use the more detailed options available in the full **try** command to deal with the error in more detail, but it just isn't that important. Feel free to elaborate the script's response to an error by using information from Chapter 12.

Lines 25–27

```
        end try
      end repeat
    end tell
```

Not a lot of explanation needed here, right?

Line 28

```
end open
```

This is the end of the **open** handler that gets invoked whenever any files or folders are dropped on the script application.

Line 29

```
on rename_me(new_script_name)
```

This is the beginning of the handler that renames the script application the first time it's run.

Line 30

```
tell application "Finder"
```

Line 31

```
set n_procs to the number of processes
```

A **process** is a running application or desk accessory. If you check the Finder dictionary, you find that the **process** value class supports plurals. You can count the number of processes this way.

Line 32

```
repeat with i from 1 to n_procs
```

This **repeat** loops over each process.

Line 33

```
if the name of process i is "wormhole" then
```

This gets the **name** property for the process number **i** and sees if it's the magic value. Only the script application is named "wormhole," unless of course some new sci-fi game comes out. This tells us which process corresponds to the script application itself.

Line 34

```
set app_file to file of process i
```

The **file** property of a process contains a reference to the file that is being run in the process. In this case, it's the script application file.

Line 35

```
set new_name to "Port to " & new_script_name
```

Here, the script builds the new name for the script application by adding the name specified in the call to the **rename_me** handler to the phrase "Port to." You can generalize this routine by having the entire file name sent via an input parameter. That way, any script can use this handler, not just a script that teleports files around your hard disk.

Line 36

```
if length of new_name > 32 then
```

On the Mac, file names can't be more than 32 characters long — file paths, which include the folder names, can be much longer. This line uses the string's **length** property to see how many characters are in the value of **new_name**. If it's more than the allowed 32 characters, line 37 is executed to trim the name down to size.

Line 37

```
set new_name to characters 1¬
through 32 of new_name
```

This sets the value of **new_name** to the first 32 characters of **new_name**.

Line 38

```
end if
```

Line 39

```
set the name of app_file to new_name
```

This script line sets the **name** property of the script application file to the value of **new_name**. This renames the file.

Line 40

```
exit repeat
```

After you've found the process corresponding to the script application, you don't need to look at the other processes. As a result, you can jump out of the repeat here. If there are 10 processes and the script application called "wormhole" is number 3, this script line makes sure that the script doesn't waste time looking at processes 4 through 10.

Lines 41–43

```
        end if
      end repeat
   end tell
```

Line 44

```
end rename_me
```

This is the end of the script, as well as the **rename_me** handler.

Pretty amazing how easy it is to dynamically rename the script application, isn't it? Not to mention the fact that you can move files all over the place with just a single Finder command — **move**. Well, actually three if you count **exists** and **delete** which you have to use to delete the orginal of the file when the destination is on another disk.

Feel free to customize this routine. You can easily check the file type dropped on the script application and use that info to decide where to route the files. For example, you can make an application that routes files whose names contain "temp" or "trash" to the trash can, those with an "arc," "back," "archive," or "save" to a back-up volume, and applications to a special disk. I tend to download lots of files from various online services. A script that takes scripting additions to the Scripting Additions folder, screen saver files to the right screen saver folder, and astronomical photos to the folder where the planetarium program I use, Voyager, can read them is nice. I bet you've got similar situations in your daily Mac agenda. So be creative and harness the power of the scriptable Finder to make moving files to far-off folders truly trivial.

Finding Scriptable Applications and Processing Every File to Boot

Next you'll see a script that searches all of your hard disks, finds all of the scriptable applications, makes an alias of each one, and moves the alias to a folder called "aliases of scriptable applications" at the top level of your startup disk. Well, that's what it would do if the Finder meant *AppleScriptable* when it says an application is scriptable. It turns out that the **scriptable** property is true if an application can receive AppleEvents, even if it doesn't have a dictionary so that it's not scriptable with AppleScript. This script actually puts aliases of all of the applications that can handle AppleEvents into the folder. You can then use the Script Editor to figure out which ones have dictionaries. Those are the really scriptable applications.

An application can receive and send AppleEvents but not be scriptable with AppleScript. That's because in order to use AppleScript to control an application, that application has to provide a dictionary so that AppleScript can understand the application's vocabulary. There are some very complex ways, although not practical, to get around this problem. One easy way around the problem is that you can send the four required events—**open**, **run**, **quit**, **print**—with the standard **tell** command to applications which show up as scriptable but which don't have a dictionary.

Even if the ability to automatically find all of your scriptable applications doesn't interest you, you should take note that this script touches every file and folder on all of your hard disks. By replacing one handler, the one called **deal_with_file**, you can completely change what this script does. For example, you can search for all files that are older than a certain date and that aren't applications, or in a folder with an application, and move those files to an archive disk. Or you can find all of the Excel files and move them to a certain folder. You can even make a simple incremental back-up program that makes a copy of every file modified in the last day and move it to a back-up folder. The possibilities are endless.

The actual script is made up of four handlers:

- ✔ **initialize:** This makes the folder to which the aliases are moved, if it doesn't already exist.

- ✔ **search_everywhere:** This searches every file and folder on every hard disk on your desktop.

- ✔ **deal_with_folders:** This one processes every folder on your disks.

- ✔ **deal_with_files:** This processes each file. By changing this handler, you can dramatically alter what the script does.

Keep that in mind as you read through this next script.

```
global new_folder
initialize()
search_everywhere()
on initialize()--this routine will get everything ready
    tell application "Finder"
        set temp to ((the name of startup disk) & ":" & "aliases of scriptable apps")
        if exists folder temp then
            set new_folder to temp
        else
            set new_folder to make folder at startup disk
            set the name of new_folder to "aliases of scriptable apps"
        end if
    end tell
```

```
end initialize
on search_everywhere() --this routine searches all of the disks
    tell application "Finder"
        --this gets a list of all of the disks that are on your Mac,
        --including network disks you've mounted via the chooser
        set all_disks to disks
    end tell
    repeat with disk_to_check_now in all_disks
        --this kicks things off by processing all the files¬
        and folders at the top level of the disk
        search_folder(disk_to_check_now)
    end repeat
end search_everywhere
on search_folder(folder_to_search) --this handles each folder
    tell application "Finder"
        set list_of_stuff_in_folder to items of folder_to_search
        repeat with some_finder_item in list_of_stuff_in_folder
            --if the item is a folder make a new copy of this handler¬
            and deal with it
            if class of some_finder_item is folder then
                my search_folder(some_finder_item)
            else
                --if the item is file process it
                my deal_with_file(some_finder_item)
            end if
        end repeat
    end tell
end search_folder
on deal_with_file(some_file) --handles each file, by changing¬
this handler you can completely change what the script does
    tell application "Finder"
        --if the file is an application
        if file type of some_file is "APPL" then
            if scriptable of some_file then
                --make a new alias for the application
                set app_alias to make alias file to some_file
                --move the alias to the folder defined in the global¬
                variable new_folder
                --should put a try here in case another alias of¬
                the same name already exists
                --in the destination folder
                move app_alias to folder new_folder
                --if the alias is copied instead of moved, because¬
                the destination is on another
```

(continued)

```
(continued)
        --disk make sure to delete the alias in this folder¬
        so it doesn't waste space
        if app_alias exists then
            delete app_alias
        end if
      end if
    end if
  end tell
end deal_with_file
```

The only really unusual part of this script is that when the handler **deal_with_folder** finds a folder, it calls itself. What actually happens is that AppleScript makes a new copy of the **deal_with_folder** handler — with its own variables and storage space. That new copy of the **deal_with_folder** handler takes the new folder as its input. This is called recursion in techno lingo. This sort of approach is nice for dealing with structures such as the file system.

Using PlainTalk

PlainTalk is Apple's speech and speech recognition technology. If you install version 1.4.1 or later, your Mac executes script applications you place in the folder called Speakable Items inside the Apple Menu Items folder in your System folder. That's right — write any script, verify that it works, put it in the Speakable Items folder, and then speak its name, and the script runs. Unlike earlier versions, you don't have to make scripts in a special editor; you can use the standard ScriptEditor. PlainTalk also adds **say,** a new command, to AppleScript. The general syntax is

```
say some_string
```

If you've got the appropriate PlainTalk software installed, then this next script speaks the words "Greetings to the future."

```
say "Greetings to the future"
```

By now, you should have an understanding of how to work with Finder in order to save yourself time. I recommend you try to keep mental track of what tasks you do with Finder and see which ones are easy and useful to automate. Then take the plunge and start saving time!

Chapter 23

Word Processors

- -

In This Chapter
▶ MacWrite Pro
▶ WordPerfect
▶ Microsoft Word

- -

MacWrite Pro

MacWrite Pro is my favorite word processor, even though its scripting support
is somewhat limited. It doesn't support any value classes. In fact, its entire
dictionary is just made up of commands. You can, however, do a reasonable
amount of stuff with them. I use MacWrite Pro to format my monthly online
column on GEnie, for example, even though I can't access many of MacWrite
Pro's functions, such as defining styles. But the commands that you can use are
sufficient for many common tasks, such as finding specific messages in large
message digests that are interesting. The MacScripting mailing list on the
Internet (see Chapter 28) generates hundreds of pages of text per month. I
wrote a script that uses MacWrite Pro to combine daily digests into larger files
and to extract the daily index of message topics into a separate file that I can
quickly peruse to look for interesting messages.

Getting information out of MacWrite Pro consists of selecting the text you want
with the **select paragraph** or **set selection** command and then using the **get
chars** command to extract the text you selected.

```
tell application "MacWrite Pro for Power Mac"
    set selection starting 0 ending 23
    set x to get chars
    select paragraph 4
    set y to get chars
end tell
```

Note that paragraph, selection, and chars aren't value classes; they're just part
of the command's name. Another thing to be careful about is that the first
character in a file is numbered 0, as is the first paragraph, so that in the

examples above the value of **x** is the first through 24th character in the file and **y** will contain the fifth paragraph.

Inserting data uses a similar approach. Define the insertion point by using the **set selection** command. Then use the **put chars** command to insert text.

```
tell application "MacWrite Pro for Power Mac"
    set selection starting 0
    put chars "this is a test " & return
    set selection starting 0
    if find "test" then
        do menu item bold
        do menu item italic
        do menu item size18point
    end if
end tell
```

After inserting text, the selection point is right after the newly inserted text. The latter part of this script uses the **find** command to locate the word "test." If "test" is found, its style is changed to bold and italic with a font size of 18 point.

If you've got MacWrite Pro, or you're thinking about buying a cheap but powerful word processor, I recommend you take a glance through the rest of the scripting commands that MacWrite Pro provides. In addition to commands that insert files and support mail merges, a bunch of commands lets you work with styles and multiple documents.

WordPerfect

WordPerfect is another word processor whose scripting support is less than complete. Unlike MacWrite Pro, it does support value classes for such things as **words, paragraphs, characters, text flows, styles,** and **pages.** You've seen its commands, such as **duplicate, make, delete,** and **set,** in other applications, so you won't find too many surprises. This script shows you how to open a file, get data from it, and count the number of paragraphs in a document.

```
tell application "WordPerfect"
    set test to choose file "pick a WordPerfect file" of type { "sPD3", "PICT", "WPD3"}
    open test
    if (count paragraphs of document 1) is greater than 9 then
        set z to every word of paragraph 3
        set x to characters 2 through 5 of paragraph 9
```

```
    end if
    set y to text of page 1
end tell
```

The file types specified in the **choose file** command correspond to templates, clip art, and standard WordPerfect documents.

Inserting text is easy too, with one small hitch. In this script,

```
tell application "WordPerfect"
    copy "this is another test" to after word 2 of paragraph 1
    copy "test 2" to after the last character of word 1 of paragraph 3
    copy "yet another test" to before word 3 of paragraph 2
end tell
```

the first copy replaces word 2 of paragraph 1 with the string "this is another test." The second copy, however, does what you expect — namely, put the string "test 2" after the last word in paragraph 3. Interestingly enough, the third copy also does what you expect, which is place "yet another test" right before word 3 of paragraph 2.

You can access WordPerfect macros, which can be very complex and powerful, from AppleScript by using the **do script** command, as shown in the following script.

```
tell application "WordPerfect"
    Do Script "test1"
    Do Script {"test", "test case"}
end tell
```

If you don't need to send any data to the macro, you can just put the macro name after the **do script** command, as in the first example. The second example shows how to send data to a macro. WordPerfect has a bunch of global variables, called ScriptVar01, ScriptVar02, and so on, which are associated with the list items 2 and beyond. In the second **do script** line, the WordPerfect global variable called ScriptVar01 is set to the string "test case." You can then use that variable in your script.

The ScriptVars are global variables whose values persist after the macro is done executing. This means that other macros see the value of the ScriptVar that is set when your script calls the macro. If you're not careful, this can cause problems similar to those discussed for global variables in AppleScript (Chapter 13). So be careful when you use the ScriptVars.

Between the built-in scripting and WordPerfect macros, you can do pretty much anything using scripts.

Microsoft Word

Microsoft products on the Mac in general tend to be fairly well designed, but idiosyncratic, like the somewhat eccentric but rich uncle every family seems to have. Word implementation of scripting is no exception. While the basic commands are nothing to write home about, complete but unexciting, you can use the **do script** command to harness the power of Word Basic to do just about anything. The bad news is that while Word does come with a reference to Word Basic commands, it doesn't come with a tutorial. Given that Word seems to ship with everything else, including the kitchen sink, the lack of a tutorial is somewhat surprising. So how do you, a regular person whose idea of fun and productivity doesn't include learning a whole programming language by reading what's effectively a dictionary, manage to overcome this slight problem and harness the full power of Word? The answer is that once again, Microsoft has done the unorthodox. It turns out that Word is recordable. It just happens that many of the scripts you'll record will be full of **do script** commands invoking Word Basic. For example, if I change the style of a text selection, I get the following script:

```
tell application "Microsoft Word"
    activate
    do script "Style \"Normal\""
end tell
```

The "activate" is there because I start recording in the Script Editor, and I then have to bring Word to the front in order to change the style. The actual work is all done by the **do script** line. Remember that the backslash (\) is used to insert quotes and other special characters inside quotes, so that the Word Basic command you're asking Word to execute is actually the following:

```
Style "Normal"
```

Although this approach is a bit odd — but then that's a Microsoft hallmark — it does work, and it's not too complex. After all, it doesn't take a rocket scientist to figure out that if you want to set the selection to a style called "Code," you should use this AppleScript command:

```
do script "Style \"Code\""
```

Of course, in the standard DOS way, many Word Basic commands have a few billion parameters — which are documented in the Word Basic Help file that comes with Word — so finding something generates the following script:

```
tell application "Microsoft Word"
    activate
    do script "EditFind .Find = \"testing\", .Direction = 0, .MatchCase = 0,
```

```
          .WholeWord = 0, .PatternMatch = 0, .SoundsLike = 0, .Format = 0, .Wrap
       2"
end tell
```

If you try to compile this script, you've got to make sure that you handle the incredibly long line correctly. The full Word Basic command has to be one line with no returns in it. You can accomplish that by using the **&** and ¬, as shown in the following script:

```
tell application "Microsoft Word"
   activate
   do script "EditFind .Find = \"testing\", .Direction = 0," & ¬
      " .MatchCase = 0, .WholeWord = 0, .PatternMatch = 0," & ¬
      " .SoundsLike = 0, .Format = 0, .Wrap = 2"
end tell
```

This script works because AppleScript just appends lines that are separated by a ¬. When AppleScript sends the **do script** command to Word for execution, it sends the whole EditFind — real intuitive name, that — as a single line, so Word doesn't have any problem with it. Many of the parameters have fairly clear names, if you can get over that . in the front, but you still should either record an example with the parameters you want or check the reference before setting any parameters.

You should plan to do lots of recordings when you're working with Word so that you can harness its power without having to learn Word Basic. Most basic word-processing functions can be done without Word Basic, though. Accessing data is easy, as these examples show:

```
tell application "Microsoft Word"
   tell document 1 of window 1
      set word1 to word 1 of paragraph 5
      set word2 to words 3 through 7 of paragraph 21
      set word3 to word 100
      set line1 to line 376
      set line2 to line 1 of paragraph 233
      set line3 to the last line of paragraph 32
      set char1 to the first character of paragraph 40
      set char2 to characters 2 through 4 of word 2 of paragraph 50
      set char3 to character 890
      return {word1, word2, word3, line1, line2, line3, char1, char2, char3}
   end tell
end tell
```

Identifying documents

In Word, you can identify documents by name, but that name is the full path, with all of the folder names, for the file. You can also use the index, document 1, for example. I use document 1 of window 1 because that's whatever document is in the frontmost window, and for making quick little examples, it's the easiest. When you use the window 1 or window 4 style to identify a window, Word numbers windows by their distance from the front. The frontmost window is 1, and if you change the frontmost window, then window 1 will point to the new frontmost window. Window 1 doesn't correspond to the file labeled 1 in the Window menu. To make sure you're working with the document you want to work with, you should use the name of the file, which you can easily get if your script opens the document.

Inserting data is similarly straightforward. Start with this text in the front window of Word:

This is a sample document designed for editing.

This is paragraph 2

this is para 3

Then run this script.

```
tell application "Microsoft Word"
    tell document 1 of window 1
        set the selection to insertion point after word 1 of paragraph 1
        set style of selection to bold
        set size of selection to 24
        set font of selection to "chicago"
        set the selection to "This is a UFO"
    end tell
end tell
```

You get the following text in the Word document:

This **This is a UFO** is a sample document designed for editing.

This is paragraph 2

this is para 3

One thing to look out for is that sometimes Word and AppleScript can count words differently. AppleScript and Word come up with different word counts for the phrase "This -- take a break -- is a test," as shown by this script:

```
tell application "Microsoft Word"
    tell document 1 of window 1
        --have Word do the counting
        set n to number of words in line 1 --> n is 9
        --set the line to a local variable so AppleScript does the counting
        set text1 to line 1
        set m to number of words in text1 --> m is 7
        return {n, m}
    end tell
end tell
```

Apparently AppleScript counts "- -" as a word, while Word doesn't.

I could devote a whole book to telling you about the various commands and value types in Word. Since I don't have room for that, you should look over this next script, which goes through a document and installs *HTML* (HyperText Markup Language), the file standard for the World Wide Web, and tags for headers as well as bold and/or italic words. While this isn't a full-fledged HTML converter, it's easily extensible. In addition, it shows you a practical example of how to open a file, how to look at all of the words and paragraphs in a Word document, how to check the style of paragraphs and words, how to insert text into a document, and how to save a file under a new name.

```
--this is the main part of the script
tell application "Microsoft Word"
    --let the user pick a Word file
    set doc_ref to choose file with prompt "Pick the file to convert to HTML" of ¬
    type {"W6BN", "WDBN"}
    -- you can open multiple files by putting multiple items in the list
    open {doc_ref}
    set doc_ref to document 1 of window 1
    set n_paras to the number of paragraphs in doc_ref
    --save typing by using this tell statement so that we can omit references to
    --the document
    tell doc_ref
        --loop over all of the paragraphs in the document
        repeat with i from 1 to n_paras
            set n_words to the number of words in paragraph i
            if n_words > 0 then
                --deal with heading style which applies to an entire paragraph
                if the ((paragraph style of paragraph i) as string) contains "Heading" ¬
```

(continued)

(continued)

```
      then
            if the ((paragraph style of paragraph i) as string) contains " 1" then
            my insert_Para_tag(i, "h1", doc_ref)
            else if ((paragraph style of paragraph i) as string) contains " 2" then
            my insert_Para_tag(i, "h2", doc_ref)
            end if
      else
            set j to 0
            --loop over all of the words looking for words that are bold or italic
            repeat while j < n_words
                  set j to j + 1
                  --deal with italic style
                  if italic of word j of paragraph i of document 1 then
                        my insert_tag(j, i, "em", doc_ref)
                        --this line makes sure that the script doesn't
                        --treat the
                        --tags as part of the document text
                        set j to j + 6
                        --the paragraph is longer because of the new tag
                        set n_words to n_words + 6
                  end if
                  --deal with bold style
                  if bold of word j of paragraph i then
                        my insert_tag(j, i, "strong", doc_ref)
                        set j to j + 6
                        set n_words to n_words + 6
                  end if
            end repeat
      end if
   end if
end repeat
set title to the name of window 1
--use the title of the document as the title for the HTML page
set selection to insertion point before paragraph 1
--put in the document header before the body of the document
set selection to "<html>" & return & "<head><title>" & ¬
   title & "</title></head>" & return & "<body>" & return
set selection to insertion point after the last paragraph
--put in the end of the document
set selection to return & "</body>" & return & "</html>"
--label the file as html(you should check to make sure the file name is <
--33 characters long
```

```
          set file_name to (the name of document 1 of window 1) & ".html"
          --save the file with its new name
          do script "FileSaveAs .Name = \"" & file_name & "\", .Format = 2," & ¬
          ".LockAnnot = 0, .Password = \"\", .AddToMru = 1, .WritePassword =
              \"\"," & ¬
          " .RecommendReadOnly = 0, .EmbedFonts = 0, .NativePictureFormat =
              0, .FormsData = 0"
      end tell
  end tell
--this handler puts a tag before and after a specified word in a given document
on insert_tag(word_id, para_id, tag, doc_ref)
    tell application "Microsoft Word"
        set selection to insertion point after word word_id of paragraph para_id of ¬
        doc_ref
        set selection to " </" & tag & "> "
        set selection to insertion point before (word word_id of paragraph para_id
        of doc_ref)
        set selection to " <" & tag & "> "
    end tell
end insert_tag
--this handler puts a paragraph level tag set around paragraph para_id of doc doc_ref
on insert_Para_tag(para_id, tag, doc_ref)
    set marker to "</" & tag & ">"
    tell application "Microsoft Word"
        set selection to insertion point after last word of paragraph para_id of ¬
        doc_ref
        set selection to marker
        set selection to insertion point before first word of (paragraph para_id of ¬
        doc_ref)
        set selection to " <" & tag & "> "
    end tell
end insert_Para_tag
```

HTML works by putting tags, special text strings that are of the form <tag> and </tag>, into a document to indicate formatting. For example, to indicate that a word is formatted to bold, you'd use this string <strong>word</strong>. Actually <strong> is a logical tag that can mean different things on different systems, but it's a reasonable way to translate the bold format. You can apply similar tags to paragraphs. In addition, every HTML document begins with a set of header information and ends with some closing tags. The majority of this script is in the implicit **run** handler that begins the script. The first handler, **insert_tag**, will insert a specified tag before and after a specified word. It works for all tag types, and hence can mark all types of styles. The second handler is **insert_Para_tag**, which is very similar to **insert_tag** except that it inserts tags around paragraphs instead of words. Feel free to extend this script to deal with other HTML elements.

The bottom line is that Microsoft Word is very scriptable. If you can't figure out how to do something, make a recording of it. Recording is the best way to figure out how to use the various Word Basic commands. If you plan to script Word a lot, you might start building up a script object library with friendlier interfaces to the various Word Basic commands. For example, the EditFind command you discovered earlier through the wonders of recording can be put into an AppleScript handler with a much more English syntax through the use of labeled parameters. Actually, it's amazing. AppleScript gives you the capability to do what millions have thought impossible: put a comprehensible interface on a Microsoft product.

Chapter 24
Other Business Applications

- -

In This Chapter

▶ FileMaker Pro

▶ Microsoft Excel

▶ DeltaGraph Pro

- -

FileMaker Pro

FileMaker Pro is the most popular non-relational database around for the Mac (the next version will sport relational features). It's easy to use and meets the needs of most users. Fortunately, it's also pretty easy to script. If you get really dedicated, you can do some fairly complex things by combining FileMaker's internal scripting language with AppleScript. Internal scripting isn't covered in this book, but you can read about it in *Macworld FileMaker Pro Bible,* published by the fine folks at IDG Books.

But even if you don't know how to script in FileMaker, you can still do a number of useful things with just AppleScript. For example, I take electronic pictures of various deep space objects, such as galaxies, open clusters, giant alien space-ships returning from making crop circles, and various nebulae. I want to put these pictures into a FileMaker database without having to manually cut and paste. By combining AppleScript, FileMaker, and a scriptable drawing program that can read in the files, I avoid manually cutting and pasting 200 images into the database.

I don't have enough room in this book to show you every FileMaker command, so instead, I show you how to do the basic tasks you'll want to do with a database. The functions I demonstrate are opening a database, sorting the database, adding a record to the database, printing a report, and finding a set of records.

FileMaker data objects

FileMaker Pro has a variety of data objects you can work with. The ones used most often are shown in Table 24-1.

Table 24-1	Commonly Used Data Objects
Data object	**Meaning**
Database	These are database files.
Layout	These are the various layouts of the database, which determine how the data is displayed.
Record	These are the individual entries in the database.
Field	These are the elements of the database records.
Cell	These are the elements of an individual record.

Figure 24-1 shows the containment hierarchy for the various data objects in FileMaker Pro.

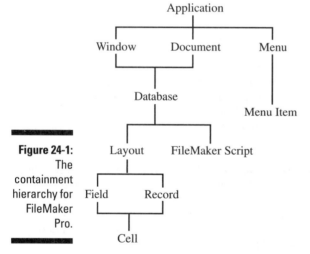

Figure 24-1:
The containment hierarchy for FileMaker Pro.

Launching FileMaker and opening a database

The first thing you need to do is launch FileMaker Pro and open the file of your choice, which is demonstrated by this little script:

```
tell application "FileMaker Pro"
   Open file "military books"
end tell
```

When you run this script, it opens a file called "military books," which resides in the same folder as the FileMaker Pro application. You can use a more general reference to a file — see Chapter 7 — such as "Hard Disk name: folder name: another folder name:military books" if the database file isn't in the same folder. When this script is run, FileMaker Pro launches, if it's not already running, opens the "military books" database, and brings it to the front.

Before going on, it's helpful if I tell you a little about this database. The database has a number of *fields*, including title, author, period, and comments.

field: You've probably heard about force fields in science fiction movies. In the even more frightening world of databases, a field is a place to stick a piece of information. A database of books may have one field that contains the title of the book and other fields that contain the author's name or comments. Fields can contain various types of data, including sounds and pictures.

record: This isn't what you get for eating 5,000 live piranhas. Nor is it the AppleScript record (see Chapter 4) you've come to know and love. It's actually a single entry in a database. For example, a database of employee records consists of a bunch of records, all having the same fields, one for each employee.

You need to know the names of fields, and the sort of data they contain, in order to understand the following examples.

Another thing that you need to keep in mind is how FileMaker Pro handles various items, such as fields and records. The most important thing to understand is that in FileMaker Pro, a field refers to the entry in all records, while a cell is an entry for a specific record.

Sorting a database

Okay, after you have a database, one of the most common activities is sorting the database. FileMaker lets you sort using one or more of the fields in a record. This means that you can sort the database by the title of the book or first by the author's name and then by the book's title to get alphabetized lists of an author's books. FileMaker makes it easy to sort records because it supplies a single command called, not surprisingly, **sort,** which lets you perform a wide variety of sorts.

Here's a simple script to sort a book database by book titles.

```
tell application "FileMaker Pro"
    Open file "military books"
    Sort Document "military books" By {Field "title"}
end tell
```

The only new thing in this script is the sort line. The general syntax of the **sort** command is

```
sort some_object by list_of_fields in order [ascending/descending/numeric/custom]
```

Some_object is a reference to a database file or a window, so you can use any of the following examples.

```
Sort second Layout of Window 3 By Field 7 of Window 3
Sort first Window By {Field "title", Field "author's name"}
```

As you see in the third example, when you want to sort by more than one field, you make a list (see Chapter 4) of the field names, which are each preceded by the keyword "field."

Getting and setting the value of a field

While some people think it's wonderful to stuff tons of data into a database, it's only useful if someone can get at the data. You may find that you want to read and change the value of various entries in databases. This little script shows you how to both set and get the value of a cell — another term for a field in this context.

```
tell Application "FileMaker Pro"
    set Cell "title" of Record 1175 to "Alamo Scouts"
    set x to Cell "title" of Record 1174
end tell
```

The first line after the **tell** sets the value of the field called "title" to "Alamo Scouts" in record 1175, while the second line sets the value of the local variable **x** to the value of the field called "title" in record 1174.

Adding a record

Another thing you may often want to do is add a record via a script. For example, you can write a really spiffy script that surfs the Internet finding articles of interest, downloads them, and puts them in a database. While the Internet scripting part may be a bit complex, the FileMaker part is a breeze. This next little script adds a new entry to the "military book" database.

```
tell application "FileMaker Pro"
    Open file "military books"
    Create Record With Data {"Texas Navy, the", "Hill", "state house press",¬
```

```
          "1937", "texas independence", ¬
          "Historical, Tactical information general history of texas navy in 1837 ¬
          prior to joining union", ¬
          "", "", "1994", "", "18.95"}
    end tell
```

The values in the list are stuffed into the fields in the database record, so that "Texas Navy, the" goes into the first field, "Hill" goes into the second, and so on.

If you don't want to put data into a field, you've still got to put a "" in the list. Otherwise, the data ends up in the wrong fields.

Finding some records

Finding records that match some search criteria is pretty easy to do, but not entirely intuitive. This script finds and selects all records whose first field contains the word "German."

```
tell application "FileMaker Pro"
    Show (Records whose first Cell contains "German")
end tell
```

One thing to keep in mind is that **whose** clauses are pretty slow with large databases. If possible, try to use FileMaker Pro's internal scripting language for searches. You'll see how to use such scripts in the next section.

Printing a report

Printing in FileMaker is a little strange because of a problem with the printing dialog box. If you use the **print** command, which you find in the FileMaker dictionary, FileMaker displays the standard print dialog box. Unfortunately, that requires someone to click on a button in the dialog in order to dismiss it, which isn't very nice if you're trying to automate something. You can use a macro utility to deal with this, as shown in Chapter 26, or you can use a FileMaker Pro script.

The basic idea is to write a script using FileMaker Pro's ScriptMaker, which you find in the Scripts menu. The print command in ScriptMaker doesn't bring up the dreaded print dialog box, so you can have your script print without human intervention. The first step is to create a new ScriptMaker script. Selecting the ScriptMaker menu item gets you the dialog box shown in Figure 24-2. Now you have to make the toughest decision. What do you call the script? Try to use something simple yet descriptive. Because the script's job is printing, let's call it Print. I'd call it Melvin, but he owes me money.

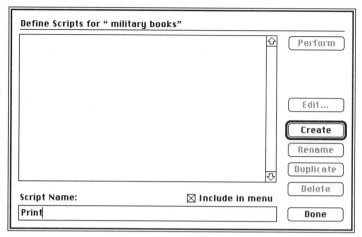

Figure 24-2:
The hardest
part of
making a
ScriptMaker
script is
figuring out
a name.

After you've typed in the script name, you're ready to start defining the script. Just click the Create button in order to get things moving. You see the dialog in Figure 24-3 — the stuff in the right-hand box, under Print, may be different. The first thing to do is delete everything in the right-hand box by selecting it and hitting Delete. Next, select "Page Setup [...]" in the scrolling list on the left-hand side of the dialog box and then click the ">>Move>>" button. What ">>Move>>" button, you may ask. Well, when you select an item in the left-hand list, the Clear button changes its name to ">>Move>>". Then select the new command in the right-hand window, as shown in Figure 24-3. You can change the way the command behaves by checking the boxes in the Options area in the lower right-hand side of the dialog box. Notice the Perform without dialog option. Seems made to order to fix our little problem, doesn't it?

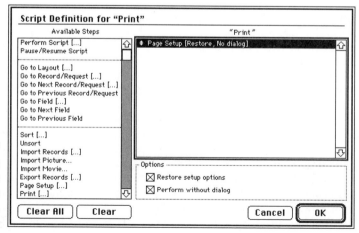

Figure 24-3:
Adding the
Page Setup
command.

The next step is to add the actual Print [...] command, as shown in Figure 24-4.

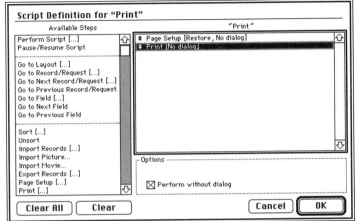

Figure 24-4:
Adding the
Print
command to
complete
the script.

With this command, you have only one option and, by George, it's the one we need. Bet you're really surprised about that, aren't you? With the script complete and perfect in all aspects, you can click the OK button. We're rewarded with a return to the original dialog box, but now, as shown in Figure 24-5, our new script — one internal to FileMaker Pro and not written in AppleScript — is proudly installed.

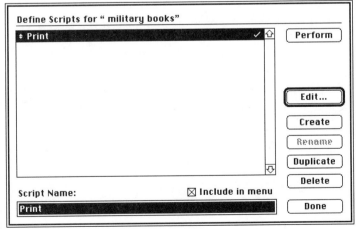

Figure 24-5:
One
complete
script ready
for action.

Now that we've got our print script, we can invoke it in AppleScript by using the **do script** command like this:

```
tell application "FileMaker Pro"
   Do Script "Print"
end tell
```

Nice and easy, isn't it? You can invoke any of FileMaker's internal scripts this way. In addition, you can call several scripts in a row if you like.

Microsoft Excel

Well, as you know, the exception proves the rule, and Excel has a very well thought-out and complete set of scripting commands and value classes, so it proves that Microsoft can never conform to anyone else's standard — see Chapter 23 for details. This program has tons of commands that let you control just about every aspect of its behavior. The value classes are natural — they reflect things you work with if you use Excel, such as cells and worksheets, and they have tons of attributes. The range class, which represents a set of cells, has more than 70 attributes. Don't let this intimidate you. Rather, realize that when you want to customize the format or content of a range, you'll probably be able to do whatever you want because you have access, via the attributes, to the relevant values.

When referring to cells in Excel, you have to use the RxCy approach where R stands for row, C stands for column, and x and y are integers. So cell A1 is R1C1, while cell B1 is R1C2. You can specify a range of cells by putting in a colon, so R1C1:R1C3 is cells A1, B1, and C1.

Getting data from Excel is pretty straightforward. If you start with a simple worksheet that has the value "3.1415" in cell A1, the formula "=a1*2" in cell A2, and "1/9/55" in cell A3, you get the results shown in this example:

```
tell application "Microsoft Excel"
   set the Name of Worksheet 1 of Workbook "Excel demo for dummies" to "test case"
   tell Worksheet "test case" of Workbook "Excel demo for dummies"
      set z to Value of Range "r1c1:r3c1" --> z is {{3.1415}, {6.283}, {2.0098E+4}}
      set z1 to text of Range "r1c1:r3c1" --> z1 is {"3.1415"}, {"6.283"}, {"1/9/55"}}
      set z2 to Formula of Cell "r2c1" --> z2 is  =A1*2
   end tell
end tell
```

The second script line shows you how to set the name of a worksheet — starting with Excel 5, you can have multiple worksheets inside a single workbook — so references to it in the script are clearer. Notice that you need to make it clear to Excel which worksheet and which workbook you want to refer to.

Setting values is also fairly straightforward with just a few complexities, as shown in these examples:

```
tell application "Microsoft Excel"
    set the Name of Worksheet 1 of Workbook "Excel demo for dummies" to "test case"
    tell Worksheet "test case" of Workbook "Excel demo for dummies"
        --set a row of values
        set the Value of Range "r1c2:r3c2" to {1, 2, 3}
        --set a single cell
        set Cell "r4c2" to "2-Jun-84"
        --set a rectangular region, each sublist is a row in the range
        --so this creates two columns, the first is 1,2,3 and the second
        --is 4,5,6
        set Range "r1c4:r3c5" to {{1, 4}, {2, 5}, {3, 6}}
        --fill a range with a value
        set Range "r1c7:r6c7" to 1
    --fill a range using autofill
    AutoFill Range "r1c7" Destination Range "r1c7:r1c10"
    --fill a range with a relative formula.
    --This computes the sum of the range with columns between 5 less
    --and 4 less than the cell the formula is in.
    --So if the cell is R1C12—L1— the formula is "=sum(g1:k1)"
    set FormulaR1C1 of Range "r1c12:r1c15" to "=sum(RC[-5]:RC[-1])"
        end tell
end tell
```

Value vs. Text

Value is the information that Excel uses internally. It can be the same as what you see in a cell — for numbers, for example — or dramatically different, as for dates. *Text,* on the other hand, is what you see when you look at the cell in the spreadsheet. For example, 1/9/55, the date Jan. 9, 1955, is represented internally as 2.0098e+4. Odds are your script would rather work with 1/9/55 than 2.0098E+4. In general, you want the text of a cell. AppleScript converts text to numbers, so you don't have to worry if the cell has a numerical value.

The one slightly complex point is that when you want to fill in a rectangular or square region, Excel wants the values in a list format where each sublist is used to set the values of the cells in one row of the region whose values are being set. In the example, a 2-cell-wide by 3-cell-high region — r1c4:r3c5 — is being set. The first sub list, {1,4}, is used to set the value of cell r1c4 — 1 — and cell r1c5 — 4. This format isn't hard to create in AppleScript. But if you're going to bring in data from other applications very often, you may create one handler that does the transformation, say from a database format, and recycle it in all your scripts. This is a good situation to use a script object.

Opening and saving files is straightforward, as shown:

```
tell application "Microsoft Excel"
    Activate
    --pick a file using AppleScript's built-in commands
    set file_to_open to choose file with prompt "excel file to open" of type "XLS5"
    set file_to_open to file_to_open as string
    --use Excel's command to let the user pick a file
    set file_to_open to GetOpenFilename Title "which excel file?" FileFilter "XLS5"
    Open file_to_open
    Save file_to_open
end tell
```

A lot of optional parameters are available, so you should look at the dictionary if you want to do anything fancy, such as using a password.

If you want to combine Excel macros with AppleScript, you can use this simple approach:

```
tell application "Microsoft Excel"
    Select Cell "R1C1"
    Evaluate "'macro test'!enter_primes()"
end tell
```

The argument to the **evaluate** command is the name of the workbook, followed by an !, the name of the macro, and parentheses.

If you use Excel a great deal, you'll find that you can easily automate just about any task without having to delve much into Excel macros.

DeltaGraph Pro

DeltaGraph Pro is designed to make it easy for you to create complex, colorful 2- and 3- dimensional plots (or charts as they're called in the business world) of data sets. You can make pie, column, scatter, hi lo final, and format plots, as well as a ton of other types. You've got extensive control over all aspects of the plot's appearance so that you can ensure that you're conveying the message you want with maximum impact.

The scripting support in DeltaGraph Pro 3.5 isn't that extensive, see Figure 24-6, but it's very useful nonetheless. The manual covers the program's scripting features and the sample scripts that come with the application. In fact, some of the sample scripts are very powerful. One shows you how to get data to plot from Excel, and another one demonstrates getting data from FileMaker Pro.

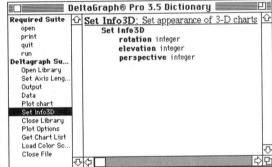

Figure 24-6:
The
DeltaGraph
Pro 3.5
dictionary.

Plotting with DeltaGraph

The basic idea for scripting DeltaGraph Pro is that you develop the plot template manually inside of DeltaGraph Pro. You then write a script that gets the data that you want to put in the plot and use script commands to fill the plot with the selected data. As a result of this concept, you can't control the detailed creation of a complex plot from a script, but you can create scripts that generate very complex plots by getting large data sets and having DeltaGraph Pro use a manually created plot template to display the data.

For example, you may want to display the price of New York gold versus time — I didn't even know they had gold mines in New York, but I guess that's because I'm a physicist, not an MBA. You first go into DeltaGraph Pro and create the plot template you want. If you just want a simple plot, you can fully define the plot inside your script. Then you write a script to get the data you want to plot, format that data for DeltaGraph Pro, and then use the DeltaGraph Pro commands to make a plot.

This little example plots some fake gold price data that's hardwired into the script.

```
on format_data_for_plot()
    -this formats the data for plotting. You can get the data from anywhere
    set day_value to {1, 2, 3, 4, 5, 6, 7, 8, 9, 10}
    --set the value of gold on a given day
    set gold_value to {384, 378, 398, 401, 200, 360, 390, 400, 410, 420}
    -- start defining the string to be plotted by adding a title
    set data_string to tab & tab & "Gold($/ounce NY)" & return
    set n_items to the length of gold_value
    --add each of the entries, a day and the value of gold on that day,
    --to the data string
    repeat with i from 1 to n_items
    set data_string to data_string & tab & item i of day_value & tab & ¬
    item i of gold_value & return
    end repeat
    return data_string
end format_data_for_plot
set data_to_plot to format_data_for_plot()
tell application "DeltaGraph® Pro 3.5"
    Set Axis Lengths for X 300 for Y 300 --set the lengths of the axis of the plot
    Data data_to_plot as type Tab Delimited
    --tell DeltaGraph which data to use and its format
    Output PICT to file "System:delta test"
    --tell DeltaGraph where to output the plot as a PICT file
    Plot chart "scatter" --make the chart and the output it
    quit --don't need DeltaGraph anymore so quit it
end tell
    tell application "SimpleText"
    --Even though SimpleText doesn't have a dictionary it can be scripted
    activate
    open file "system:delta test" --open is one of the required events so it works
end tell
```

This little script generates a file, in PICT format, with the graph shown in Figure 24-7. The **format_data_for_plot** handler formats the data into the tab-delimited format that DeltaGraph Pro likes. For scatter plots, that format starts out with a tab, followed by the first label, another tab, the second label, and then the Return key. In this example, I didn't use the first label, so I didn't put anything between the tabs. After the return, every point is entered as a tab followed by the **x** value, followed by a tab, followed by the **y** value, followed by the Return key. This type of format is called tab delimited, and most databases can export data in this format. Instead of building up a string, as this example shows, you can also read the data in from a file, which can be in any one of several formats. After the data is formatted, the script starts using various DeltaGraph commands to set up, create, and save the chart.

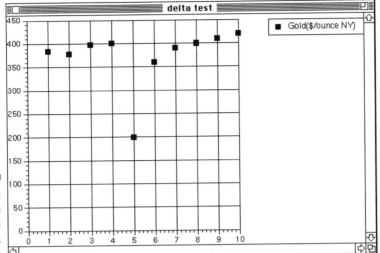

Figure 24-7: Day 5 was bad for the gold market.

PICT: This is a standard format for pictures on the Mac. Just about any painting or drawing program is able to read PICT files, although you have to open them using the Open or Import command item rather than double-clicking them.

In order to get DeltaGraph to plot the data, you need to use the **data** command to tell DeltaGraph which data to plot, the **output** command to tell where to send the graph when its made, and the **plot** command to actually generate the plot.

The data command

The **data** command, whose full syntax is

```
data string [as type Tab Delimited | Comma Delimited | Space Delimited]¬
[from file file_alias]
```

defines which data is plotted and what format the data is in. If the data is tab delimited, you can leave off the **as type** part of the command. You can also read the data from a file by using the **from file** option. This is convenient if you read in a gold price each day and then store it to a file. You need all the points to make the plot, and the best place to save them is a file.

The output command

The **output** command has to come before the actual command to plot the data. It defines where the output goes, but it doesn't actually route the plot. A better name for it is *define output destination*. You can pick from five formats — PICT,

PICT with embedded Postscript, EPSF, Adobe Illustrator 3.2, and PICT for TeachText 7.0. If the file doesn't exist, it can be created.

The plot command

The **plot** command defines the type of chart — you can use the **get chart list** command to get a list of available chart types — and tells DeltaGraph to create the chart and save it to a file. You can't view the chart in DeltaGraph Pro; you have to view the file that's created. If you've failed to define the data with a call to the **data** command, or the plot destination with a call to the **output** command, and you try to call the **plot chart** command, then you get an error. Other calls to define plot parameters, such as **set axis lengths**, are optional.

As you can see, it's pretty easy to make charts using DeltaGraph Pro. The manual has a lot of information about scripting, and the sample scripts that come with it are very powerful and demonstrate useful scripting techniques, not only for DeltaGraph Pro, but for FileMaker Pro and Excel as well.

Chapter 25

Layout and Illustration Applications

. . . .

In This Chapter

▶ QuarkXPress

▶ Photoshop

. . . .

QuarkXPress

While QuarkXPress isn't recordable, it's one of the most scriptable applications around. It's got a dictionary that can choke a digital horse and tons of value classes that represent the types of things you use every day when working with a page layout program, things like **page**, **master document,** and **image.** In addition, QuarkXPress comes with a sample script, called Document Construction, that, surprisingly enough, builds an entire document, including custom colors and other fun features that you can use as a cheat sheet for automating tasks, such as building a catalog from a database. For some reason, that script and two Quark documents nearly a megabyte long, which describe Quark's AppleScript support, are in a folder called "For Advanced Scripting." Don't let that faze you. Aside from one or two small things, scripting Quark is straightforward — assuming, of course, that you know how to use Quark in the first place. That's the big hurdle for me. My idea of page layout is what happens when you let a 2-year-old play with a book with a weak binding.

One important thing to keep in mind: Quark has many value classes that sometimes aren't what they seem, as you can see from this example. The quote after the number, 1.75", signifies that the value is in inches. You can use other units, such as cm, as well.

```
tell application "QuarkXPress™"
    make document at beginning --make a blank document
    make text box at beginning of document 1
    --put in a text box for the rest of the script to use
    set z to the bounds of window 1 --get the outer limits of the window
                                                        (continued)
```

```
(continued)
    set y to the class of z --find out what type of data z is
    --y is list as you'd expect
    tell document 1
        set z to bounds of text box 1 of page 1 --get the boundary of the text box
        set y to the class of z --find out what type of data z is
        --y is measurements rectangle not list, z is {3", 1.75", 10.667", 7"}
        set x to left of bounds of text box 1 of page 1
        --get the left edge of the text box
        set y to the class of x --see what type of data x is
        --y is horizontal measurement not number or integer, x is 1.75"
    end tell
end tell
```

Accessing a measurement rectangle's values

Because a **measurement rectangle**, which shows up in the dictionary as a **fixed rectangle**, isn't a list, you need to access its values using its properties, such as **left**. Those values are in turn not numbers, but another value class. It turns out that QuarkXPress stores measurements in the form of a number, followed by a quote (to indicate that the measurement is in inches). QuarkXPress converts inputs if you put them in the proper string format, "1.23\"." As a result, these two handlers let you convert numbers to a format QuarkXPress understands, and they also convert QuarkXPress measurements to numbers.

```
on get_number(q_value) --converts a Quark measurement("1.34\"" or 1.06 cm) to a
        real (1.34 and 1.06)
    set q_value to q_value as string
    --this character is used instead of a space when the units are cm
    set special_character to ASCII character 202
    if q_value contains "\\" then
    --double \ required for one \ to actually show up see Chapter 4
        set n_chars to the number of characters in q_value
        set value to (characters 1 through (n_chars - 1) of q_value) as string
        --remove the "
        --this handles 1.06 cm where the special character is between the 6 and the c
```

```
        else if q_value contains special_character then
            set n to offset of special_character in q value --find the special character
            set value to (characters 1 through (n - 1) of q_value) as string
        end if
        set value to value as real
    end get_number
    on make_q_number(value) --converts a number(3.14) to a Quark value(3.14")
        set value to value as string
        set value to value & "\""
    end make_q_number
```

The one very unusual thing is that if you print to the log file a measurement value and the units are cm, even though it appears to have a space between the number and the cm, it's really a different character that doesn't print. Another thing to note is that if you want to put a \ in quotes, you have to use two backslashes because the \ is a special character used to insert things like quotes, \", inside of quotes. If you put just one backslash, AppleScript assumes the next character is part of a backslash special and then treats that backslash as a special character.

Modifying document contents

Getting and modifying the contents of a document is straightforward, as you can see here. The next script will only run if you create a document that has all of the pages and text boxes and so on that are used in the script. It turns out that you can use the Advanced Scripting Document that comes with QuarkXPress 3.3. You will also need to replace the two hardwired paths: The first —"System:test" — points to a Word document or any other text file that QuarkXPress can read while the second — "System:test picture" — points to a PICT file with paths that work on your Mac.

```
tell application "QuarkXPress™"
    tell document 1 --save some typing
        set the_text to the text of text box 2 of page 2
        set the_text to line 1 of paragraph 1 of text box 2 of page 4
        set the_text to story 1 of text box 2 of page 2
        tell page 1 --this saves more typing
            set story 1 of text box 2 to "this is a test"
```

(continued)

```
(continued)
       set the size of story 1 of text box 2 to 24 --24 point font
       set the style of story 1 of text box 2 to italic
       copy "just kidding" to after word 2 of paragraph 1 of text box 2
       set story 1 of text box 2 to alias "System:test" --import a Word file
       --notice that you can use cm units as well as inches
       make picture box at beginning ¬
         with properties {bounds:{"1cm", "4cm", "8cm", "20cm"}, name:"a picture"}
       --read a picture in from a PICT file
       set image 1 of picture box "a picture" to alias "System:test picture"
     end tell
   end tell
end tell
```

This makes it clear that you can do some pretty powerful things with scripts. Make sure you check out the Document Construction script from Quark, which shows you all of the steps necessary to build a document from scratch. Doing so gives you ideas of how to do other types of data manipulation.

Photoshop

Photoshop is the world's most popular painting program, with more tools than the average grease monkey. It's also one of the slowest tools, not because it's not well written, but because it just takes lots and lots of calculations to process millions of pixel pictures, which use 32 bits of color for each pixel. As a result, you'd think that Photoshop would be scriptable, so that you can auto- mate it, right? Wrong. Photoshop has no scripting support. Fortunately, the American system came to the rescue. Sensing a profit, Daystar developed a tool called Photomatic. Photomatic is a Photoshop *plug-in,* a little program that can extend the feature set in Photoshop, and it lets you record scripts in Photo- shop. The resulting scripts are in AppleScript, and you can enhance them by editing the file — in text editor, not the Script Editor — by putting in AppleScript stuff, like **if** and **repeat** statements.

Scripting for nothing

Until recently, you had to pay for Photomatic, but for some reason, Daystar has released version 2.0 for free. You can get Photomatic 2.0 by going to Daystar's World Wide Web page at http://www.daystar.com. Make sure you also get the manual for version 1.0 from the same site. The documentation that comes with 2.0 makes it clear how to install Photomatic. When you run Photoshop after you install Photomatic, you'll find a new menu, shown in Figure 25-1. This menu is your one-stop shopping center for working with scripts in Photoshop.

Figure 25-1: The Photomatic script recording menu in Photoshop.

Record
Start Recording   ⌘⇧R
Pause Recording
Script Functions   ▶
Play   ▶
Continue Playing   ⌘⇧P
Preferences   ▶
Register...

The first step of automating Photoshop is to record a script. Just click the Start Recording menu item. Photomatic then watches what you do and builds a script of it. My experience is that Photomatic does a great job of capturing menu commands and keystrokes, but it has some problems with mouse actions, such as dragging to select a region. You have to experiment with Photomatic to see what you can reliably record. You can record the application of a series of filters, which can save you time because you don't have to sit around waiting for one filter to finish before going to the next. It also handles opening files pretty well.

When you're done doing whatever it is you want recorded, you go back to the Recording Menu, which looks like Figure 25-2, and tell it to stop recording. The script functions, shown in Figure 25-2, are special functions you can insert in the script. When you stop recording, you get a standard Mac Save File dialog box, which lets you save the script as a compiled script file. Any compiled script file in the Script folder shows up in the Record menu under the Play menu item. The next script inverts an image, sharpens its edges, and then saves it as a file with the name "new file name."

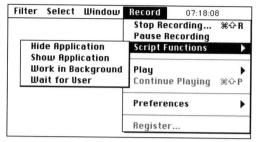

Figure 25-2:
Other
options
you'll find
while
recording.

```
-- 2.0 PhotoMatic™ Sat, Oct 14, 1995 13:40
select menu "Map;Invert"
select menu "Sharpen;Sharpen Edges"
select menu "Save As…"
wait for window change
type string "new file name"
type special key return
wait for window change
wait for window change
type special key return
wait for window change
```

As it stands, this is a useful script. But because Photomatic understands AppleScript, you can improve it. You can add **if** and **repeat** statements, or you can use some of Photomatic's built-in automation to apply scripts to multiple files. You can also change the file name based on such things as the time and type of processing used.

Automating Photoshop: another option

You can automate applications like Photoshop in another, potentially nicer and easier-to-use way. You can build up a script object with a bunch of handlers that invokes macros in a friendly way. For example, the following script defines a script object called **photoshop_commands**, which is saved to a file:

```
script photoshop_commands
  on activate {}
    tell application "Adobe Photoshop™ 3.0.4"
      activate
    end tell
  end activate
```

```
    on invert()
       tell application "!Tempo Assist"
         Do Script ("play invert")
       end tell
    end invert
end script
store script photoshop_commands ¬
   in file ¬
   ("Mary:Files:AppleScript for Dummies Book:scripts under construction:" & ¬
      "photoshop:photoshop_commands") replacing yes
```

That script object can be loaded into a script and used as in the following example, which launches Photoshop and moves it to the front:

```
set photoshop_commands to load script file ¬
   ("Mary:Files:AppleScript For Dummies Book:scripts under construction:" & ¬
      "photoshop:photoshop_commands")
tell photoshop_commands
   activate {}
end tell
```

The **invert** handler shows you how to invoke Tempo II macros from a script. Just use a **do script** command, with the argument being a string that starts with "play" and then has the name of the macro. You can only call *universal macros,* ones that are available everywhere, not macros that are associated with a specific application. But because you can save macros recorded in Photoshop as universal macros, this limitation isn't a major problem. You can use handlers like **invert** once you've opened a file in Photoshop. OSA Menu, discussed in Chapter 28, is a great way to launch scripts in an application.

While the **invert** handler is a trivial example, it shows how you can hide all the complexity of invoking macros by putting them into script objects. If you grow your script object by adding new handlers every time you run across a task that you generate a macro for, then you'll find that by combining handlers from the script object, you'll be able to do more and more complex and powerful automation. In addition you'll find that because you can recycle macros you've recorded before, you'll have to record fewer and fewer new macros as time goes on. This approach can also be used with applications, such as PageMaker, that have built-in scripting languages. But in those cases, instead of building handlers around macros, you build handlers around **do script** calls, which invoke scripts in the application's internal scripting language. This scripting method is a very, very, very, powerful approach to automation because it allows you to use AppleScript with applications that have little or no scripting support built in.

Chapter 26

Miscellaneous Applications

● ●

In This Chapter

▶ America Online

▶ HyperCard and FaceSpan

● ●

America Online: Using Macro Utilities

In a perfect world, every application is scriptable and recordable. In a totally messed up world, every computer is running Windows 1895. The real world is in the middle. Unfortunately, because it takes a reasonable amount of effort to make an application scriptable, a lot of software tools, which are otherwise very nice, aren't scriptable. America Online, the most popular online service as I write this book, has a very Mac-like interface — in fact, AOL started life as AppleLink Personal Edition with Apple as a key player, and I've got the beach towel to prove it — but a very minimal scripting interface. But you can auto-mate your e-mail so that you can write e-mail offline — that's when your computer isn't talking over the phone to AOL — and then use a script to send your e-mail when convenient. The only hitch is that the AOL script implementa-tion has a bug, so the command that sends e-mail doesn't fill in the subject field. In addition, AOL doesn't send e-mail without an e-mail subject. Sounds grim, doesn't it? No script commands will save us. Our only hope is to call on one of the Mac's super-macro utilities, such as QuicKeys, Tempo II, PreFab Player, or the new kid on the block, OneClick. These utilities work by fooling applications into thinking that a real live human user is clicking the mouse and typing in things. Super-macro utilities are designed to work with applications that aren't scriptable. They lack AppleScript's powerful control structures, things like **if** and **repeat**, but they're good tools to use when an application absolutely, positively has to be automated by tomorrow.

You record *macros* — a set of instructions for selecting menu items, typing text, and that sort of stuff — by completing the steps for the task you want to make a macro for. The macro utility watches you and makes a macro that duplicates your actions. PreFab Player is the only one that doesn't let you record a macro. It requires you to manually build up macros.

Here's a script that uses the ever-popular QuicKeys to enter the e-mail subject on AOL:

```
--The wait handler just causes the script to delay for t_in_seconds seconds
on wait(t_in_seconds)
    set start_time to current date
    set delta_time to 0
    repeat until delta_time > t_in_seconds
        set delta_time to (current date) - start_time
    end repeat
    return delta_time
end wait
tell application "America Online v2.6"
    --launch AOL and/or move it to the front
    activate
    set success to 0
    set number_of_tries to 3
    --send some mail, just one message in this case
    repeat with i from 1 to 1
        Mail to "trinkos" subject "test" content "Eureka"
        --Use QuicKeys to take care of the fact that AOL won't put "test" in the
        --subject field
        tell application "QuicKeys™ Toolbox"
            --Play a macro which makes AOL think the user clicked the mouse in the
            --subject field
            PlayByName "ClickinSubject"
            --Have QuicKeys type the string into the now selected subject field
            TypeTheString "Another mindless test" & i
            --Play another macro, which tells AOL to save the changes
            PlayByName "Clicksavechange"
        end tell
    end repeat
    my wait(5)
    repeat until success > 0 or success ≤ -number_of_tries
        try
            --Sometimes AOL is slow, so give it two minutes to log on
            with timeout of 120 seconds
                --use the AOL command to sign on to AOL
                SignOn name "trinkos" password "cuttaxes"
                my wait(10)
            end timeout
            set success to 1
```

```
     on error
        set success to success - 1
        --if a problem occurs and a dialog box shows up, use QuicKeys to select
        --the default button,
        --by hitting return, so we can try to log on again.
        tell application "QuicKeys™ Toolbox"
          TypeTheString return
        end tell
     end try
  end repeat
  if success > 0 then
     my wait(5)
     --After the script logs on, it can use this command to send the mail that's
     --been created
     mailout
     my wait(5)
     SignOff
  else
     display dialog "Couldn't connect"
  end if
end tell
```

You've seen most of the stuff used in this script before. The basic approach I used in this script is

1. **Launch the AOL software.**

   You need version 2.6 or later.

2. **Use the AOL command** mail **to create one or more new mail messages.**

3. **Use QuicKeys macros to enter a subject in each mail item's subject field.**

4. **Log on using AOL's** sign on **command.**

   And, yes, I have changed my password!

5. **Send the mail using AOL's** mailout **command.**

6. **Sign off using AOL's** sign off **command.**

The **wait** handler, which works by checking the time when it's first called and continually checking the time until the number of seconds of delay you asked for has elapsed, is used to pause script execution in several places to allow AOL to finish one AOL command before racing on to the next one. An interesting use of QuicKeys is to deal with the dialog box that AOL puts up if you fail to connect. If the script doesn't use QuicKeys to type a Return, the script will stall until someone takes care of the dialog box that AOL puts up when you fail to connect. By using the macro, the script can automatically retry connecting to AOL. The exact number of times the script tries to connect is determined by the value you set the variable **number_of_tries** to at the start of the script.

One thing you have to be aware of is that the first macro "ClickInSubject" is more complex than it sounds. I tried to just record clicking in the subject field, so that the text typed by **TypetheString** would end up in the subject field, but for some reason I was unable to determine, the script would stall at that point. In order to get things to work, I had to record a macro that first clicks on the Subject field, then clicks on the Address Book icon, and then clicks on the OK button in the dialog that comes up because you can't use the Address Book with the subject field. With that macro, things work just fine. While this is a bit strange, it works, so just record the macro and don't worry about it. The second macro, "Clicksavechange," is just a single step, which is clicking on the icon labeled "Save Changes."

PreFab Player is a set of AppleScript scripting additions that gives you the capability to click at a specified location on the screen or on a specific menu item or button from inside a script. PreFab Player is designed to be used by scripters, and it's cheaper than the macro utilities, if you plan to distribute your script. The next script shows how you can use PreFab Player to fill in the subject of an AOL message.

```
tell application "America Online v2.6"
    activate
    Mail to "trinkos" subject "test" content "Eureka"
    tell application "PreFab Player™"
        click location {124, 72} --put insertion point in subject field
        type "This is a test of player"
        --type in the message subject at the insertion point
        click location {37, 126} --click send later button
    end tell
end tell
```

The click location is easy to determine with PreFab's tools. Using PreFab has the advantage of avoiding the need to learn how to work with another utility. On the downside, you can't record a macro in PreFab.

One last note. The current AOL World Wide Web browser, Web Browser 1.0, seems to have a reasonable number of commands in its dictionary. If you use the Web a lot, you may want to see if you can automate some of your most common tasks.

HyperCard and FaceSpan: Putting On a Friendly Face

HyperCard is Apple's programming environment for the rest of us. It makes it easy for nonprogrammers to create useful applications and games on the Mac. I can't cover HyperTalk, HyperCard's scripting language, but version 2.2 and later of HyperCard give you the ability to completely control HyperCard stacks with AppleScript. Stacks, or HyperCard documents, that are saved as applications are fully scriptable with AppleScript. You can also use AppleScript scripts inside HyperCard, as shown in Figure 26-1.

All you have to do is select AppleScript as the scripting language by using the pop-up menu at the top of the script window. Notice how you put the names in a *card field* — that's just a text display area. Placing names in a card field is very similar to the corresponding HyperTalk syntax. The easy integration of AppleScript and HyperCard makes HyperCard a great tool for creating user interfaces for AppleScript. AppleScript is really lacking in good user interface tools. The most complex interface is a dialog box with three buttons and one text entry area, but with HyperCard, you can have extremely rich multiwindow interfaces. If your script has a lot of user interaction and you're familiar with HyperCard, it's a very good candidate for building the user interface.

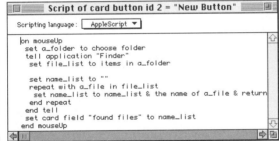

Figure 26-1:
Displaying
file names in
HyperCard.

In a similar vein, FaceSpan 2.0, originally called Frontmost, was designed from the beginning to be a user interface and application construction tool for AppleScript. With FaceSpan, you draw your interface and then put AppleScript's — or any OSA-compliant language's — scripts in buttons, menu items, or other user interface items, which are activated when the user clicks a button or performs other actions. FaceSpan ships with a wide spectrum of sample applications, including a game, which gives you good examples of how to use it. One example application lets the user integrate any of several database programs with one of two data-graphing applications to provide a financial display package. Unfortunately, I can't cover FaceSpan in detail here, but you'll find it easy to use and you won't need to learn any new scripting language in order to use it. If you're serious about scripting, you should have both of these tools available for use.

Part IV
The Part of Tens

In this part . . .

Someone once said, "No man is an island." The same is true of scripting. You'll find that your ability to automate tasks will be enhanced by various scriptable applications as well as additional sources of information about scripting. In this part, I list some of the available scriptable applications and some resources for more information (that don't call for having to buy more books). I even cover how to install AppleScript in the first place, and I tell you what tools are available to make your scripting jobs easier.

Chapter 27

More Than Ten Scriptable Applications

ACT! (personal information manager): It's very scriptable, and you can even replace menu items with scripts. It comes with a bunch of sample scripts.

Anarchie (Internet FTP tool): Very scriptable. It comes with many sample scripts.

BBEdit 3.5 (text/program editor): This utility provides good scripting support. The CD contains several sample scripts, and there's a Script menu in the application so that you can easily access scripts.

Canvas (paint/draw program): This application has some scripting capabilities, but the dictionary contains errors.

ChemDraw,Chem3D (chemical analysis): Good scripting support should enable effective automation.

Claris Impact (presentation/charting): This program is essentially unscriptable, but you can close and save documents via AppleScript.

ClarisWorks 4 (integrated word processor/paint/draw/database/spreadsheet/ telecom): This application has limited AppleScript support, but you can do useful stuff with the **do script** command. ClarisWorks also has a very nice macro language. This is another application that greatly benefits from the script object approach discussed in Chapter 25

clip2GIF (graphic conversion/viewer utility): Very scriptable. It's often used when writing scripts for World Wide Web pages.

CodeWarrior (C/C++/Pascal programming): This utility features complete scripting for project management. It comes with several sample scripts.

DragStrip (application launcher/miscellaneous utilities): You can use scripts to build palettes of buttons that launch applications, open folders, and so on. You can also control and configure existing palettes.

Eudora (Internet mail utility): Very scriptable. Scripting will help you manage your Internet mail.

InfoDepot (configurable information manager/planner): Completely scriptable. This is almost a toolbox rather than an application because of its extensive scripting support.

Informed Manager (forms management): This application has a good selection of commands and value classes. The CD has a manual just for AppleScript that covers the basics as well as the commands and value classes for Informed Manager.

JMP 3.0 (statistical analysis program): This product's scripting support is still not complete, but even so, many tasks are scriptable. Future versions will probably extend the scripting support.

JPEGView 3 (JPEG image viewer/file format converter): Very scriptable. I wrote a script that used this shareware program to move a folder full of PICT files into a FileMaker Pro database. Best of all, you only have to send the author a postcard!

MacProject Pro 1.5 (scheduling/project management): This program has relatively limited scripting, though you can get and set data. A reasonable number of value classes and **do script** are supported.

netOctopus (network administration/monitoring): Very scriptable. It comes with sample scripts, and it should be easy to automate some standard tasks.

Netscape (World Wide Web browser): This browser offers reasonable scripting support, but I haven't been able to test it.

PageMaker (page layout): This DTP program has very limited scripting support, but you can use the **do script** command to access the powerful, built-in scripting language. It's a great application for using script object libraries.

Panorama 3 (database): This application has reasonable but sparse scripting support sufficient for most needs. It supports **do script** command access to scripts written in Panorama 3.

PhotoFlash (image management/manipulation): Very scriptable and recordable. It comes with useful scripts, and it's great for automating the management of your images.

PowerKey Pro (power control): You can use scripts to control the power to peripherals and to turn off your Mac.

Retrospect 3 (backup program): This utility offers some scriptability. Basic tasks can be scripted, and you can use the **execute** command to run scripts written in EasyScript, Retrospect's own scripting language. You can script what Retrospect will do when certain events occur, which is a very powerful feature.

Route 66 (route planner on American roads): Very scriptable. It also comes as an OpenDoc part.

Shrink II (works with files compressed on the Apple II): This program has limited scripting, probably sufficient to automate the translation of compressed archives.

SITComm (telecommunications): Very scriptable and recordable. It's ideal for automating telecommunications sessions.

Square One 3.0 (application/script/macro launching utility): This utility offers decent scriptability so that you can automatically build palettes of icons. Other functions, such as making sure that palettes are up-to-date, are also scriptable.

StuffIt Deluxe (data compression): Very scriptable. I use this program to manage all of the files I download from online services.

Symantec C++ Development System (C/C++ programming): This application is very scriptable and recordable. It comes with several sample scripts, and it has a script menu for easy access to scripts. You can also create scripts that run on startup, shutdown, and when a project is opened. There's also a section in the manual about how to use AppleScript.

Virex (virus detection/eradication): Basic scripting support allows reasonable automation.

White Knight 12.0 (telecommunications): Very limited scriptability. This program only supports **do script** and the four basic events. It's another case where a script object library is called for because the internal scripting language is very powerful.

This is only a partial list. I've left off tons of applications, including many specialty applications such as, for example, Mac Thermal and Label Designer.

Chapter 28

More Than Ten Scripting Resources

In This Chapter

▶ Ways to get AppleScript-related help and info

Where to Get AppleScript

The most common way to get AppleScript is to buy System 7.5 or higher. You can also buy a CD-ROM from APDA — Apple's in-house store for programmers and scripters. The CD-ROM is called the AppleScript Software Development Toolkit version 1.1, and it includes version 1.0 of FaceSpan and tools for adding Finder scripting to System 7.1 and System 7 Pro.

Information Sources

In general, vendors don't provide free support for scripting their applications. There are a number of places to look for help, though. If you can access the World Wide Web, you should check out ScriptWeb with its links to tons of good scripting stuff — information, sample scripts, and scripting additions for example — at http://www.gz.com/scriptweb/.

A really valuable source of information is the MacScript mail list. It generates hundreds of pages per month of script-related messages. You can subscribe by sending an e-mail message to LISTSERV@dartmouth.edu with the subject being "subscribe" and the message text being "subscribe macscrpt (your name)." Leave out the quotes and replace (your name) with your name. Once you've subscribed, you'll want the digest, the day's mail in one file, so send another message to the same address with the subject of "digest" and the message text being "set macscrpt digest."

Most of the online services — such as America Online, GEnie, and CompuServe — have areas where scripting is discussed as well. These services are also good places to find the latest and greatest scripting additions. In general, these services have better descriptions of files than what you'll find on the Internet, and the files are checked for computer viruses.

You can contact me, but I can't guarantee that I'll be able to respond quickly, at

> GEnie: T.Trinko
>
> America Online: Trinkos
>
> eWorld: trinkoteam
>
> AppleLink: trinkos
>
> CompuServe: 72147,3723

Tools

OneClick: This is a new product that's a macro utility like QuicKeys or Tempo II, but it comes with a full internal scripting language and the capability to run AppleScript scripts. It also has a nice floating palette interface.

OSA Menu: This is a freeware utility that puts a little icon in your menu bar. When you click on it, you get a menu of scripts you've put into a special folder. You can run the scripts by just clicking on the script's name. This is a very nice tool to allow you to run scripts inside of applications.

Script Editor: This nice, easy-to-use script editor/debugger allows you to step through scripts and monitor the values of global variables. It also has a cool dictionary display window that automatically builds inheritance graphs and element graphs for applications. It includes a large set of scripting additions, which come in handy.

Script Wizard: This utility has a nice dictionary approach, which makes it easy to see the basic AppleScript commands' syntax. It also lets you step through scripts and monitor global variables.

Scriptor: Scriptor is designed to make it easy for beginners to write scripts. For power users, it allows you to track local variables as well as global variables. Surprisingly, I found its interface less intuitive than Script Editor's, primarily because it tends to use key combinations and key and mouse click combinations more than Script Editor. If you need to get one tool, though, this is probably the best choice at the moment. If, however, you're an experienced scripter, you might find that Script Editor is better.

Text Machine: This is a set of scripting additions from the folks who brought you PreFab Player. It makes it easy to perform complex searches and replacements on text files.

Chapter 29

Ten Tips (More or Less) on Installing AppleScript

· ·

In This Chapter

▶ Just what the title says

· ·

*T*here are several ways to get AppleScript, but the most common for non-programmers is with System 7.5 or later. Before you start to worry about how to install AppleScript, you need to see if it's already there. If you did a full install of System 7.5 or probably any later version, AppleScript will be installed. If you're not sure or you want to check, take a look inside your System Folder. You'll find a folder called Extensions. Open that folder up and look for files called AppleScript, ObjectSupportLib, AppleScriptLib, and Finder Scripting Extension. There should also be a folder called Scripting Additions. These items, along with some of the other extensions on my system, are shown in Figure 29-1.

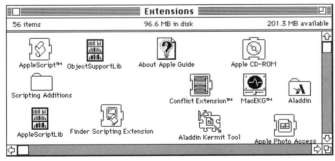

Figure 29-1:
The stuff on the left brings you AppleScript.

If these items aren't present, then AppleScript isn't running on your computer right now.

One thing to watch for is that if you've used an extension-controlling utility such as Now's Startup Manager or Conflict Catcher 3, you might have the files you need but they could be disabled. If you think that you should have AppleScript, then use your extension-controlling utility to see if you've disabled some or all of the AppleScript items. If so, reenable them and restart your Mac.

If AppleScript isn't installed, you should get your System 7.5 CD or disks and start up the installer application (see Figure 29-2). Click on the Continue button in the first window.

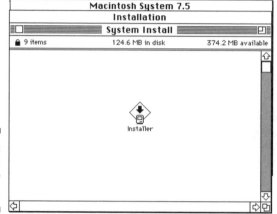

Figure 29-2:
The System
7.5 Installer
on the CD.

In the next window, don't use the Easy Install option. Instead, pick the Custom Install option as shown in Figure 29-3.

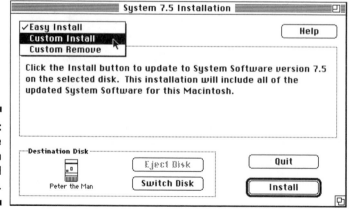

Figure 29-3:
Choose the
Custom
Install
option.

Then look through the list of options and find the one called Utility Software and expand it by clicking on the little triangle to the left of its name. You'll see three different utilities including AppleScript. Check the box next to AppleScript as shown in Figure 29-4. Then click on the Install button. That'll install AppleScript on your Mac.

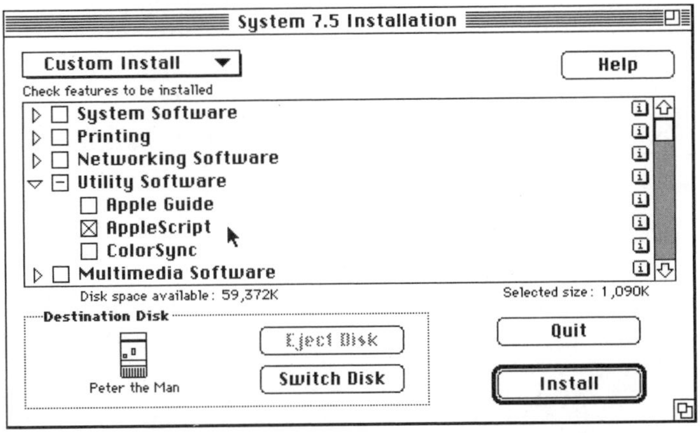

Figure 29-4:
Selecting
AppleScript
for
installation.

When it's done, you'll find that the files I mentioned at the beginning of this chapter are all installed in your Extensions folder. In addition, you'll find a folder called Apple Extras installed at the top level of your hard disk, as shown in Figure 29-5.

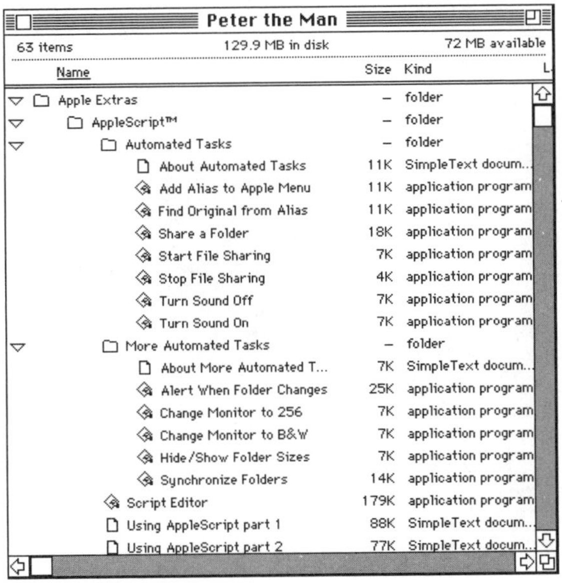

Figure 29-5:
Non-
extension
AppleScript
files installed
by System
7.5.

If you're working with a version of the system that is newer than version 7.5, the procedure you follow will probably be similar, but since I don't have a working crystal ball, I can't give you any better instructions. Sorry.

If you've moved things around since you installed System 7.5, use the Find command in the Finder's File menu to look for Script Editor because you'll be needing it. It also wouldn't hurt to glance through the two Using AppleScript files.

The 5th Wave   By Rich Tennant

Re·al Pro·gram·mers

At a football game, the Real Programmer is the one comparing the plays against his simulation printout.

Index

• R •

• *W* •